UNDERSTANDING TR

Discourse, power an

Ruth Pearce

P

First published in Great Britain in 2018 by

Policy Press
University of Bristol
1-9 Old Park Hill
Bristol
BS2 8BB
UK
t: +44 (0)117 954 5940
pp-info@bristol.ac.uk
www.policypress.co.uk

North America office:
Policy Press
c/o The University of Chicago Press
1427 East 60th Street
Chicago, IL 60637, USA
t: +1 773 702 7700
f: +1 773-702-9756
sales@press.uchicago.edu
www.press.uchicago.edu

© Policy Press 2018

British Library Cataloguing in Publication Data
A catalogue record for this book is available from the British Library

Library of Congress Cataloging-in-Publication Data
A catalog record for this book has been requested

ISBN 978-1-4473-4235-9 paperback
ISBN 978-1-4473-4233-5 hardcover
ISBN 978-1-4473-4236-6 ePub
ISBN 978-1-4473-4237-3 Mobi
ISBN 978-1-4473-4234-2 ePdf

Cover design by Robin Hawes
Front cover image: istock
Printed and bound in Great Britain by CPI Group (UK) Ltd, Croydon, CR0 4YY
Policy Press uses environmentally responsible print partners

This book is dedicated to the memory of

Deborah Lynn Steinberg,

who made it possible, in so many ways.

Contents

List of abbreviations   vi
Acknowledgements   vii

Part One: The context of care   **1**
one   Introduction: coming to terms with trans health   3
two   Condition or movement? A genealogy of trans discourse   19
three   Trans health in practice: conditions of care   51

Part Two: Navigating health services   **81**
four   (Re)defining trans   83
five   Trans temporalities: imagining a future in the time   119
       of anticipation

Part Three: Changing trans health   **157**
six   The politics of trans health: negotiating credible knowledge   159
seven   Towards affirmative care   197

Appendix: notes on fieldwork, methods and ethics   209
List of key terms   219
References   227
Index   247

List of abbreviations

CCG	Clinical Commissioning Group
CRG	Clinical Reference Group
DSM	American Psychiatric Association, *Diagnostic and Statistical Manual of Mental Disorders* (followed by edition number)
FTM	female-to-male
GATE	Global Action for Trans★ Equality
GIC	Gender identity clinic
GIRES	Gender Identity Research and Education Society
GMC	General Medical Council
GP	general practitioner
GRA	Gender Recognition Act 2004
GRC	Gender Recognition Certificate
HBS	Harry Benjamin Syndrome
HRT	hormone replacement therapy
ICD	World Health Organization, *International Classification of Diseases and Related Health Problems* (followed by edition number)
LGBT	lesbian, gay, bisexual and trans
MTF	male-to-female
NHS	National Health Service
PCT	Primary Care Trust
RLE	Real Life Experience
WPATH	World Professional Association for Transgender Health

Acknowledgements

How to begin?

In this book, I talk a lot about the collective work that goes into bringing about change, and also touch upon how often people's actions are erased when a single author effectively takes credit for an enormous group effort.

This book is my own work, the result of seven years of hard graft: research, writing, revisions. I have kept working as friends have died, due in part to failures in the NHS; I have kept working to pull myself out of a deep depression as the emotional impact of these deaths intersected with the stresses of precarious employment.

Nevertheless, I could not have done this without the support of so many incredible people. If you have been in my life during this time: thank you. I could not have done this without the inspiration of my trans siblings, past and present: if you have written super-cool theory or poems or songs, if you have spoken out or protested or organised or simply survived on your own terms and lived to tell the tale for a few glorious years: thank you. I could not have done this without the contributions of so many research participants who bared their soul and permitted me to tell their stories, and from the healthcare practitioners who have dedicated their lives to helping others. Thank you.

I could not have done this without the support of academic colleagues who believed in me and made me believe in myself. Deborah Lynn Steinberg, Maria do Mar Pereira and Karen Throsby provided vital guidance and mentorship. Mick Carpenter and Nickie Charles offered me important opportunities and – on more than one occasion – righteous and pure political solidarity. Igi Moon, Kat Gupta, Hel Robin Gurney and Mark Carrigan were partners in crime as we plotted excellent events and collaborative writing that helped me develop my own ideas and deepen my understanding of the field. Zowie Davy, Surya Monro, Sally Hines, Gaví Ansara, Michael Toze, Noah Adams, Jaimie Veale and Beth Clark have inspired me to broaden my academic horizons. Fellow PhD students Helen Anderson, Anna Reynolds Cooper, Joanna Cuttell, Louise Ellis, Izzy Gutteridge, Morteza Hashemi, Nazia Hussein, Michelle Kempson, Milena Kremakova, Ana Paula Magalhaes, Joelin Quigley-Berg, Monae Verbeke and Reva Yunus were true friends, from whom I learned so much. Thank you.

I could not have done this without the support of Policy Press, who have provided me with robust support and genuinely believe in the work they are doing. In particular, I have benefited enormously from the advice, feedback and general cheeriness of editor Victoria Pittman, production editor Jess Mitchell and editorial assistant Shannon Kneis. Thank you.

I could not have done this without the support of numerous people who read various early versions of this text, sometimes over and over again. Maria, I have already mentioned you once, but truly you were the queen of constructive feedback and none will best you. Freja Sohn Frøkjær-Jensen, you were a harsh and unrelenting proof-reader and I love you for it. Ro Bevan, Joanna Cuttell, Daniel William Kerr, Frederique Retsema and Ben Vincent, your feedback was invaluable. Thank you.

I could not have done this without the support of my friends, particularly those with whom I lived, partied, schemed and/or played music. Helen Thomas, I miss you immensely, now and forever, but will never forget your joy and warmth. Jo Oldham, you are a beautiful human being and an incredible friend. Greg the cat, you'll never read this because you're a cat, but I'm grateful anyway. To you and all the denizens of Trans Manor, and all my bandmates in Not Right, Abandoned Life, Bad News Everyone, and Dispute Settlement Mechanism, and all the people who came to Revolt and all the queers and freaks and riot grrrls and rockers and revolutionaries and glorious weirdos in the Midlands and beyond: thank you.

I could not have done this without the support of my parents, John and Yvonne Pearce. I don't know if you ever really understood what I was studying or why, but I always knew I had your unconditional love and backing regardless. Thank you.

Finally, I could not have done this without the support of my partner, Dr Kirsty Lohman, the woman with a PhD in Punk. You have been the most incisive academic colleague, the most dedicated reader, the most excellent bandmate, the best of friends and true family. Thank you.

Part One
The context of care

ONE

Introduction: coming to terms with trans health

> No social study that does not come back to the problems of biography, of history and of their intersections within a society has completed its intellectual journey. (C. Wright Mills, 1959)

Trans health ... who cares?

The origins of this book lie in the emergence of sexology in the late 19th century as learned doctors sought to describe and categorise the deviant behaviour of those who failed to conform to norms of sex and gender.

The origins of this book lie in the emergence of transsexualism in the 20th century as a means by which individuals desiring social and physical transitions from one gender to 'the other' could be identified and managed.

The origins of this book lie in the emergence of the trans movement in the 1990s, which sought to redefine and recognise a great range of gender-variant identities and experiences as an aspect of human diversity, rather than as conditions requiring treatment.

The origins of this book lie in the emergence of my own trans identity in the early years of the 21st century, as a lonely teenager reaching out for solace, support, understanding and community on the internet.

The origins of this book lie ... in a warm Birmingham meeting room gently devoid of character, in which I sat listening to a talk in March 2009. Spring was (in theory) just around the corner, but that wasn't apparent on this overcast day, with its blustery wind and occasional showers of rain. I was attending a seminar entitled 'LGBT Health ... Who Cares?' as a representative of internet-based advocacy and support group Trans Youth Network.[1] The short walk to the seminar venue from the train station had been somewhat challenging; I was in the latter months of a gruelling recovery from surgery undertaken the

3

previous summer, in what I imagined at the time to be the final stage of my long transition from 'male' to 'female'.

I sat through numerous fascinating presentations on LGBT (lesbian, gay, bisexual and trans) health that day, delivered variously by practitioners, social researchers and community activists. What played on my mind after the event, however, was not any particular item of information I had picked up. Rather, it was the expressed *lack* of information on *trans* experiences of healthcare in the UK, as exemplified in a report launched by Catherine Meads and colleagues during the day.

> [T]rans health research was originally going to be included in this systematic review. Unfortunately, having trawled through all of the literature, no peer-reviewed and published UK-specific information was found on the general health of trans people. (Meads et al, 2009: 81)

Meads and colleagues used **trans** as an umbrella term, incorporating a range of identities and experiences such as 'transsexual', 'transgender', 'transvestite' and 'crossgender'. This approach links 'trans' to both medical accounts and collective social movement, with connections forged on the grounds of shared marginalisation. The Trans Youth Network conceptualisation of 'trans' was wider still, reflecting a move towards open-ended accounts of gender-variant possibility within the connected worlds of trans activism and academia. Similarly, Stephen Whittle (2006: xi) describes trans identities as accessible 'to anyone who does not feel comfortable in the gender role they were attributed with at birth, or has a gender identity at odds with the labels "man" or "woman" credited to them by formal authorities'.

It is this 'open' definition of trans possibility that informs my own use of the term throughout this book. I use it to refer to a wide repertoire of identities, experiences and modes of gender presentation. The trans possibilities found within this repertoire are frequently – but *not always* – linked to a notion of social and/or physical **transition**. Transition refers to a move away from the gender that was assigned to a person at birth and towards to an alternative preferred, desired or felt state of gendered (or non-gendered) being.

I learned from Meads and colleagues that studies on trans health typically focus only on the transition process; indeed, the authors' extensive review of UK literature failed to uncover a single peer-reviewed article looking at trans health more widely. Moreover, I would soon discover that research on the UK's **gender identity**

services, which facilitate physical transition through the provision of hormones, surgeries, hair removal and voice therapy, is also rare outside of medical journals. This is because the intellectual field of trans health has historically been shaped by the health professionals who oversee gender identity services. However, in recent years a range of alternative academic approaches to understanding categorisation, diagnosis and treatment have begun to emerge from the trans rights movement, reflecting and drawing upon similar contestations in the realms of queer and feminist health (Hanssmann, 2016). It is within this tradition that this book is located.

I left 'LGBT Health … Who Cares?' feeling inspired and motivated to address some of the gaps that exist in our knowledge. As both a trans patient and an active member of trans community groups, I felt intimately connected to the challenges faced by trans people in accessing healthcare services. My transition had been a lengthy process, mediated by multiple appointments, assessments and waits. Having first approached my general practitioner (GP) for help with feelings of severe dysphoria at the age of 16, I eventually attended a first appointment at London's Charing Cross Gender Identity Clinic over three years later. I received approval for hormone therapy around the time of my 20th birthday, and acquired my first hormone prescription after a further wait of around four months. I was nearly 22 by the time I underwent an operation to surgically reconfigure my genitals. In the meantime, I found my GP to be indifferent at best and obstructive at worst; he was dismissive in appointments, denied me access to the regular blood tests required by the gender clinic and continued to refer to me as male in my medical records.

This book is written from a sociological perspective. Like many sociologists, I am interested in the connection between 'personal troubles' and wider 'public issues' (Mills, 1959: 8). Back in 2009, I had yet to embark on my training as a researcher, but was already aware that my own frustrating experience of long waits, extensive assessment procedures, ignorance and rudeness within healthcare settings paled in comparison to challenges faced by many of my peers. I felt that my transition, long and difficult as it was, had been a relatively straightforward process. This was facilitated by my luck in the 'postcode lottery' of local public health commissioning bodies, and the manner in which my relatively normative (white, middle-class, abled, English) female gender identity happened to 'fit' the existing diagnostic models and modes of assessment. By contrast, I knew trans people who had spent years fighting for access to specialist care, and others – particularly those whose gender identities could not be categorised straightforwardly into a male/female binary – who had trouble meeting the clinical criteria for treatment even as they experienced severe dysphoria. Within the wider realm of healthcare beyond the gender identity services, an enormous number of trans people I knew had been insulted or harassed (sometimes sexually) by health professionals, and denied routine treatments for all kinds of ailments due to their trans status.

I therefore realised there was a vital need to better understand why and how this happened, in order to address the issues reported by trans patients. I embarked on a research project that came to define my life for many years. I immersed myself in trans people's stories and experiences, their (our) hopes, fears and dreams. I followed passionate arguments and heated debates within online activist groups and carefully read health practitioners' accounts of working with trans patients. This book is the culmination of that project. It offers an insight into some of the narratives and contentions that characterise conversations around trans health, and I hope that it will be useful to patients as well as practitioners, activists as well as academics.

While my research focused primarily on trans healthcare services in a UK setting, many of the ideas and debates I draw upon and discuss in this book have a wider relevance. In addressing issues of power, identity, language and contestation with regard to health, I draw upon and contribute to international conversations about trans rights and access to services. This book will be particularly relevant to readers in countries with a strong tradition of public health and institutionalised gender identity services, but also speaks to ideas and concerns identified by scholars and activists in other contexts, particularly the United States. I also draw upon insights from wider critical health literatures, having noted parallels between patient activism in trans health and in other arenas, such as AIDS and cancer care. In turn, this book will be useful to social scholars of health working outside of the specific arena of transgender studies.

This book is *not* concerned with establishing what gender 'is' (or, for that matter, what sex 'is'), or how this relates to trans identities, experiences and bodies. I regard both gender and sex as socially constructed categories with a complex relationship to biological difference, following theorists such as Judith Butler (1999) and Julia Serano (2007). My deeper thoughts on the matter of gender, sex and trans discourse would form the basis of an entirely separate book! However, this work is based on an acknowledgement that trans people are real, valid and deserving of affirmation, and the observation that trans people experience health inequalities that require specific attention.[2]

Discourse, power and possibility

I soon came to realise that it is insufficient to merely fill a perceived 'gap' in academic knowledge on social experiences of trans health. If it was enough simply to note that trans people face widespread discrimination and ignorance in public life, then many of the troubles trans people face might have been tackled decisively some time ago. Instead, I began to seek a deeper understanding of how and why the troubles that trans people face have emerged.

Many such troubles are not rooted in malice on the part of health professionals, but can instead by linked to different **understandings** of what it *means* to be trans and/or gendered. For example, the broad scope of trans possibility as understood by writers such as Whittle and grassroots organisations such as Trans Youth Network contrasted with more rigid forms of categorisation employed by the health professionals who assessed me for gender dysphoria at the gender clinic. Similarly, my understanding of myself as a *woman* contrasts with my former GP's view that I was 'really' a man, as evidenced by his use of male pronouns to refer to me in my medical notes.

This book therefore goes beyond simply chronicling the challenges faced by trans patients. I ask *why* differences of perspective occur, *how* they might be characterised and in *what ways* they might be linked to the complex interaction of 'medical' and 'trans' ideas both historic and contemporary.

The main concept I use to make sense of this is **discourse**. Discourse refers to the authoritative ways in which we talk about ideas within and as a society. This concept can be linked to the operation of *power*, and the manner in which some ways of living might seem *possible* while others do not. Discourses do not simply describe the world: they also work to reproduce how the world is seen and experienced (Foucault, 1978). This does not necessarily mean that discourses come from a place of power. While some discourses are 'hegemonic' – meaning that they hold sway as the predominant way of seeing the world within a particular social context – counter-discourses may also emerge from the social margins. For example, the hegemonic discourse around gender within Western society holds that there are *two* and *only two* genders – female and male – and that everyone 'fits' into only one of these categories. This is not simply an idea that describes how the world works: it is an *idea with power*, shaping *how* the world works.

By contrast, trans, feminist and decolonial counter-discourses of non-binary gender draw attention to the diversity and complexity of both biology and social life, enabling us to recognise a world that is not divided simplistically between two overarching ideals of sex and gender (Kessler and McKenna, 1978; Bornstein, 1994; Patel, 2017). As I shall show in this book, such ideas have come to challenge the hegemony of binary gender discourse.

Through analysing discourse, I seek to centre the importance of narrative in generating possibility and mediating relations of power. In doing so, I employ a poststructuralist framework. Poststructuralism 'asks us to consider the ways in which subjects are constituted in and through social institutions and the language employed by these ... bodies', thereby enabling scholars to 'examine the constitution of subjectivity in social life' (Namaste, 2000: 16–17). However, I also follow poststructuralist transgender studies scholars such as Surya Monro (2005), Sally Hines (2007) and Zowie Davy (2011) in looking beyond language in and of itself, linking my discussion of discourse to an acknowledgement of the *material conditions* of trans health.[3]

Condition and movement

In this book, I ask two key questions about discourses of trans health:

1. How are 'trans' possibilities produced, reified and legitimated through health discourses and practices?
2. How are discourses of trans health *negotiated* within and between trans community groups, trans activists and health professionals? How are they disseminated, and how are they contested?

These questions aim to uncover how trans identities and experiences, along with conceptualisations of trans health, are understood in multiple contexts. My purpose is to grasp the social processes at play in encounters where trans patients feel marginalised, misunderstood and/or discriminated against. With these questions I also recognise that (like this book) the term 'trans' and concepts of 'trans health' have multiple points of origin and definition.

The first question asks how trans meanings and possibilities are produced, reified and legitimated through health discourses and practices. In unpacking and responding to this question, I describe 'trans' in terms of two intersecting discursive repertoires: 'trans as condition', and 'trans as movement'.

Discourses of **trans as condition** frame 'trans' as fixed and fix*able*. 'Trans' in this sense is also *resolvable*: whether as medical condition or social condition, it can be clearly defined and delineated, while the problems it raises can be addressed and managed in a particular way. Fixing or resolving 'trans' typically entails a certain level of expertise: in this context, 'trans' can be understood as *conditional*, in that it requires identification from a qualified expert such as a health professional, with reference to a set of quite static criteria that are usually rooted in binary conceptions of gender.

Discourses of **trans as movement** recognise the potentiality and actuality of changes to theory, subjectivity, embodiment, space and time taking place through continual creation, fluidity and world-building. Rather than being a categorical matter, 'trans' in this context describes an open-ended 'movement across a socially imposed boundary away from an unchosen starting place' (Stryker, 2008: 1). Trans as movement can hence refer to collective social movements – that is, 'politicised communities of identity' (Stryker, 2006: 5) – but I also use the phrase to describe queer discourses of individual identity and experience. Expertise on 'trans' possibility is in this context typically located in 'the movement', be that social movement or individual subjectivity (Green, 2017).

Movement-oriented understandings of trans identity and experience – in particular, the notion of *trans* itself – emerged from critiques of trans as condition by academics such as Sandy Stone (1991) and activists such as Silvia Rivera (2002) and Leslie Feinberg (1992). These interventions are often said to have heralded a change in medical paradigm. For instance, Walter Bockting (2009: 104) describes 'a shift from a disease-based model (something went wrong during the individual's development that needs to be corrected) toward an identity-based model of transgender health'. However, accounts such as this risk creating a simplistic binary, in which 'trans' is understood as disease/pathology on the one hand, or social/political identity on the other. While the research findings discussed in this book *do* broadly support Bockting's account of a discursive shift, I also show how conditional notions of trans as pathology continue to powerfully frame both the provision of healthcare services *and* the construction of trans subjectivity. Moreover, through the wider concept of 'condition', I seek to explore the discursive links between medical accounts of disease and pathology, trans notions of fixed and definable identity and, briefly, gender essentialist and radical feminist accounts of trans *im*possibility. In describing 'discursive repertoires', therefore, I intend to broadly categorise ideas on the basis of discursive similarity, while also creating space for difference and contestation *within* categories.

The second question asks how discourses of trans healthcare provision are **negotiated** within and between trans community groups, trans activists and health professionals. Like Maria do Mar Pereira, I regard negotiation as an ongoing social process in which change arises from *constant* and *continual* interventions.

> Negotiation is formed by the [Latin] particle *neg* (translating as 'not'), and *otium* ('leisure' or rest) ... and so literally means 'there is no rest'. Thinking of [the negotiation of meaning] as something that allows no rest helps to underscore the fact that its production is continuous and never complete, and also that it demands active (boundary-)*work*. (Pereira, 2017: 61)

Trans health can be negotiated on a personal level as patients and practitioners navigate practical, emotional and temporal challenges within healthcare systems; it can be negotiated on a collective level as community members engage in identity work and/or practices of mutual support and care; and it can be negotiated on a political level as various parties seek particular changes or continuities within the realm of service provision. In light of these complexities, I follow Kyra Landzelius (2006: 536) in understanding 'patienthood' not simply as a site of 'affliction, treatment and research' but also as a 'field of contention' and the possible basis for 'experiment[s] in power-sharing'. When I refer to people as 'patients', therefore, I do not simply regard them as passive recipients of care, but as active agents involved in the work of negotiation.

The research project

My account of the discursive repertoires of 'trans as condition' and 'trans as movement', plus the negotiation of these discourses by multiple groups, is grounded in the findings of an ethnographic research project undertaken between 2010 and 2017. **Ethnography** involves immersive participant observation within a particular social context, with the aim of understanding and providing an account of the culture and behaviour in this setting.

The fieldwork for this project was undertaken on the internet, in recognition of the great importance of online communities for bringing together the largely disparate and frequently invisible trans population

(Whittle, 1998; Shapiro, 2004). Internet ethnography is a well-established form of social research (Hine, 2000; Kendall, 2002), and this approach enabled me to observe conversations taking place within trans community spaces and activist groups over an extended period of time. It also provided me access to a wide range of blogs and media articles written by trans people, alongside websites and documents produced by and for health professionals and service providers.

With ethnography requiring immersive participation on the part of the researcher, I acquired data in a manner informed by the networked nature of the internet, through pursuing the connections that *could* be made by any individual navigating trans spaces online. I therefore allowed myself to also encounter new research sites as I followed links from one internet space to another. In contrast to the rigid sampling techniques typically used within quantitative 'big data' exercises, this was a form of intentionally *human* mediation, reflecting the 'messiness' of everyday social interaction (Postill and Pink, 2012; Lohman, 2017). In this sense, my behaviour as researcher was shaped by my role as a participant in trans spaces and discourses; a situation both aided and complicated by my pre-existing connections to trans communities. I used one primary criterion to prevent information overload and ensure focus in my findings: I focused on posts, comments, articles and documents that related specifically to *healthcare provision* for trans people, in terms of the provision of medical services by a public or private individual or institution.

A number of sites and spaces operated as 'starting points' for research. Two of these were UK-based trans web forums, which I selected from the first page of results displayed by a search engine. I also started my fieldwork from a small number of Facebook activist groups in which I was already a member. To ensure a range of voices and perspectives from across the trans spectrum, this original selection included forums and groups that, together, hosted a diverse range of trans users. From these starting points, I acquired links to over 100 websites and social media spaces, including additional activist Facebook groups, Twitter hashtags, blog posts, media articles, National Health Service (NHS) websites, reports and documents. These constituted the ethnographic field for the purposes of participant observation and analysis.

In discussing my research findings, I divide the areas in which fieldwork took place into three broad sub-'spheres' from within what I regard as a wider 'transphere' of online spaces. These are the 'activist' sphere, the 'community' sphere and the 'practitioner' sphere. I do not intend to claim that there is any necessary distinction between either individuals or text within these three areas; indeed, there are plenty of activists who participate in community groups or have written documentation as/for practitioners. Instead, I use these overarching groupings to make sense of broad trends and some of the ways in which particular spaces and platforms might facilitate particular activities at a particular point in time.

The **activist sphere** consists of social media space and blog/media articles created with the explicit intention of discussing political issues for trans people and/or organising collective action. For the purposes of this project, the field included seven Facebook groups, the Twitter hashtag #transdocfail (along with related hashtags such as #transdocwin), and a great many articles written for blogs and media organisations. A wide range of political tactics were discussed and/or implemented by individuals organising within these spaces, including protests/pickets, letter-writing campaigns, petitions, information/ awareness drives, event organisation, event disruption and the lobbying of politicians.

For research within the **community sphere**, I primarily followed discussions taking place on two internet forums (also known as message boards). Some of the activist spaces discussed in the previous section were also arguably communities in their own right (or one constituent part of a larger community). However, I use 'community' in this context to refer to the manner in which the forums visited for fieldwork primarily operated as social spaces: their purpose was *specifically* to provide a basis for community in terms of people with a shared experience being able to gather and talk in a casual manner. This differed from the more purposeful, action-oriented nature of spaces within the activist sphere.

The **practitioner sphere** consists of information written both by and/or for medical practitioners on the subject of trans health. I encountered relatively little public discussion involving practitioners. Within this sphere I therefore focused largely on informative websites and documents addressing issues around trans health from the perspective of health professionals within the UK. These included guidance and advice documents for NHS staff and patients, clinical guidance and protocols, gender clinic websites and information on public consultations. The majority of this material was, therefore, written by non-trans professionals who work with trans people. However, there were a number of key documents written and/or influenced by trans professionals and activists.

This book includes a number of indicative quotes from trans people talking about their experiences, used to illustrate common discursive themes present within the field. These are drawn from across the activist and community spheres, as well as from a number of publications produced by other writers. All participants in this project were adults, meaning that I focus largely on adults' experiences and accounts of healthcare services in this book. However, some younger adults (particularly those in their late teens) did reflect on recent experiences of child and adolescent services. While some of these accounts are now a few years old, I have ensured that the quotes used in this book reflected discourses and contemporary reported experiences that I continued to observe into late 2017.

I obtained informed consent from these research participants to reproduce quotes from the web forums as well as Facebook and Twitter. I have taken care to provide anonymity to participants from private spaces, which include the web forums and several 'closed' and 'secret' Facebook groups. I use pseudonyms to refer to these individuals, and in some cases have redacted certain information or quoted my fieldwork diary to ensure that their privacy is protected. In contrast, I wish to openly acknowledge the contribution of individuals writing in *public* contexts such as Twitter, blog posts and media articles. I therefore refer to these individuals with the usernames they chose themselves. All quotes have been reproduced faithfully where possible in order to retain the original 'feel'. For instance, in some cases a limited use of punctuation serves to potentially reflect an individual's anxiety. Further discussion of my methodological decisions in these matters can be found in the Appendix.

I myself am present in the research findings. My data corpus includes blog posts, Facebook comments and tweets that I wrote at various points in the past, observed for the project in instances where they were linked to by other participants. I am further present in my interaction with the field as researcher, my creation of meaning through analysis of data and my own experiences as a trans woman who has accessed a range of healthcare services in the UK, and I draw analytic insight from this. In this sense, my research project was also *auto*ethnographic. **Autoethnography** combines 'ethnography' with 'autobiography', thereby drawing upon personal experience to understand the social world (Ngunjiri et al, 2010). Like Heewon Chang (2016), I seek to combine the artful, emotive insight of 'evocative' autoethnography with a committedly 'analytic' approach to the social world. I thus position myself as a full participant in the research setting, becoming visible as such through personal vignettes such as the story about my experiences at the 'LGBT Health … Who Cares?' event. This approach draws upon a substantial intellectual tradition of autobiographical insight from trans academics,[4] and provides an important contribution to our theoretical (and, by extension, material) understandings of social phenomena (Anderson, 2006).

I do not regard ethnography (let alone autoethnography) as a means to absolute authority in describing the material world; after all, the data generated through the project described in this book broadly represents what *is said* about trans health. However, I work from the foundational assumption that '[l]anguage and speech do not mirror experience; they *create* experience' (Denzin, 1994: 296, emphasis in original). In conducting this study, therefore, I set out how understandings of trans health that shape people's experiences of the world are constructed *through* discussion and representation, in both everyday and institutional contexts.

Structure of the book

This book is located within the field of transgender studies. The field coalesced in response to the othering of trans people within academic literatures prior to the 1990s, with trans people presented as deviant bodies, medical curiosities and/or metaphorical figures stripped of agency in a range of disciplines (Stone, 1991; Stryker, 2006). Transgender studies therefore speaks to discourses around trans possibility and the lived experiences of trans people, but also looks beyond these in demonstrating the relevance of 'trans' insights for wider understandings of social and political phenomena (Stryker and Aizura, 2013). It is an interdisciplinary field, and this is an interdisciplinary book: while I write from a broadly sociological perspective, I also draw upon feminist theory and speak to literatures of trans health within psychological, psychiatric and therapeutic fields.

The next two chapters of this book provide some initial responses to the questions I have raised about discourse, power and possibility. Like this chapter, they provide an important context for later discussions, by describing the historical and social background to activist, community and practitioners' discourses and experiences of trans health.

Chapter Two offers a genealogical account of the discursive repertoires of trans as condition and trans as movement. In this chapter, I describe the negotiation of differing positions on trans condition and movement by health professionals and radical feminists as well as trans patients, activists and academics. In addition to providing a roughly chronological history of ideas, I explore how contemporary trans possibilities have emerged through categorisation and contestation, and explain why medical discourse has played a particularly important role in this process.

Chapter Three focuses on UK healthcare provision in the 2010s. In this chapter, I describe the material context of my research project in terms of both public and private healthcare provision, making visible the systems that trans patients must negotiate to access care. I outline the medical pathway and extensive assessment procedures for the trans 'condition' with reference to clinical guidance and public health documents, while also examining the challenges faced by patients outside of trans-specific services. I show how this context has been shaped by recent political events such as the passage of the Equality Act 2010 and the Health and Social Care Act 2012, as well as by international guidance such as the World Professional Association for Transgender Health (WPATH) *Standards of Care*. The discussion is framed by a description of the power differentials that persist between practitioner and patient.

Two chapters then draw on my research findings in depth, to show how trans people navigate medical discourses and systems. Chapter Four looks primarily at how a considerable number of the ideas and conflicts discussed within Chapter Two remain relevant, as the discursive repertoires of trans as condition and trans as movement continue to operate within the contemporary settings of trans health in the UK. I examine how trans possibilities are both constructed and constrained within and between health services and trans community groups. I draw upon the concept of cisgenderism to show how some trans narratives are rendered *im*possible within certain healthcare settings, due to the power differential between practitioner and patient. I link this process to the challenges that many trans patients encounter in accessing treatment in a range of settings, with reference to the discursive clashes that can occur when health professionals and trans patients subscribe to different notions of trans possibility.

Chapter Five focuses on transitioning patients' collective temporal engagements with systems of healthcare provision that prioritise understandings of trans as condition. This chapter unpacks the emotional experience of waiting, theorising this through a model of 'anticipation'. I examine how the temporal and emotional process of anticipation can shape patients' hopes, worries and despairs, as well as a common mistrust of health professionals. My analysis here utilises theories of trans and queer temporality to show how transitioning patients draw upon community discourses in negotiating the often stringent requirements of assessment and diagnosis.

The last two chapters of the book look at processes and possibilities of change for trans health. In Chapter Six I provide an analysis of 'epistemic politics': that is, the politics of knowledge production. I focus particularly on the process of trans patient advocacy, looking at how individual interventions may contribute to collective efforts for discursive and material change. Drawing on examples from the depathologisation movement, I further examine how trans activists have sought to challenge the practitioner/patient power differential in both the micro-setting of the healthcare encounter and the macro-setting of medical discourse. I demonstrate that these challenges are most successful when trans knowledges are reproduced and established as credible through continual acts of mutual recognition and iterative citation across multiple spaces and contexts.

Finally, in Chapter Seven, I conclude the book with a summary of my arguments, relating these to the two main questions raised in this introduction. I also take a further look at the discursive power wielded by gender identity specialists, and relate this to the manner by which 'trans health' is constituted through the operation of this power. I argue that to best meet the needs of trans patients it is necessary for healthcare service providers to take a more affirmative approach that empowers trans people to more easily take decisions about their own lives.

A transgender tipping point?

The 2010s have been a time of both great change and considerable continuity for trans people. Even as I emerged from a seminar into the grey Birmingham streets with a sense of optimism back in 2009, I could not have anticipated the shifts in public, medical and trans discourse that were to take place over just a few years. The Equality Act 2010 enshrined in law protections from harassment and discrimination for a great many trans people in most areas of public life. The once quite private concerns of trans community and activist groups have become very public, buoyed by the opportunities afforded to them by new platforms in the mainstream and social media. Terms such as trans, genderqueer and non-binary have found their way into dictionaries and newspaper columns, as trans people appear more regularly on television and in film, in dramas, on reality television and in news programmes. In 2014, US magazine *Time* featured out trans woman and *Orange Is The New Black* actress Laverne Cox on its front cover, and declared that 'the transgender tipping point' was at hand; a claim that has since been repeated or interrogated by numerous columnists within the UK media. As I shall show, this very public emergence of trans has also been accompanied by the growing presence and influence of trans people and trans ideas within the sphere of health.

However, as I cast my gaze back, the recent past disappointingly resembles the decades which preceded it. Yes, the present 'tipping point' is perhaps unprecedented in offering some acknowledgement of contemporary movement-oriented trans discourse (as opposed to the more condition-oriented discourses of transvestism and transsexualism that dominated popular discussion in the 20th and early 21st centuries). However, the emergence of high-profile US trans celebrities only echoes the media frenzy over 'GI turned blond bombshell' Christine Jorgensen in the 1950s, whose transition attracted more attention in the news than either the Korean War or the development of the polio vaccine (Stryker, 2008). Moreover, an increased public awareness of trans people and the establishment of new legal rights have not necessarily led to an immediate improvement in the lives of many trans people, particularly with the realm of health. As Aren Aizura (2017: 607) argues, 'recognition may have arrived, but justice for transgender people has not yet begun'. Where gains have occurred, they been uneven, mediated by geography, national and clinical politics and intersecting inequalities on the grounds of class, ethnicity/race, dis/ ability and sexuality (Raha, 2017).

It is no coincidence that I write this book as a white, middle-class person. I have encountered significant difficulties as a trans woman within the academic world as in healthcare systems, but my class and race privilege have aided me enormously in overcoming these challenges. To ensure real, progressive change, it is vital that those of us with any form of privilege use it to lift others up, rather than simply to pursue our own personal goals. I hope that my work within and beyond this book might contribute in some small way to the erosion of intersecting inequalities, helping us to build collectively towards trans liberation.

The very gradual, complex process of change described in the chapters that follow highlights the difficulty and constant challenges of this collective work. There is not one easy narrative in my tale of trans health, with a clear beginning and a neat set of findings and conclusions. However, I identify stories that can help us to understand the shape of the field, the origin and journey of ideas, the interplay of discourse and material experience. The 'tipping point' is too blunt a narrative for this task, denoting as it does a supposed point in time where one state simply gives way to another. By contrast, the threads of 'condition' and 'movement' – and negotiation within and between the two – enable a coherent and productive story to emerge, even as this book delves deep into the myriad investments and multiple complications of trans health.

Notes

[1] Trans Youth Network was a semi-autonomous branch of Queer Youth Network, a primarily internet-based activist and community support group run by and for young LGBTQ people in the UK during the 2000s. A different network with a similar name (The National Trans Youth Network) was created by an alliance of youth groups in 2013.

[2] I do, however, regard 'reality' as socially constructed too, a matter discussed in detail in later chapters of this book. This approach does not undermine the fundamental importance of recognising and affirming people's experiences: rather, it is a philosophical claim about how we perceive the world and generate knowledge.

[3] I generally use 'transgender' interchangeably with 'trans' in this book, as both are employed in a range of settings as umbrella terms and/or fluid categories in a manner similar to that described by Whittle (2006). While my own preference is for 'trans', context occasionally dictates that 'transgender' is more appropriate. For instance, given the great range of words that include the prefix 'trans-', 'transgender' is often used for cataloguing academic work within contemporary online databases and search engines; hence 'transgender studies'. Similarly, as I discuss in Chapter Two, the 'trans movement' initially used 'transgender' to denote solidarity between gender-variant people.

[4] For examples, see Prosser (1998); Ravine (2014); cárdenas (2016); Nicolazzo (2017); Raha (2017).

TWO

Condition or movement? A genealogy of trans discourse

> Here on the gender borders at the close of the twentieth century, with the faltering of phallocentric hegemony and the bumptious appearance of heteroglossic origin accounts, we find the epistemologies of white male medical practice, the rage of radical feminist theories and the chaos of lived gendered experience meeting on the battlefield of the transsexual body: a hotly contested site of cultural inscription, a meaning machine for the production of ideal type. (Sandy Stone, 1991)

Discursive repertoires: unpacking trans possibility

The language of trans identities and experiences is multifaceted and contested. Trans – along with related identities such as non-binary and genderqueer, and concepts such as transition, gender dysphoria, gender diversity and gender-nonconformity – can be variously used to describe individual or collective bodies and histories, medical diagnoses and treatments, social and political phenomena, feelings and emotions. The term 'trans' may be used an adjective (describing an *aspect* of personhood, as in 'they are a trans person') or as a verb (describing what people *do*, as in 'to trans'); it is sometimes also employed as a noun.

While the introduction to this book offered a brief definition of 'trans', this chapter unpacks the multiple, competing and sometimes contradictory means by which the term might be understood. I look at how differing models of trans possibility (and *im*possibility) have arisen from the historical interplay of medical literatures, radical feminist theories and an emergent trans social movement.

'Trans' is historically and socially contingent (Enke, 2012): that is to say, like any other social category it is historically located, and is therefore meaningful in a specific time and place. We might be able to *recognise* experiences and behaviours in a different time and place as somehow trans, but this doesn't mean that they *are* straightforwardly trans, particularly if they weren't or aren't recognised as such by the individuals having these experiences and exhibiting these behaviours.

The language of gender diversity I use in this book emerged largely in the West, primarily within the English and German languages; the stand-alone 'trans' effectively evolved from identities/diagnoses such as 'transsexual' and 'transvestite', while also incorporating political and social influences from lesbian, gay, drag and queer subcultures (Pearce et al, 2018).[1]

This chapter therefore traces a genealogy of trans language in the Western world, exploring where contemporary UK understandings of trans health 'came from'. A genealogical approach acknowledges and examines how subjectivities are *constructed* through social processes: '[w]here a positivist assumes that better science or a more nuanced history could accurately identify and distinguish between categories of sexuality or gender, a genealogist refuses the assumption that individuals exist apart from the historically changing categories that made them' (Rubin, 2003: 483).

In taking a genealogical approach, I do not seek to abstract trans identity through discussion of socio-historical context, nor do I engage extensively in debates around what trans might mean for the supposed naturalisation or destabilisation of binary gender. Rather, I focus on the discourses that have made trans language – and by extension, trans lives as we might understand them today – *possible*. I am interested in how trans lives can become comprehensible, imaginable and liveable. This is necessarily a story about trans health: in terms of the medical discourse from which contemporary trans language has evolved, in terms of the counter-discourses that have emerged from trans communities and in terms of scholarly critiques of medical research from the humanities and social sciences.

Repertoires of possibility

In the previous chapter, I identified two main discursive repertoires of trans possibility: trans as condition, and trans as movement. The repertoire of condition entails understandings of trans as fixed, fixable and/or conditional. Trans in this sense can be clearly defined and also *resolved*, often (but not necessarily) through some form of cure or treatment. In this chapter, I explore understandings of trans as condition in the context of evolving medical discourses, 'transgenderist' subjectivities and radical feminist accounts.

The repertoire of movement entails a continual potential for and actuality of change, being linked to queer notions of fluidity and the constant *work* of negotiation (Green, 2017; Pereira, 2017). This can entail individual movement – through identities that are not necessarily fixed or resolvable – as well as collective social movement; I explore the relationship between the two through a discussion of transgender studies and the notion of trans solidarity.

In addition to exploring difference and diversity *within* these broad categories, I examine how the two repertoires intersect and influence one another. The final two sections of this chapter work to avoid the limiting notion of a condition/movement binary by respectively exploring the place of 'condition' within understandings of trans as movement, and of 'movement' within understandings of trans as condition. The former section looks at how recent sociological studies incorporated condition-oriented identities within broadly movement-oriented accounts of trans community, focusing particularly on Surya Monro's concept of 'gender pluralism'. The latter shows how recent interventions from health professionals have sought to acknowledge movement-oriented trans identities and experiences.

Condition and cure: fixing trans

Sexual inversion

Late 19th century and early 20th century accounts of gender diversity often conflated experiences that we now describe as 'trans' with wider forms of gendered and sexual difference, including intersex bodies, gay, lesbian, bisexual and/or asexual preferences, and acts of gender nonconformity. Sexologists such as Richard von Krafft-Ebing (1877 [2006]) sought to account for gender/sexual diversity through an extensive process of differential categorisation, identifying a myriad of deviant traits such as 'androgyny', 'gynandry' and 'defemination'. However, 'umbrella terms' also emerged to more broadly refer to individuals who deviated from sexual norms by behaving (or identifying their behaviour) in a manner associated with the 'opposite' sex. One such term was **invert**, popularised by sexologist Havelock Ellis (Stryker, 2008) For example, a 'female invert' – that is, a gender-variant individual assigned a female gender at birth[2] – might have a 'male' frame, dress and smoke like a man, be assertive, uninterested in needlework and sexually attracted to (or active with) women (Prosser, 1998; Rubin, 2003).

While his views on the matter were to shift with time, Krafft-Ebing initially regarded individuals exhibiting what we might now understand as lesbian, gay, bisexual or trans behaviour as 'profoundly disturbed', and described any desire on their part for 'self-affirming transformation' as psychotic (Stryker and Whittle, 2006: 21). Henry Rubin (2003) argues that such accounts laid the groundwork for treatments that aimed to 'cure' inverts of their 'condition'. From the 1930s through to the 1950s, endocrinologists drew upon the emerging science of hormones to administer hormone therapy to inverts. If the inversion was considered 'acquired' (through social factors such as nurture), then a 'homo-sexual' hormone regime – 'oestrogens for [assigned] females and testosterone for [assigned] males' – was seen as necessary to restore normal sexual behaviour (Rubin, 2003: 489). Conversely, if the inversion was considered 'innate', then 'hetero-sexual' hormones could be used to 'hormonally castrate inverts and prevent them from acting out their pathological nature' (Rubin, 2003: 498). 'Hetero-sexual' hormonal treatments were most often employed in the administration of oestrogen to assigned male patients.[3] The provision of testosterone to 'female' inverts was seen as risky, as it could increase their libido, thereby undermining the normative role of women as sexually passive.

The apparent failure of endocrinology to cure inversion informed a shift towards psychological and psychiatric treatments in the 1950s, including psychoanalysis and aversion therapy. With reference to a corpus of case notes from the 1950s and 1960s, Rubin (2003: 493–496) contends that nascent female-to-male (FTM) accounts can be identified in these notes, with a number of patients requesting access to hormone therapies in order to facilitate a physical transition from female to male.[4] However, as in the early work of Krafft-Ebing, the health professionals in these instances typically regarded their patients as deluded. Rubin (2003: 496) describes a range of practices that misgendered and pathologised patients: '[t]he use of the female pronoun throughout these cases, plus the ubiquitous comments on the normal physiological condition of these patients, indicates the psychologists' beliefs that these patients are delusional'. This attitude towards perceived gender deviance can be understood as one just part of a wider pathologisation of all and any gendered behaviour that departed from upper- and middle-class white male norms. As Jemma Tosh (2016) observes, psychiatric terminology and treatments for 'abnormal' sexual expression evolved alongside diagnoses such as 'hysteria', which pathologised and punished women both for conforming to social norms and expectations regarding appropriate feminine behaviour and for rejecting these norms too strenuously.

The logic of inversion could, however, also be used to *affirm* the gendered experiences of those who deviated from the norm. The most prominent example of this can be found in Radclyffe Hall's (1928) novel *The Well of Loneliness*, which sees (assigned female) protagonist Stephen Gordon struggle at length with normative expectations of gender and sexuality, due to her desire to live as a boy and her sexual attraction to women. Upon reading Krafft-Ebing's *Psychopathia Sexualis*, Stephen comes to regard her[5] difference as pathological and herself as inherently damaged; however, she later comes across the more affirmative work of Havelock Ellis, who regarded inversion as a form of natural difference. Although Stephen arguably never fully comes to terms with her deviance from sexual norms, the book functions to both promote the category of inversion and reflect the sexual identity of its author (Prosser, 1998; Rubin, 2003). Inversion is, of course, as much a historically and socially contingent identity as trans, which is illustrated in Jay Prosser's (1998) reading of Stephen as a trans man. However, the important point here is that inversion could be embraced as a productive identity and account of selfhood in a similar manner to the 'trans' terminologies of transvestism, transsexualism and transgenderism that would follow. As a *condition*, inversion did not simply entail invasive medical management; it also opened up certain *possibilities*, providing a basis for self-understanding and stable non-normative subjectivity.

Transvestism and transsexualism: grounds for transition?

Magnus Hirschfeld's book *The Transvestites* offered an alternative model to inversion, which recognised a difference between what we might now refer to as sexuality and gender expression. In a forerunner of feminist work on the sex/gender distinction, as well as trans and intersex accounts of sex/gender complexity, Hirschfeld's (1910 [1991]) theory of sexual intermediaries distinguishes four distinct aspects of sexual difference: 'sexual organs', 'other physical characteristics', 'sex drive' and 'other emotional characteristics'. This account contrasts with the conflation of these characteristics within discourses of inversion, and provided grounds for distinguishing between transvestites and homosexuals. Moreover, Hirschfeld seeks to highlight the social contingency of certain gendered norms: for instance, he provides a proverbial account of a young, naked boy unable to recognise similarly naked girls *as* girls because they were undressed. That is to say: it is the girls' clothing that *makes* them girls in the eyes of the young boy. This aspect of Hirschfeld's work foreshadows later trans-positive feminist accounts of the role that gender presentation plays in shaping presumptions about genital status. For example, Suzanne Kessler and Wendy McKenna (1978) draw on the work of Harold Garfinkel to discuss how an individual's gender is socially assigned on the basis of their (assumed) genital status. Since genitals are not usually seen in Western society, observers rely on an individual's (imagined) 'cultural genitals', which are in turn shaped by how an individual appears to 'do' gender. Talia Mae Bettcher (2007: 54) expands on these observations, noting that 'the very gendered attire which is designed to conceal [the] body ... represents genital status'.

In contrast to later uses of the term **transvestite**, however, Hirschfeld's work does not simply refer to individuals who desired to engage in gender-variant *behaviour* such as cross-dressing. For Hirschfeld, 'transvestite' signals a range of subject conditions that might – according to patient need or desire – be affirmed and/or cured. In 1919 he founded the Institut für Sexualwissenschaft (Institute for Sexual Science) in Berlin, which both employed transvestites and – in collaboration with endocrinologists and surgeons – provided some of the first tailored medical procedures for patients seeking to transition from male to female or vice-versa (Stryker, 2008: 39).

Later writers sought to delineate different forms of gender-variant condition. Where transvestism came to refer specifically to the practice of (and/or an identity centred on) cross-dressing, **transsexualism** (or transsexuality) – popularised by Harry Benjamin (1966) in *The Transsexual Phenomenon* – specifically described individuals who sought to live permanently in the 'opposite sex'. The figure of the transsexual emerged through extensive negotiation between practitioners and patients across a number of decades as individuals actively sought treatment by approaching health professionals – including Hirschfeld and his one-time colleague Benjamin – to request medical interventions such as hormone therapy and genital or chest surgeries (Stone, 1991; Meyerowitz, 2002; Rubin, 2003). Benjamin's work represented an attempt to take these patients seriously, with his 1966 book in particular providing a guide for both the diagnosis of transsexualism and the management of transition. Consequently, 'transsexuals became recognizable' – *possible* – and treatments became more widely available (Rubin, 2003: 489).

As with Radclyffe Hall's experience of inversion, the transvestite and transsexual models have provided a liveable identity for many (Namaste, 2000; Ekins and King, 2006; Hines, 2007; Davy, 2011). This was particularly the case with transsexualism after the 'male-to-female' (MTF) transition story of Christine Jorgensen – a patient of Benjamin's – received a great deal of media attention in 1952 (Stryker, 2008: 48–49). Jorgensen's sudden fame served to popularise a terminology and language by which gender-variant individuals might come to describe themselves and reify their experiences, particularly as Benjamin ultimately used the incident as an opportunity to promote his model of a supposed transvestite/transsexual distinction. Both

Jorgensen's story and Benjamin's work ultimately provided a language by which individuals wishing to transition could understand themselves *as transsexual* and seek treatment accordingly. I explore contemporary examples of this in Chapter Four.

However, many health professionals continued to regard transsexualism, like inversion, as the product of a deficient mind and/or body. For example, David Cauldwell (1949: 274) describes the 'psychopathic transexual [sic]' as 'an individual who is unfavorably affected psychologically [and] determines to live and appear as a member of the sex to which he or she does not belong'. While Cauldwell – citing Hirschfeld – acknowledges that transsexual individuals can live productive and 'useful' lives, his own account (drawing upon a single FTM case study) portrays the transsexual as a figure prone to lies and deceit, misleading practitioners, his family and – most of all – himself.[6] The trope of the 'deceptive transsexual' would later populate large parts of the medical literature (Stone, 1991), and has also become common within wider social and political discourses (Bettcher, 2007; Serano, 2007).[7] In this way, transsexualism can be regarded as a condition associated with wider mental health issues, requiring psychological, psychiatric and/or psychotherapeutic management rather than medically mediated physical interventions.

Benjamin, by contrast, acknowledged that many of his patients could benefit from physical transition. He regarded transvestism and transsexualism as complex phenomena, and sought to distinguish the different ways in which these conditions might manifest. He initially outlined three forms of MTF desire and behaviour. The 'principally psychogenic transvestite' does not 'want to be changed, but wants society's attitude towards him [sic] to change', seeking typically to dress 'in the clothes of a female' and 'lead a woman's life' (Benjamin, 1954: 48–49). The 'somatopsychic transsexualist', however, exhibits an 'intense and often obsessive desire to change the entire sexual status including anatomical structure' (46). Therefore, while the MTF transvestite '*enacts* the role of a *woman*, the transsexualist wants to *be* one and *function* as one' (46, emphasis in original). Recognising that his patients didn't always fit neatly into these two categories, Benjamin also noted the existence of 'the intermediate type', who 'inclines towards transsexualism, but is at other times content with merely dressing and acting as a woman' (49). While the transvestite and the intermediate type can, according to Benjamin, generally be provided with psychotherapy to help them manage their condition, this is not the case with the transsexualist, for whom this is a 'waste of time' (51). It is for this reason that Benjamin advocates for the provision of 'conversion surgery' for such individuals, with hormone therapy to follow in order to mitigate the impact of physical castration. However, he also argued that psychiatrists should play a role in assessing patients to ensure their psychological suitability for the procedure. This laid the groundwork for a mode of treatment that continues to this day.

By the 1980s, 'a routine set of procedures and protocols for medically managing transgender populations had fallen into place' (Stryker, 2008: 112). In 1979 the Harry Benjamin International Gender Dysphoria Association (later the World Professional Association for Transgender Health, or WPATH) was created by clinicians working broadly within the paradigm Benjamin had established. They issued a document entitled *The Standards of Care*, which outlined how transsexualism could be assessed and managed. A year later, in 1980, differential diagnoses for transsexualism – as 'gender identity disorder' – and transvestism were published in the third edition of the American Psychiatric Association's internationally recognised *Diagnostic and Statistical Manual of Mental Disorders* (DSM-III). An updated version of this diagnosis – **gender dysphoria** – can be found in the current edition of the manual, DSM-5.

A number of gender identity disorders (including 'transsexualism' and 'dual role transvestism', along with 'fetishistic transvestism' as a 'disorder of sexual preference') are also included in the 10th edition of the World Health Organization's (1992) *International Classification of Diseases and Related Health Problems* (ICD-10). At the time of writing, this is the current edition of the ICD: however, ICD-11 is due to be published in 2018. This will replace the current gender identity diagnoses with a new category, gender incongruence.

The power of a diagnosis

The creation of gender identity disorder (and gender dysphoria) diagnoses has had four important consequences for trans people. Firstly, it placed a capstone on the process of pathologisation that had gradually unfolded for over a century. In seeking to categorise gender-variant conditions, sexologists succeeded in framing deviation from (binary) gender norms as pathological – that is, a disease, illness or medical condition – even when the deviating individuals in question do not seek a medical intervention of any kind.

Secondly, gender identity disorders have relied on binary divisions between female and male, transvestism and transsexualism that persist to this day, even as 'intermediate types' (Benjamin, 1954) proliferate within trans communities and medical accounts. While the actual term 'transvestite' is less popular as a contemporary form of identification, a line continues to be drawn between trans people who 'require' physical transition and those who (supposedly) do not, within both medical and social contexts. This has placed an onus upon trans people to prove themselves 'trans enough' within both community and healthcare settings (Catalano, 2015; Vincent, 2016), informing the emergence of hierarchies of trans identity that sometimes valorise medical interventions and other times celebrate the 'transgressive' nature of those who do not desire physical transition (Bornstein, 1994; Serano, 2007).

Thirdly, while many health professionals who are *not* gender identity specialists continue to echo Cauldwell (1949) in regarding transsexualism primarily as a mental health issue that cannot be treated through physical intervention (Schonfield and Gardner, 2008; Bailey and McNeil, 2013), *formal diagnoses can ensure that treatment is available.*[8] In the UK, access to gender identity services through the NHS is a legal right, following a number of important court victories for trans rights advocates in the 1990s and 2000s. A number of trans health specialists have argued that the existence of gender identity diagnoses underpins this right, providing a clear basis for public funds to be allocated to gender identity services (Richards et al, 2015; Barrett, 2016; Drescher et al, 2016).

Fourthly and finally, the creation of gender identity disorders has worked to construct a professional class of gender identity *experts*, who may act as **gatekeepers** for trans-specific healthcare. These individuals are variously responsible for assessing and managing patients seeking physical transition, discussing quantitative research and case studies in the clinical literatures, preparing protocols and care pathways for patients and peer-reviewing these studies, protocols and care pathways (Lev, 2009; De Cuypere et al, 2013; Bouman et al, 2014). This process of knowledge production has granted health professionals power not only over medical processes, but also over the *trans identities that emerge from these processes* (Stone, 1991; Davy, 2015). It can also work to delegitimise accounts emerging *from trans people* working in the social sciences and humanities, reflecting wider epistemic hierarchies in which work on gender from marginalised peoples (as in feminist scholarship) is framed as partially outside the realm of proper knowledge (Hird, 2003; Pereira, 2012). This can be observed in an imbalance of citation between the interdisciplinary field of transgender studies – in which the medical literatures are frequently referenced – and the medical literatures of gender identity, in which authors often only cite and speak to others in the field (although this is beginning to change, as I discuss later).[9] Similarly, Zowie Davy describes how the DSM-5 workgroup 'disregarded the plethora of work in feminist social science which criticizes the inherency of gender roles, gender identities, and sex differences, as well as research in transgender studies that depicts non-dysphoric transpeople, desires for different embodiments, non-conventional transitioning trajectories, and sexualities' (Davy, 2015: 1170).

There are, nevertheless, multiple discourses of trans possibility present within the medical literatures (Richards et al, 2014). For example, in recent years many specialists working with transitioning patients have argued against the pathologisation of trans identities and experiences (Bockting, 2009; Bouman et al, 2010; Richards et al, 2015). An alternative medical model instead emphasises psychological *distress* for the purposes of diagnosis (Nieder et al, 2016). Some writers have focused upon the distress of gendered incongruence (such as Nieder and Strauss, 2015), while others have emphasised the distress of belonging to a marginalised social group: 'it is the discrimination rather than the membership of this specific group which is psychopathogenic' (Richards et al, 2016: 97). These positions are, however, complicated by the maintenance of assessment procedures that continue to centre expert diagnosis conducted by gender identity specialists (Ahmad et al, 2013; Royal College of Psychiatrists, 2013). Endocrinologist Leighton Seal argues that psychiatric assessment and diagnosis of transitioning patients is necessary to ensure that:

> other possible diagnoses are excluded where hormonal and surgical intervention is not of benefit, such as psychosis, bipolar depression, or dysmorphia. With a rise in queer culture and exploration of gender identity, medical treatment is not always in the patient's best interest in people with gender non-conformity. (Seal, cited in Morgan, 2016: 207)

The resulting tension between **depathologisation** and the role of clinical expertise can be seen for instance in Version 7 of the WPATH *Standards of Care* (Davy et al, 2018). Furthermore, misunderstandings continue to play out within clinical settings between gender identity specialists and patients who do not easily 'fit' diagnostic categories, as well as those who object to the strict criteria and extensive process of assessment associated with physical transition pathways (Bauer et al, 2009; Burke, 2011; Davy, 2011; Ellis et al, 2015).

In contrast to these tentative moves towards *de*pathologisation, misgendering practices comparable to those described by Henry Rubin have persisted within the literatures of psychology and psychiatry. Y Gavriel Ansara and Peter Hegarty (2012) describe how the practice of casting trans patient experiences into doubt by disregarding their stated gender identities and/or preferred gendered pronouns has been maintained in the field of psychology by an 'invisible college', centred around prolific American-Canadian author Kenneth Zucker. The invisible college consists of a network of collaborating authors who work to maintain their collective academic profile through co-authorship, mutual peer review and publishing in one another's journals. This has enabled authors such as Zucker to represent forms of ethnocentric, anti-trans 'aversive conditioning' as good practice; examples include working with parents to restrict gender expression in children (Hird, 2003; Ansara and Hegarty, 2012), or 'shaming' children and parents into pursuing conformity (Pyne, 2014). In this way, Zucker – a co-author of DSM-5 and the Version 7 WPATH *Standards of Care* – maintained his academic credentials and role as head of a Toronto gender clinic for many years, even as numerous allegations of unethical, controlling or otherwise inappropriate behaviour were made by academics, activists and former patients (Hird, 2003; Tosh, 2011; Pyne, 2014).[10]

Medical diagnoses can therefore work to both make trans lives *possible* and limit the liveable scope of these possibilities. The following chapters of this book demonstrate how the interaction of the outlined four consequences of diagnosis has complexly impacted upon the liveability of trans lives.

An 'intermediate type': the transgenderists

I have previously noted that sexological categories of condition – including inversion, transvestism and transsexualism – provided the basis for personal identity claims through the reification of gender-variant experience. I now turn to examine how *non-medical* condition-oriented trans identities can emerge, through an examination of US activist, academic and community organiser Virginia Prince's work. This discussion accordingly draws upon the wider notion of 'condition' outlined in the introduction to this book; a fixed or resolvable, yet conditional mode of being.

Prince (1973 [2005]) draws upon the work of Magnus Hirschfeld and the ideas of the fledgling women's liberation movement to argue for a distinction between 'sex' and 'gender' within accounts of MTF experience. Like Harry Benjamin, she seeks to distinguish between transsexuals and transvestites, arguing that while both groups 'do' the same thing – that is, wear the clothes of the 'opposite' gender – they do so for different reasons. She further distinguishes between transvestites who cross-dress for sexual reasons (a category inclusive of both gay men and the 'fetishistic transvestite' who was later to appear in the DSM and ICD) and 'femiphile' transvestites. While MTF transsexuals seek a sex *change* to live as women, femiphile transvestites seek *recognition* as women without having to physically transition: 'my gender, my self-identity is between my ears, not between my legs' (Prince, 1973 [2005]: 30).

As Prince's thinking developed, she came to regard some femiphilic transvestites – including herself – as 'transgenderists'.[11] She outlines her thinking in this regard in an article entitled 'The "transcendents" or "trans" people' (Prince, 1978 [2005]); an early example of the stand-alone 'trans' being used as an umbrella term for a range of gender-variant identities and experiences. In contrast to those femiphiles who shifted between 'female' and 'male' modes of living and gendered presentation (later to be termed 'dual role transvestites' in ICD-10), transgenderists 'are people who have adopted the exterior manifestations of the opposite sex on a full-time basis but without any surgical intervention' (Prince, 1978 [2005]: 43). In this sense, they are an alternative form of 'intermediate type' to that described by Benjamin (1954).

Prince's writings – distributed largely through her magazine *Transvestia* – are therefore important in offering an alternative form of *knowledge* to medical accounts of trans phenomena. However, her works also resemble these accounts in providing a categorical, prescriptive sense of trans possibility. The bounds of femiphile and transgenderist possibility are quite clearly delineated: such people are assigned male at birth, necessarily sexually attracted to women, do not (in the long term) have a sexual motivation for cross-dressing and do not wish to physically transition. These are, therefore, accounts that ultimately rely upon the binary divisions of male/female and masculine/feminine while working to exclude FTM and non-binary expressions of gendered possibility, reflecting the strict rules by which Prince controlled membership of the social groups she oversaw (Stryker, 2008: 55; Hill, 2013). Moreover, the dissemination of Prince's writings within the professional realm was limited by the aforementioned positioning of medical practitioners as 'trans experts' who presided over both the transition process *and* wider expressions of trans identity. Susan Stryker (2005) notes that in a preamble to Prince's first-known article in a formal academic journal she is 'vouched for' by Harry Benjamin. This demonstrates the manner in which expertise was historically located not simply in the medical professions, but also within the detached perspective of *non-trans* writers. As Susan Stryker (2005: xvi) notes, '[Prince] was a superbly well-educated person with medical credentials of her own … yet, because she was openly a transvestite, Prince could speak "only" as a transvestite, and not as a medical expert whose professional knowledges and competencies were respected by her professional peers.'

Shadows of the empire: radical feminist critiques

An alternative non-medical model of trans as condition is articulated by a particular branch of radical feminist thinking. During the 1970s, a number of feminists began to critique what they saw as an unquestioning reification of sexist gender norms by trans people and health professionals alike. This is exemplified in Janice Raymond's (1979) *The Transsexual Empire*, a book that Sandy Stone (1991: 223) characterises as arguing that 'transsexuals are constructs of an evil phallocentric empire and were designed to invade women's spaces and appropriate women's power'.

In a similar manner to the poststructuralist trans theorists I cited towards the beginning of this chapter, Raymond (1979: xv) notes the historical contingency of the transsexual phenomenon, and the manner by which practitioners such as Benjamin 'make transsexualism a reality' by offering treatment. However, she differs in positing that transsexualism has been constructed as an 'individual solution' to the social problem of rigid sexual stereotyping within 'a patriarchial society, which generates norms of masculinity and femininity' (Raymond, 1979: 70). Instead of fighting these norms, surgeons and psychologists have reified them by creating a means by which 'men' can be 'transsexually constructed' into women.

Raymond (1979: 26–27) ultimately regards transsexualism as a *male* activity: 'a creation of men, initially developed for men', with the 'female-to-constructed-male transsexual' being 'the *token* that saves face for the male "transsexual empire"' (emphasis in original). She observes that the vast majority of authors writing within the contemporaneous medical field of transsexualism were men, even as psychiatric accounts of the transsexual condition frequently attributed its genesis to the role of unruly women, with (for example) overbearing mothers held responsible for feminising children assigned a male gender at birth.[12] Moreover, she draws upon interview data, anecdotes, media reports and transsexual autobiographies to argue that trans women define themselves as female 'in terms of the classic feminine stereotype' (78).

This entails passive, nurturing behaviour, an interest in feminine clothes and make-up, a belief in traditional heterosexual gender roles and a preference for occupations such as housework and secretarial employment. The exception to this can be found in the 'transsexually constructed lesbian-feminist', who brings 'masculinity and masculinist behaviour' into women-only feminist spaces (101). In this way, the activities of stereotypically heterosexual, feminine trans women *and* the behaviour of lesbian-feminist trans women represent different means by which 'men' might problematically occupy womanhood: '[a]ll transsexuals rape women's bodies by reducing the real female form to an artefact, appropriating this body for themselves' (104). Raymond therefore asserts that '[t]ranssexuals are *not* women … they are *deviant males*' (183, emphasis in original). With Raymond taking the view that gender is socially and biologically determined in line with (binary) designations at birth, she recommends an alternative, *feminist* solution to this deviant condition: that of counselling and peer support through feminist consciousness-raising.

The Transsexual Empire provides an ideological and analytic basis for a strand of 'trans-exclusionary' radical feminist thought that continues to be represented in both academic and popular media contexts to this day. Writers such as Bernice Hausman (1995) and Germaine Greer (1999) argue that trans women embody and reify sexist stereotypes of womanhood; Sheila Jeffreys (2014) echoes Raymond in accusing transsexuals of 'invading' women's spaces; Julie Bindel (2009) has called for hormone therapies and genital surgeries to be replaced with counselling and therapy. However, these accounts have done little to build upon Raymond's (1979) theoretical and empirical work. Moreover, they have been largely superseded by trans-affirming and trans feminist accounts in terms of wider ideological resonance and praxis within contemporary feminist scholarship and activism (Bettcher, 2009; Elliot, 2009; Bunch, 2013).

Ironically, for all that Raymond and her followers criticise the medical establishment, their accounts also echo certain medical discourses of trans possibility. Even as they denounce transsexual people and health professionals for reinforcing sexist stereotypes, they subscribe to a binary notion of sex and gender rooted in biological determinism, through asserting that trans women will always *really* be men, trans men will always *really* be women, and that sex/gender can be understood only in terms of a male/female binary. This perspective goes beyond the somewhat binary thinking of Benjamin (1966), who at least provides some narrative space and clinical provision for the possibility of movement through sex *change*. It ultimately echoes the view of the

1950s psychologists described by Rubin (2003), and informs a practice of misgendering and misrecognition similar to that described within contemporary psychological and psychiatric literatures by Ansara and Hegarty (2012). In taking this perspective – and in effectively outlining a form of *treatment* for transsexual deviancy – Raymond and her followers thereby similarly regard trans as condition: definable, resolvable, fixable, curable. Furthermore, they position *non-trans* expertise as the appropriate basis for knowledge about trans lives, thereby effectively objectifying and silencing trans voices (Namaste, 2000; Serano, 2007).

'A movement whose time has come': the emergence of 'trans'

Sandy Stone's (1991) *The Empire Strikes Back: A Posttranssexual Manifesto* provides a nuanced response to Raymond. Stone rejects many of Raymond's more outlandish claims, but also accepts and expands upon her arguments regarding sexism and the reification of traditional gender roles within medical systems. Together with works such as Leslie Feinberg's (1992) influential pamphlet *Transgender Liberation: A Movement Whose Time Has Come*, this laid the groundwork for the emergence of transgender studies (Stryker, 2006). Drawing upon the insights of feminist and queer theories, the embodied realities of marginalised trans peoples and the extensive medical literature of transsexualism, transgender studies enabled the 'establishment of subjects in new modes, regulated by different codes of intelligibility' (Stryker, 1994: 248). I characterise these as modes of *movement*, shaped by new codes of individual and collective trans understanding.

Individual movement: the gender outlaws

Stone (1991) argues that Raymond's portrayal of transsexual women as intentionally complicit in upholding and reifying gender norms is both simplistic and misleading. She focuses her analysis particularly on the role that gender identity specialists play in socially constructing transsexualism. Raymond (1979: 135) states that gender identity specialists engage in 'behavioural modification' procedures, but she does not analyse these processes in any depth, nor does she link this discussion back to her earlier account of passive, stereotypically feminine heterosexual trans women. Stone therefore examines Raymond's claims with reference to a wider field of evidence. She focuses upon the gendered discourses present within transsexual women's autobiographies, noting that – at first sight – the concerns raised by Raymond and her followers seem quite legitimate:

> All these [transsexual] authors replicate the stereotypical male account of the constitution of woman: dress, makeup, and delicate fainting at the sight of blood. Each of these adventurers passes directly from one pole of sexual experience [male, attracted to women] to the other [female, attracted to men]. If there is any intervening space in the continuum of sexuality, it is invisible…. No wonder feminist theorists have been suspicious. Hell, *I'm* suspicious. (Stone, 1991: 227, emphasis in original)

Later trans feminist theorists such as Julia Serano (2007) argue that Raymond's account holds trans women to a different standard to *non*-trans women, as plenty of women from all backgrounds adhere to gendered norms. Others have noted the restrictive cultural conditions under which these accounts were published: '[u]p until the last few years, all we'd be able to write *and get published* were our autobiographies, tales of women trapped in the bodies of men or men pining away in the bodies of women … the romantic stuff which set our image as long-suffering, not the challenging stuff' (Bornstein, 1994: 12–13, emphasis in original).

Stone's critique, however, focuses on the role of medical literature and practice in constructing the **traditional transsexual narrative** found within autobiographical accounts. Acknowledging that the early gender clinics were ultimately 'in the business of helping people', Stone (1991: 227–228) explains how their treatment criteria nevertheless favoured patients who seemed most likely to 'succeed' in navigating the world in their new gender role: '[i]n practice this meant that the candidates for surgery were evaluated on the basis of their *performance* in their gender of choice' (emphasis in original); a performance that extended to autobiographical accounts. Stone further examines how the publication of Benjamin's *The Transsexual Phenomenon* effectively provided a manual for patients seeking to transition. This created a discursive feedback loop in which many patients met the expectations of health professionals (or pretended to do so) in order to access treatment, thereby reinforcing the idea that 'true' transsexuals necessarily conform to such stereotypes. The resulting situation was clearly not conducive either to the advancement of medical knowledge or to the long-term possibility of gender fluidity for those who transitioned.

Stone therefore concludes her article by calling for the creation of a 'posttranssexual' counter-discourse. Where the traditional transsexual is 'totalized' by conditional discourses, Stone advocates for posttranssexual identities and experiences that are diverse and complex. Where the traditional transsexual is 'programmed to disappear' by undertaking an appropriate gender performance, she calls upon the posttranssexual to 'forgo passing, to be consciously "read", to read oneself aloud – and by this troubling and productive reading, to write oneself into the discourses by which one has been written' (Stone, 1991: 232). In this way, Stone imagines a new mode of being: a form of living that acknowledges and embraces movement in terms of gendered discourse, identity and embodiment. Further posttranssexual accounts of gendered possibility would follow. Like Stone, these works typically drew upon recent innovations in feminist and gender theory, including the cyborg feminism of Donna Haraway (1991) and Judith Butler's (1999) account of gender as performative: that is, constructed and reified through continual social (inter)action.

In response to an invocation of Frankenstein (and his monster) by Raymond (1979) in her discussion of the medical construction of transsexual bodies, Susan Stryker (1994) theorises transsexualism as 'monstrous' in her paper 'My words to Victor Frankenstein above the village of Chamounix: performing transgender rage'. While the paper does not explicitly reference her work, Stryker effectively echoes Haraway's (1991) 'Cyborg Manifesto' in celebrating the revolutionary feminist potential in transformative technologies of the body: '[t]o encounter the transsexual body, to apprehend a transsexual consciousness articulating itself, is to risk a revelation of the constructedness of the natural order' (Stryker, 1994: 250). This process of articulation is grounded in transgender rage, a 'queer fury' that arises in response to the *unliveability* of normative gender roles. Stryker illustrates the origins of transgender rage with a story about the birth of her lover's baby. As the baby is born, somebody declares, 'it's a girl'. In this utterance, Stryker locates an important moment of gendered violence: the *non-consensual* assignment of gender at birth. At this moment various norms are imposed upon the gendered body; norms that form the basis of patriarchal power relations, norms that will eventually compel the trans subject to enter 'a domain of abjected bodies, a field of deformation' (Butler, 1993: 16). Transgender rage provides a means of revolt against this 'naturalized order': 'by mobilizing gendered identities and rendering them provisional, open to strategic development and occupation' (Stryker, 1994: 248). Transgender rage therefore responds to the fixity of binary gender norms – *and* to the seeming fixity of the transsexual condition – through reimagining notions of gendered identity, imbuing them with a sense of fluidity and movement that reflects the constructedness of the transsexual body.

An altogether more playful account of identity as *movement* can be found in Kate Bornstein's (1994) book *Gender Outlaw*. Like Stryker (1994), Bornstein draws extensively upon her personal experiences of transition to illustrate an account of gendered possibility through revolt against the 'natural' order. 'Standing outside of a "natural" gender', she explains, 'I thought I was some kind of monster, I thought it was my fault' (Bornstein, 1994: 12). Building on Butler's description of gender performativity, Bornstein questions how she might render the artificial bounds of gender visible, and furthermore seek to live beyond these bounds as neither female *nor* male. Having originally transitioned from male to female in line with the traditional transsexual narrative, Bornstein finds herself feeling that her experience is neither that of a 'man' *or* of a 'woman'. Her account therefore paves the way for a multiplicity of gendered possibilities beyond the male/female binary: 'there are as many truthful experiences of gender as there are people who think they have a gender' (Bornstein, 1994: 8). While an acceptance of gendered multiplicity, complexity and fluidity is portrayed by Bornstein as a potentially liberating means to make 'gender outlaw' lives more liveable, she does not have a clear account of how this might be achieved. 'I love the idea of being without an identity, it gives me a lot of room to play around', she states, 'but it makes me dizzy, having nowhere to hang my hat' (Bornstein, 1994: 39). I therefore move next to explore how Stone, Stryker and Bornstein's imagined 'different codes of intelligibility' (Stryker, 1994: 248) were *implemented* through the collective action of a new social movement.

Social movement: collective transgender solidarity

The term **transgender** certainly existed prior to its use by Leslie Feinberg. However, it tended to refer to individual relationships to gender diversity, as in Prince's (1978 [2005]) 'transgenderist', which specifically described male-assigned individuals seeking to live permanently as women without medical intervention. In calling for *transgender solidarity*, Feinberg played an important role in popularising transgender – and later, the stand-alone 'trans' – as the basis for a *social movement*, a politicised version of Prince's (1978 [2005]) 'trans people'.

Feinberg argues that a language is needed to bring together people with a shared experience of marginalisation on the grounds of gender variance, while also recognising differences between these people.

This would be a language *by and for* trans people, as an alternative to externally imposed terminologies.

> When I first worked in the factories of Buffalo as a teenager, women like me were called 'he-shes' … There are other words used to express the wide range of "gender outlaws": transvestites, transsexuals, drag queens and drag kings, cross-dressers, bull-daggers, stone butches, androgynes, diesel dykes … We didn't choose these words. They don't fit all of us. It's hard to fight oppression without a name connoting pride, a language that honours us. (Feinberg, 1992: 206)

Notably, Feinberg lists the medical terms 'transvestite' and 'transsexual' alongside a range of other stigmatised identities. There is a racial and class dimension to this divide between medical and non-medical terminology, particularly within the US context in which Feinberg was writing. The cultural and financial capital required to access medical literature and/or a formal diagnosis was historically more likely to be held by white, middle- and upper-class trans people (Koyama, 2004; Stryker, 2008). Subcultures such as drag scenes, sex worker collectives and butch/femme communities therefore offered a means by which more marginalised individuals could build community around gender diversity (Munt, 1998; Rivera, 2002; Valentine, 2007; Ware, 2017). There also tended to be a divide between the more restrained, assimilationist advocacy undertaken by relatively privileged individuals such as Virginia Prince, and the more militant activism undertaken by economically and racially marginalised trans people through groups such as New York's Street Tranvestite Action Revolutionaries.

Feinberg's priority is *unity* between transgender people, regardless of their background. In stating that '[g]enuine bonds of solidarity can be forged between people who respect each other's differences', sie argues from a Marxist perspective for a single trans movement, united through shared but diverse experiences of oppression (Feinberg, 1992: 220). In this way, hir work incorporated movement away from strictly delineated identities and externally imposed gender identities in a similar manner to Stone, Stryker and Bornstein, while also seeking to incorporate these individual movements into a collective *social movement* inspired by the activism of working-class trans people, trans people of colour, sex workers, drag kings and drag queens. While inversion, transvestism and transsexualism each came to represent a somewhat monolithic categorical account of gendered possibility and impossibility, 'trans' as imagined by Feinberg enables a myriad of identifications and experiences within its loose, unbound contingent category.

The transsexual condition: rejecting movement?

In explicitly including transsexuals, Feinberg's notion of a trans movement theoretically creates space for the inclusion of individuals who regard their gender movement – the act of transitioning – as resolvable; those who 'do not seek to queer or destabilize categories of gender but to successfully embody them' (Elliot, 2009: 11). These are traditionally men or women who seek to live permanently in a 'binary' gender role that contrasts with the gender they were coercively assigned at birth, following a physical transition.

Prior to the 1990s, the traditional transsexual narrative – incorporating a particular form of social and medical transition – was the primary mode of identity available to 'binary' trans men and women. With the advent of transgender studies, writers such as Prosser (1998), Namaste (2000) and Rubin (2003) sought to create space within poststructuralist theory for a transsexual subjectivity defined neither by the conditional demands of the medical literature nor by the emerging queer language of transgenderism with its focus on fluidity and change. They warn that trans theory grounded purely in discourses of movement 'erases transsexual specificity' (Namaste, 2000: 62), and therefore aim to account for the particular individual and social experiences of the transitione*d* subject, as well as the means by which they might traverse the 'borderlands' between genders to find a gendered 'home' (Prosser, 1998): an embodied sense of belonging and resolution. Trans feminist writer Julia Serano – a biologist by profession – would later build on this work with her account of the physical and psychological changes wrought by hormone therapy, linking the alleviation of dysphoric feelings through this process to an innate sense of 'subconscious sex' (Serano, 2007). While these accounts provide an alternative to the medical literature, they can be understood as grounded in discourses of trans as condition in a similar manner to Virgina Prince's models of femiphile transvestism and transgenderism. At the same time, they also provide for the possibility of movement – albeit *resolvable* movement – in the 'migration' (Prosser, 1998; Ekins and King, 2006) from one gender role to another. This can also be coupled with a pointed feminist rejection of sexist stereotypes (Namaste, 2000; Serano, 2007).

A substantial debate unfolded during the late 1990s and early 2000s as queer 'transgender' and binary 'transsexual' theorists critiqued one another's accounts of trans possibility and authenticity. Where many transgender theorists argued that transsexual accounts were rooted in a form of biological essentialism, transsexual theorists stated that transgender accounts left little room for the lived experience of transsexual individuals (Halberstam, 1998; Elliot, 2009). However, even as this conversation unfolded, Feinberg's model of a *collective trans social movement* increasingly informed all sides of the debate. Namaste (2000) and Serano (2007) both write of 'transsexual and transgender' experience, while Jack Halberstam (2005) – positioned largely within the queer/transgender camp – increasingly sought to acknowledge and account for experiences of lived physical transition. Moreover, ideas of affirmative sexed embodiment have increasingly been taken up by individuals seeking to undergo a queer physical transition without a traditional binary resolution, thereby creating a 'home in the borderlands' (Vähäpassi, 2013).

Trans movement language and activism

The internet provided a vital catalyst for the trans social movement to grow and change, as a formerly largely invisible and geographically dispersed population was empowered to come together and organise on an unprecedented scale. Within communities of marginalised people, solitary 'experiences' can be converted into accounts of 'being', 'through the construction of *stories of identity*' (Plummer, 1995: 118, emphasis in original). Stephen Whittle (1998) notes that diverse trans communities on the internet provide valuable space for the negotiation of Stryker's (1994) 'new modes' and 'different codes' of (trans)gendered possibility. I understand these modes and codes as reproduced through mutual recognition, and an iterative citation of emergent language by community members. Writings by Stone, Feinberg and Stryker have played a role in this broad process of discursive change, having been made available by their authors and/or by others on web pages and in e-zines, while more extensive works such as *Gender Outlaw* (Bornstein, 1994) are commonly recommended within community spaces and easily available in online bookstores. However, as access to the internet has increased and trans communities have grown, the sophistication of *informal* theorisation and the rapid distribution of ideas have increased also. Trans theory within community and activist spaces is increasingly intersectional and reflexive, reflecting the growing prominence of a diversity of voices. As Natasha Curson (2010: 142) argues: 'some thinking and writing on the nature of gender by trans individuals, often in non-academic contexts, goes beyond the current level of thinking and sophistication in transgender studies itself'. I have therefore sought to acknowledge the theoretical work of certain non-academic trans writers (including research participants for this project) in my discussion of research data in following chapters.

Eve Shapiro (2004: 166–167) observes that online connectivity has enabled trans activists to more easily 'educate themselves and others ... make contacts' and 'foster collective identity'. In the UK, this increased level of education and connectivity intersected with offline activism for trans legal rights by groups such as Liberty and Press For Change, in what Whittle (1998: 393) has described as the 'street-Net-street effect'. Trans activists have successfully fought for inclusion within LGBT organisations, the universal provision of trans-specific medical services through the NHS and legal recognition in legislation such as the Gender Recognition Act 2004 and Equality Act 2010.[13] The internet has also facilitated shifts in language, with trans people seeking to create an inclusive terminology for the purposes of community organising and activism. The shift from 'transgender' to 'trans' is an example of this. So too is the emergence of non-binary and non-gendered forms of language, which provide a means by which the fluidity Bornstein sought can be achieved. For instance, in *Trans Liberation* Feinberg describes hir use of gender-neutral pronouns in the context of the normative language of binary gender.

> I am a human being who would prefer not to be addressed as Ms. or Mr., ma'am or sir. I prefer to use gender-neutral pronouns like *sie* (pronounced like '*see*') and *hir* (pronounced like '*here*') to describe myself. I am a person who faces almost insurmountable difficulty when instructed to check off an 'F' or an 'M' box on identification papers ... I simply do not fit the prevalent Western concepts of what a woman or a man 'should' look like. (Feinberg, 1999: 1, emphasis in original)

The adoption of gender-neutral pronouns – in the form sie/hir as used by Feinberg, or in other forms such as the singular 'they' used by numerous participants in this project – has limited impact as an individual act. However, the *collective* adoption of new pronoun systems within trans communities on the internet provided a means by which new forms of trans language could first be implemented (and experimented with) in affirmative environments.

Interventions such as the introduction of gender-neutral pronouns are most commonly undertaken by and for individuals who, like Feinberg, do not consider themselves to be (straightforwardly, exclusively or at all) female *or* male. A myriad of terms have been coined to describe these gendered (and/or non-gendered) possibilities, such as agender, bigender, boi, enby, genderblender, genderfluid, genderfuck, neutrois and polygender, to name just a few. These sit alongside older identities that predate the contemporary trans movement, but can be incorporated into it, such as the 'transvestites … drag queens and drag kings, cross-dressers, bull-daggers, stone butches, androgynes [and] diesel dykes' described by Feinberg (1992: 206).

The most common such terms at the time of writing are **non-binary** and **genderqueer**, which are also frequently employed as umbrella terms for the wider repertoire of identities described above (Yeadon-Lee, 2016). Like Feinberg's interpretation of trans/transgender, and in contrast to the fixity of both traditional medical terminology and social identities such as 'transgenderist', neither non-binary nor genderqueer has an absolute, clearly delineated meaning. Instead, they denote personal and/or collective gendered movement in terms of rejecting binary gendered norms. For instance, the edited collection *Genderqueer* addresses a great number of differently gendered subjectivities belonging to individuals who might previously have been categorised as transsexual, as cross-dressers or as gender nonconforming gay, lesbian and/or bi people utilising terms such as butch, femme or boi (Nestle et al, 2002). In this way, space is created within non-binary and genderqueer identity categories both for individuals intending to physically transition and those who have no desire to do so.[14] Non-binary and genderqueer language therefore creates a means by which collective movement *can* occur – in terms of social understanding and political recognition – even as traditional categorical boundaries are broken down, reassembled and broken down again. This collective movement is beginning to achieve the political goal of social affirmation through recognition in numerous settings, having successfully campaigned for the inclusion of non-binary identifiers in contexts ranging from United Nations reports to the formal records of the UK's Royal Mail (Richards et al, 2016).

Feinberg's vision of a collective trans movement has been enabled through the wide dissemination of writing by hirself and others, academic and non-academic. Trans has become both a 'politicized identity category' and something that people *do* (Enke, 2012: 236).[15] Trans language is forged through intersections of the academic, the political and the everyday, facilitated greatly by the internet. The trans movement is collectively succeeding in challenging the hegemonic discourse of binary gender, and in gaining forms of social and legal recognition. Such achievements are intrinsically linked to the advancement of increasing options for movement-oriented identities, providing a basis by which more liberated individual engagements with gender might be rendered possible. In these social and political changes, and in alternatives to condition-oriented models of trans possibility, a wider range of trans lives become possible and liveable.

Naming oppression: transphobia and cisgenderism

Having named 'trans' – along with numerous related possibilities – the trans movement worked to name how trans people find themselves marginalised in various spheres of society, including within the realm of healthcare provision. Two of the most important interventions in this arena are the naming of 'transphobia' and of 'cis' norms.

Transphobia resembles related terms such as homophobia in describing prejudicial 'anti-trans sentiments' underpinning acts of violence, harassment and discrimination (Hill and Willoughby, 2005). Transphobia can therefore denote an individual negative attitude towards a trans person, but can also represent a wider rejection of gendered movement, thus describing a 'fear of the subject in transition' (Prosser, cited in Heyes, 2007: 201). Attempts to name transphobia can be traced to the 1990s, with Bornstein (1994) considering the term and Feinberg (1992) proposing 'genderphobia'. Since then, the term transphobia has achieved a discursive stability and social recognition through regular use within trans community spaces and, increasingly, beyond. In this book I follow Bettcher (2007: 46) in regarding transphobia as 'any negative attitudes ... harboured towards transpeople on the basis of our enactments of gender', while also acknowledging that this can intersect complexly with other forms of prejudicial attitude and behaviour, including homophobia, racism and sexism (Lamble, 2008; Richardson and Monro, 2010).

A more complex genealogy can be attributed to **cis**, a term utilised by trans people for the purpose of 'decentralizing the dominant group' (Koyama, 2002). Cis – along with related words such as cisgender and cissexual – has been attributed with a number of overlapping but separate meanings. Most simply, cis can be regarded as an antonym of trans: that is, people who are 'not trans' are cis. Cis may also operate as a means by which non-trans privilege can be named – that is, if you are not trans, you hold a form of cis privilege (Serano, 2007) – and/or it can be used to describe the state of 'living a life in congruence with static medico-juridical determinations of one's sex/gender' (Enke, 2012: 236). Biologist Dana Leland Defosse is generally credited with coining 'cisgender' in 1994, in an online discussion about transphobia on university campuses (Enke, 2012: 234); the term was later further popularised in the 2000s following the publication of Julia Serano's influential book *Whipping Girl*. Like trans, cis is derived from a Latin root; where 'trans-' is a prefix meaning 'across from' or 'on the other side of', 'cis ' is a prefix meaning 'on the same side as' (Ansara and Hegarty, 2012: 152). According to Defosse, the use of cis within the social realm of gender was originally intended to reflect the use of the prefix 'cis-' within scientific disciplines such as molecular biology and organic chemistry (Enke, 2012: 235).

While cis enables nuanced conversations around gender, transition, privilege and hegemony (Serano, 2007), recent critics have noted the risks of creating a trans/cis binary that precludes the possibility of figurative, narrative and social movement both past and present, between and within these categories (Ansara and Hegarty, 2012; Enke, 2012). For example, popular conceptions of cis that position an individual as *either* trans *or* cis leave little space for an individual to be 'somewhat' trans or cis, to 'become' trans or to 'no longer be' trans. In this binary opposition, trans/cis become absolute categories of selfhood where the individual is always (and has always) been one or the other, thereby stripping 'trans' of movement. Ironically, the trans/cis binary also poses a challenge for understandings of trans as condition. Finn Enke (2012: 242) describes the example of surgeon and gynaecologist Dr Marci Bowers, who transitioned in the past but now regards herself simply as 'a woman' rather than as 'a transsexual' or as 'a transsexual woman'. In this way, the use of trans/cis as fixed categories does not leave space for trans to be resolvable. In this book, therefore, I regard cis – like trans – to be a broad, unstable, *social* category with fluid boundaries, denoting a range of social experiences or modes of moving through the world, rather than any kind of fixed, absolute identity.

This use of cis as a contingent category enables a discussion of **cisgenderism**. In Ansara and Hegarty's (2012: 141) account, cisgenderism – in contrast to transphobia – 'describes a prejudicial *ideology*, rather than an individual *attitude*, that is systemic, multi-level and reflected in authoritative cultural discourses'. In this sense, it is comparable to terms such as 'ableism' and 'heterosexism' in denoting a means by which society happens to be organised to privilege particular bodies and behaviours. Cisgenderism thus describes the structuring of social norms and institutions *around the assumption that everyone has a cis experience of the world*, thereby offering a means to analyse 'the difficulties faced by transgender people in a culture simply not constituted to account for our existence' (Kennedy, 2013: 3). For Ansara (2015), the cisgenderism framework further enables conversations around gendered oppression that can move beyond a simplistic trans/cis binary. Nevertheless, I continue to use the terms trans and cis in my discussion of cisgenderism, because even as these terms are historically contingent, they denote social roles, identities and inequalities that are very much experienced as real.

Transphobia, cis and cisgenderism are therefore examples of language that has emerged from the intersection of transgender studies and internet communities, and in the context of this discussion they are linked to understandings of trans as movement. In the following chapters of this book I occasionally use 'transphobia' to refer to individual acts of prejudice towards trans people in general and trans patients in particular. More prominently, however, I employ 'cisgenderism' to describe the social *processes* by which trans people are marginalised.

Condition as movement: towards gender pluralism

Surya Monro (2005: 10) echoes transsexual critics in noting that movement-oriented accounts of trans subjectivity from queer theorists such as Butler and Bornstein frequently fail to acknowledge specifically transsexual 'experience[s] of sexed embodiment'. In seeking to queer *all* approaches to gender, such theorists risk leaving little space for those who desire to resolve their transness and identify straightforwardly as women or men, and for political action that centres transsexual specificity. At the same time, Monro argues, it is vital to acknowledge the gendered politics and experiences of those who seek to understand gendered subjectivity beyond the male/female binary.

Monro therefore advocates **gender pluralism** as an approach that can incorporate diverse approaches to trans/gendered possibility while maintaining a strategic incorporation of identity labels.

> [T]his involves building models of gender that include gender diversity at every level, not just at the level of representation and discourse, as is the case with postmodernist and poststructuralist approaches. … [W]e need a pluralist model of gender that supports intersex, androgynous, gender-fluid, transsexual, cross-dressing, multiply-gendered, and non-male/female people as (1) physical, embodied people, with the biological foundationalism that this implies; (2) social people, who may change genders despite having a fairly static physical appearance; (3) psychological people, who may have an experience of themselves which is different to their social and physical identities and mainstream male/

female norms; (4) political actors, who require changes in social structures and institutions to enable them to have basic human rights; (5) academics, who may seek to critique current gender theory and develop pluralist alternatives. (Monro, 2005: 14)[16]

Gender pluralism understands the social reality of gender as constructed, but also provides space for individuals to feel a deep-seated need to physically transition and find a 'home' in their transitioned body. As trans activist Roz Kaveney argues, 'we are caught in a contradiction – and must embrace this' (cited in Monro, 2005: 13).

Gender pluralism provides a frame by which the political movement envisaged by Feinberg might be understood as theoretically coherent *through* its embrace of apparent contradiction. Monro's account provides for an incorporation of condition-oriented identities into a model of *social movement* that itself draws upon understandings of trans *as* movement, incorporating transitions and diversities both physical and social. This approach is effectively taken by edited collections such as *Genderqueer* (Nestle et al, 2002) and *Gender Outlaws: The Next Generation* (Bornstein and Bergman, 2010), which bring together an array of trans, non-binary and/or genderqueer perspectives on gendered subjectivity, as well as in the inclusive approach of many contemporary trans activist groups. It is here that I also locate my own work, writing from a poststructuralist, constructivist perspective while also seeking to acknowledge the diverse lived and embodied realities of trans people.

Movement as condition: towards a more inclusive model of trans health?

A small but growing number of health professionals have authored publications within the medical literatures that speak directly to transgender studies. This move reflects calls for increased affirmation of new trans identities in medical contexts, following years of work from trans movement activists opposed to the paternalism and psychopathologisation of traditional medical models, as well as the growing presence of trans people *within* health professions (Richards et al, 2014). Through this process, understandings of trans as movement have arguably been *incorporated* into models of trans as condition, particularly in the UK context.

An example of this incorporation of movement into condition can be seen in the growing recognition of non-binary and genderqueer identities within the medical literatures. For instance, Version 7 of the WPATH *Standards of Care* notes that some individuals 'no longer consider themselves to be either male or female' and that they may therefore 'transcend a male/female binary understanding of gender' (Coleman et al, 2012: 171). Christina Richards and colleagues (2017) build upon this to outline how physical transitions for non-binary and genderqueer people might be managed in clinical settings through the provision of affirmative mental health support, hormone therapies and re-/de-gendering surgeries. Nevertheless, the provision of this treatment for individuals engaged in movement away from the male/ female binary remains linked to diagnostic categories such as gender dysphoria, with gender identity specialists providing clinical oversight (Richards et al, 2016). Richards and colleagues argue that this continued adherence to pathologising diagnostic models is essentially a pragmatic move, as 'the healthcare funding systems in many countries are set up in such a way as to make it effectively impossible to assist trans people with hormones and surgeries if they do not have a diagnosis which relates to those interventions' (Richards et al, 2015: 310).

It is perhaps necessary to regard trans as in some sense resolvable. This can be as much the case for individuals who seek to undertake a non-binary transition – oriented towards movement and fluidity – as it is for those such as Enke's (2012) example of Marci Bowers, who sought to position herself as 'just' a woman. In regarding treatment as a pragmatic move (both in political terms, and in terms of meeting the needs of patients) it is possible to partly reconcile understandings of trans as condition with understandings of trans as movement.

However, the approach employed by Richards and colleagues – who are effectively working to incorporate non-binary understandings into the UK's existing gatekeeping model of care – is not necessarily the only way to bridge the gaps between condition and movement. Recent legal changes in Argentina assert trans people's right to access specialist state healthcare services without requiring a specific diagnosis (Davy et al, 2018). Moreover, clinics in Australia, Canada and the United States have pioneered medical pathways that centre patients' informed consent to receive care, rather than a psychiatric assessment of their gender dysphoric feelings. This is commonly referred to as the **informed consent model** of trans healthcare (Deutsch, 2012; Reisner et al, 2015; Cundill and Wiggins, 2017). In later chapters of this book I show that significant tensions remain between trans patients and those health professionals who purportedly embrace trans complexity while continuing to employ a gatekeeping model of care. A shift towards the provision of specialist services on the basis of informed consent may help to address these tensions.

Conclusion: negotiating medical discourse

In two recently published interventions written (or co-written) by health professionals working at the UK's Charing Cross and Nottingham gender clinics, the authors propose that sociological accounts of trans health focus too much on constructing a rigid and overwhelmingly negative account of 'medical discourse' (Richards and Lenihan, 2012; Richards et al, 2014). They argue that terms such as '"the medical approach to/discourse of" trans' work to create 'a straw figure, whereby any [negative] reported experiences of trans healthcare, or views of one professional, is presented as a monolithic' (Richards et al, 2014: 254). Moreover, contemporary gender clinics are diverse spaces with multidisciplinary teams and trans employees, 'dedicated to providing quality, pragmatically useful, care for trans people' (Richards and Lenihan, 2012), with clinicians 'rarely relish[ing] the *exercise of power*, or the role of "gatekeeper"' (Richards et al, 2014: 255, emphasis mine).

Some past accounts of 'medical discourse' from sociologists have perhaps indeed been guilty of flattening complexity; as, indeed, have past accounts of 'trans' from medical practitioners, radical feminists and trans people themselves. In this chapter I have therefore sought to recognise the multiplicity and complexity of trans discourses. In referring to intersecting discursive *repertoires* of trans possibility, I account for the ongoing negotiation of manifold understandings of 'trans'. In categorising these discourses according to an orientation towards condition and/or movement, my aim is to highlight similarities and comparisons between ideas both within and beyond trans and medical literatures, while also acknowledging difference and diversity. This is particularly important because the evolution of trans language has not resulted in one paradigm neatly replacing another. Instead, multiple understandings of trans possibility remain relevant to this day.

The *story* that these collective discourses tell, however, does suggest that the positive picture of trans-affirming healthcare provision presented by Christina Richards and colleagues is somewhat misleading. This is not because health professionals are power hungry or uncaring (although undoubtedly a minority engage in unprofessional, unethical or otherwise inappropriate behaviour). Rather, it is because the historical and contemporary discursive *processes* by which trans possibilities have been negotiated ultimately centre professional expertise and credibility in a manner that can side-line or silence patient perspectives.

The progress of medical science – like all science – is not neutral (Foucault, 1978; Collins and Pinch, 1998). While some trans people have been involved in the creation of categories of diagnosis, and these categories have undoubtedly played an important role in making many trans lives *liveable* through the provision of gender identity services, they ultimately work to interpellate[17] a class of health professionals as 'expert'; not simply in matters of service provision, but also in matters of *gendered possibility*. This has granted an enormous amount of power to the health professions over the past century, resulting in a discursive power differential that was only significantly challenged following the emergence of the post-1990s trans movement.

Importantly, even critiques of trans medical models – along with suggested alternatives – have ultimately been *defined against them*. This can be seen in interventions from both cis radical feminists such as Janice Raymond and trans theorists such as Virgina Prince and Sandy Stone. It is for this reason that transgender studies scholars – including sociologists – seek to critically engage with medical discourses, and to interrogate health professionals' exercise of power through diagnosis and discourse alike. In doing so, we reflect and draw upon similar critiques of medical discourse that have emerged from feminist and queer theory and activism.[18]

The following chapters of this book therefore offer an empirical account of the *ongoing* negotiation of discourses of trans health at a time of both continuity and change. I provide an in-depth examination of how discourses of trans health have been understood, contested and reimagined through the interaction of patients, activists and practitioners. I follow Surya Monro (2005) in taking a gender-pluralist approach to understanding and acknowledging trans possibility, reflecting an overarching concern with centring the *liveability of trans lives*, rather than debates over authenticity or transgression (Vähäpassi, 2013; Davy, 2018). In this way, I broadly subscribe to a model of trans as movement; however, in doing so, I also seek also to acknowledge and affirm some research participants' own understandings of trans as condition.

Notes

[1]   While this book focuses largely on contemporary, Western approaches to gender diversity, it is important to note that non-binary gender categories have been imagined and experienced across a range of times and places. A century ago, Edward Carpenter observed that, 'the varieties of human type, intermediate [sic] and other, are very numerous, almost endless … and cannot be dispatched in sweeping generalisations' (Carpenter, 1919: 164). Present-day Majority World and/or Indigenous gender identities that elude strict male/female divisions include Native American two-spirit identifications (Jacobs et al, 1997; Wesley, 2014), *fa'afafine* within Samoan societies (Roen, 2001), *tom*, *dee* and *khatoey* in Thailand

(Jackson, 2004; Ravine, 2014), *travesti* in Latin America (Vek, 2010), *hijra* and *kothi* in a number of South Asian countries (Monro, 2007; Dutta and Roy, 2014), and *mak nyah* in Malaysia (Goh and Kananatu, 2018), to name just a few. Complex intersections and discursive flows can be traced between these subjectivities (all of which of course have different socio-historical origins and cultural meanings), and the Western language of 'trans'. Understandings of gender diversity from the global South and Indigenous peoples have influenced white trans thinkers such as Leslie Feinberg and Kate Bornstein, but Western 'trans' language can also operate as a colonising vernacular, usurping existing languages of gendered difference (Bhanji, 2013; Gramling and Dutta, 2016).

[2] I refer to 'assigned gender' – rather than, for instance, 'natal sex' – in order to describe the gender individuals were assigned at birth in a manner that recognises the social contingency of binary gender/sex in this assignment.

[3] This is mostly famously seen in the tragic case of computer scientist Alan Turing. Following a conviction of gross indecency for engaging in a sexual relationship with another man, Turing was required to take injections of a synthetic oestrogen as a condition of his probation. He died two years later, in a case of probable suicide.

[4] The 'FTM spectrum' incorporates trans men, cross-dressing women, transmasculine non-binary and genderqueer individuals, and other movements towards 'male' and/or 'masculine' from individuals who have been assigned a female gender. The phrases FTM and MTF have been commonly used within trans communities for many years, but now are increasingly falling out of favour, especially among younger trans people.

[5] My use of the female pronoun here reflects the author's use of female pronouns in the text, along with the character's identity as a female invert.

[6] I use male pronouns here to reflect the individual's explicitly expressed gender identity in Cauldwell's case notes. Cauldwell, however, refers to his patient as female.

[7] The wider impact of the 'deceptive transsexual' trope is perhaps exemplified by fierce public debates over trans people's access to public toilets in countries such as South Africa and the United States (Patel, 2017). Trans activists and their allies advocate for access to public toilets in line with an individual's gender identity, in order to affirm trans genders and somewhat alleviate the risk of gendered violence, which is particularly high against trans women and trans people of colour. Opponents of this approach – including legislative bodies, conservative commentators and radical feminist activists – frequently argue (without evidence) that it will afford 'men' the opportunity to spy on and perhaps commit sexual violence against young (white) girls. This argument typically draws upon transphobic, homophobic and racist discourses of threat towards cis white womanhood (Koyama, 2004; Patel, 2017).

[8] That is, for those who succeed in proving themselves 'trans enough'. I touch upon this issue further in Chapter Three, and analyse it in detail in Chapters Four and Five.

[9] I further noted that exceptions to this could usually be found in cases where health professionals who are themselves trans are involved in co-writing the papers in question (for example, Bouman et al, 2010; Richards et al, 2016).

[10] In December 2015 Zucker's Gender Identity Service at Toronto's Centre for Addiction and Mental Health was closed, following an extensive review undertaken by the Centre. A report published as part of the review indicated that Zucker may have been practising reparative or 'conversion' therapies on gender-variant children: 'We cannot state that the clinic does not practice reparative approaches ... with

respect to influencing gender identity development' (Zinck and Pignatiello, 2015: 22).

[11] While Prince is frequently credited with coining 'transgenderist' (and indeed, 'transgender') she was not in fact the first person to use these terms (Williams, 2014). However, her historic analyses are useful for understanding how this language came into use and the role it played in expanding gendered possibility.

[12] This imbalance has shifted significantly since the 1980s. While authors are still predominantly male, there is a growing body of articles in the medical literature of transsexualism in which women professionals are first authors. Moreover, I informally observed that roughly half of the attendees at WPATH's 2016 Symposium were women (although this was not reflected in the choice of plenary speakers for the event, among whom men were very much over-represented).

[13] Albeit somewhat limited in scope and implementation, as discussed by Davy (2011) and in later chapters of this book.

[14] It is important to note, however, that while all of these non-binary and genderqueer identities can be recognised under the trans umbrella, not all individuals identifying with them necessarily regard themselves as trans.

[15] This assessment echoes sociological accounts of how we all 'do' gender in everyday life (Kessler and McKenna, 1978; West and Zimmerman, 1987).

[16] In Monro's (2005) discussion of biological foundationalism, she outlines research participants' descriptions of sexed 'bodymaps', in a similar manner to Serano's (2007) later theorising of 'subconscious sex' to account for the desire to physically transition.

[17] Interpellation 'refers to the ways in which we are, on the one hand, inserted into discourse ... and, on the other, insert ourselves into discourse' (Steinberg, 2015b: 138).

[18] For examples, see Epstein (1996) on HIV/AIDS; Franklin (1997) on assisted conception; Steinberg (2015a) on genetics; Jain (2007) and Steinberg (2015b) on cancer.

THREE

Trans health in practice: conditions of care

[I]t is clear from our inquiry that trans people encounter significant problems in using general NHS services due to the attitude of some clinicians and other staff when providing care for trans patients. This is attributable to lack of knowledge and understanding – and even in some cases to out-and-out prejudice. (House of Commons Women and Equalities Committee, 2016)

As a result of rigid and strict procedures around gender presentation within Gender Identity Clinics many of our respondents found their experiences in these clinics quite traumatic. (Sonja Ellis and colleagues, 2015)

Not worth the trouble?

A few years back I switched GP practice. Looking back on it, I wonder why it took me so long to do so.

The first signs of trouble were subtle. Appointments with my GP felt short and his attitude was sharp. I assumed he was just a busy man, pressured by the demands of his job. I initially went to see him about being trans, as it happened. I registered with his practice around the time of my second appointment at Charing Cross gender clinic, in which I received a formal diagnosis of transsexualism. At this point I had transitioned socially and had been living 'full time' as a woman for over a year. Having already changed my name and received a new NHS card, I joined the practice as 'Ruth', with a female gender marker on my records.

My GP followed the instructions of the Charing Cross clinicians in signing off on my oestrogen prescription. However, it rapidly became apparent that he wasn't particularly interested in monitoring my health after this. The regular blood tests required by the endocrinologist at Charing Cross didn't happen; my GP argued that he 'wouldn't understand what the results meant' and refused to speak to the rest of his team, ask for help or look up guidance on the matter. I never pursued the issue. 'It isn't worth the trouble', I felt; moreover, I didn't feel like I had the power to challenge my doctor. I wasn't aware at the time that I could seek support from the clinicians at Charing Cross, or patient advocacy bodies such as the NHS Patient Advice and Liaison Service.

During my recovery from surgery my GP signed me off as 'fit to work' at a point where I could still barely stand. I considered challenging this, but again thought it 'wasn't worth it'. I felt powerless, and didn't know how or where I might have recourse against his decision.

Matters quietly came to a head when I sought help with a mental health referral following the suicide of my housemate, a good friend. Again, my GP's response felt quite unhelpful. As I sat there in his office, something in my patient notes caught my eye on his computer screen. My GP referred to me entirely with male pronouns in the notes. 'Ah', I thought. He clearly did not respect that I was a woman, or that I was trans. Did this inform his more general attitude of dismissiveness towards me? I didn't dare directly accuse him of transphobia and was exhausted by the grief of my recent loss. I quietly registered with a different practice, and never saw him again.

My experience was in no way unusual. In the opening chapter of this book, I noted that trans patients face numerous challenges in accessing healthcare services. In this chapter, I unpack the context of the challenges. I describe the material context of trans health in the UK, thereby setting the scene for a deeper analysis that follows in Chapters Four to Six. This is a context that very much constructs trans *as condition*, with patients receiving (or failing to receive) treatment according to health professionals' understanding of what this condition might mean.

Firstly, I look at the issues that trans patients can face within wider healthcare settings, including both primary health and specialist services that do not specifically address trans health needs. I build on the above vignette to show how the *power* associated with professional capital might lead trans patients to feel *powerless* to oppose instances of ignorance and/or discrimination, even in the wake of legislation such as the Equality Act 2010.

Secondly, I explore the public pathway(s) available to trans people who want to undergo a medically mediated physical transition. At the heart of this account is a description of the NHS patient's (conditional) journey from referral to treatment. Power is once again a key theme here: specifically, the manner in which UK gender identity services are characterised by the operation of control and judgement on the part of health professionals. I also look at the role of binary logic within the diagnostic process, the persistence of lengthy waits for treatment, and changes that have taken place in recent years. I then move on to describe the alternative options available for physical transition, which include both private healthcare services and self-medication.

Finally, I explain why many trans patients experience mistrust towards healthcare professionals, with reference to the difficulties that they might encounter in all areas of healthcare service provision.

Throughout this chapter, I draw largely upon examples and evidence from social studies of trans health, clinical guidance and protocols, minutes, reports and legislation. However, I also refer to findings from my ethnographic fieldwork. I return to discuss these findings in more depth in later chapters.

The wider context of trans health

Trans people often face challenges accessing general health services; a matter that is particularly troubling given the high prevalence of mental and sexual health issues, substance abuse and experiences of violence among the trans population (Reisner et al, 2016). These challenges can frequently be attributed to a lack of knowledge pertaining to trans people among non-specialist health professionals. In the previous chapter of this book, I showed that trans languages have emerged and developed to account for and accommodate people's gender-diverse desires, interests and needs. However, the ideas and knowledges associated with these languages have not necessarily been adopted extensively beyond trans communities and gender diverse spaces. Furthermore, transphobic prejudice and discrimination remain all too common within a range of healthcare settings.

One in five participants in the 2007 *Engendered Penalties* study described their GP as 'not trans friendly' (Whittle et al, 2007: 44). More recently, Jay McNeil and colleagues (2012: 45) found that a majority of trans people had experienced at least one form of negative interaction within general health services. These findings are reflected in my own qualitative data; inappropriate behaviour from practitioners was frequently discussed within community forums and activist spaces. Sometimes – as with my own experiences with my GP – this behaviour involved the quiet denial of services and/or transphobic microaggressions, as can be seen in the below quote from research participant Warren.

> I did say that I want a referral to a gender specialist/clinic but my GP seemed to ignore it for some reason, I don't think she's dealt with transgender folks before. (Warren)

Non-specialist health professionals providing treatment for trans patients often lack relevant knowledge of trans issues (Schonfield and Gardner, 2008; Hunt, 2014). Trans people frequently find themselves having to educate healthcare providers about any trans-specific health needs they might have, as well as more general etiquette surrounding (for instance) the use of their correct name and appropriate gendered pronouns. These issues are underpinned by a lack of training in trans issues for health professionals, both in medical schools and in terms of continuing professional development (Women and Equalities Committee, 2016).

A minority of health professionals engage in direct acts of discrimination against trans patients (McNeil et al, 2012; Belcher, 2014; NHS England, 2015a). Such acts can be attributed to the circulation of 'enduring and mistaken and highly offensive stereotypes about trans people among the public at large' (cliniQ, cited in Women and Equalities Committee, 2016: 36). In some cases, inappropriate behaviour can include abuse, harassment or sexual violence. An example follows below, in an account posted by the anonymous Twitter handle TransDocFailAnon.

> GP wouldn't file my regular hormone prescription without examin[ing] my genitals [which included] traumatic penetration. (TransDocFailAnon)

Ignorance, prejudice and discrimination towards trans patients is underpinned by – and feeds into – an institutional resistance to change. This is powerfully illustrated by Louis Bailey and Jay McNeil's 2013 report on a project commissioned by NHS North West. The researchers intended to work with GP surgeries to generate a better evidence base for understanding trans health, and to improve access to primary care for trans people. However, they 'encountered a series of barriers which proved both insurmountable and demoralising', most often from practice managers and administrators (Bailey and McNeil, 2013: 4). These barriers included information being withheld from researchers, 'a lack of awareness or understanding about trans people' and, in some cases, explicitly 'negative attitudes towards trans people' (5–6). GP surgeries were also resistant to the distribution of posters designed to both show support for trans patients and signpost relevant services. This lack of cooperation severely undermined the project and limited its impact.

Both a dearth of knowledge and anti-trans prejudice can have severe consequences for trans patients. For example, ignorance can lead some practitioners to connect irrelevant health issues to a patient's trans status.

This can result in trans patients being denied treatment. In the quote below, research participant Dylan – a trans man – describes how he was denied a hysterectomy on the day his surgery was due to take place, and was not subsequently provided any support by his GP.

> The letter from my GP was something along the lines of 'they will not fund the surgery as they do not see you as a priority compared to others in a similar situation' ... what the fuck?! It did say I can appeal if I wish but she's dead against me having it anyway telling me its unnecessary surgery. By the way I had it booked last year, on the day of surgery my surgeon was on leave and the stand in refused to do it. He said the 'computer just bounces back a male name'. (Dylan)

As a person with a uterus, Dylan had a right to access a hysterectomy through the NHS through the same referral processes as anyone else. However, this access was blocked by the transphobic prejudice of his stand-in surgeon, GP and (assuming the GP was being honest) NHS commissioners. Moreover, the programming of the computer system meant that it couldn't accommodate a male hysterectomy patient.

Trans patients and their advocates frequently feel powerless to challenge inappropriate care. Health practitioners hold a great deal of professional capital, which makes it difficult for trans patients to feel able to challenge instances of ignorance or discrimination; like myself, many research participants in this study felt that it 'wasn't worth' doing so. In 2013, trans rights advocate Helen Belcher attempted to tackle this issue by collecting accounts of alleged medical malpractice. These accounts included 'allegations of sexual abuse, physical abuse, verbal abuse, inappropriate and sometimes damaging treatment, treatment withheld, threats of withholding treatment, poor administration, and acting against patients' best interests' (Women and Equalities Committee, 2016: 41). A dossier of 98 such cases was presented to the General Medical Council (GMC) by Belcher. The GMC later confirmed that at least three of these were eventually formally submitted as complaints, but all were eventually dismissed. In a submission to the House of Commons Women and Equalities Committee's Transgender Equality Inquiry, representatives of the GMC explained that:

> For us to pursue a complaint, we will also usually need the patient to identify themselves and to consent to disclosure of their complaint to the doctor. This is an unavoidable

part of due legal process, but we acknowledge it may be a disincentive to some to pursue complaints. (GMC, cited in Women and Equalities Committee, 2016: 42)

Challenging inappropriate care through formal channels can be an adversarial pursuit; one that many patients are unwilling to follow. This situation is no doubt compounded by the high prevalence of mental health issues and economic marginalisation among trans patient populations (Reisner et al, 2016). Patients who do challenge instances of prejudice or marginalisation often find themselves facing further barriers put up by those who are supposed to help, as can be seen in the response of Dylan's GP. Moreover, attempts by action researchers such as Bailey and McNeil (2013) to advocate on *behalf* of trans patients can similarly result in an adversarial relationship between advocates and providers, due to the barrier of entrenched cisgenderism and transphobia.

A right to good care?

While negative experiences were more commonly discussed, many research participants in the community sphere were also keen to recount *good* experiences of treatment. The NHS was generally very well regarded, with a great number of individuals describing how they value the organisation itself, as well as the helpful attitude of many healthcare professionals.

I'm a big supporter of the NHS. (Sam)

[The doctor] was very welcoming and friendly, and I got on with her really well. I was made to feel at ease and she listened closely to everything I said. (Warren)

My GP is great. She's been wonderful to me and very supportive and understanding from the very beginning of my transition – though she immediately told me that she had not supported a transperson before and as far as she was aware had never even met one. (Ellie)

Much of the positive feeling towards health service providers was no doubt due to the helpful and professional attitude of 'good' doctors, nurses and gender clinicians. However, participants' positive experiences are also shaped by a growing body of professional guidance and laws written to support practitioners and/or protect the rights of trans patients.

Since the beginning of the 2000s, numerous documents have been published that aim to help providers meet the general needs of trans patients, many of which were written by (or in collaboration with) trans professionals or activists (examples include Burns, 2008; Curtis et al, 2008; Ahmad et al, 2013). The last two decades have also seen the passage of three key equality laws. The **Gender Recognition Act 2004** (widely known among trans groups as the **GRA**) enabled trans people to change the name and gender on their birth certificate, on the condition that they intended this change to be permanent and could prove that they had been living 'full time' in their preferred gender for at least two years with some form of medical supervision. The Sex Discrimination (Amendment of Legislation) Regulations 2008 prohibited discrimination against individuals with the protected characteristic of 'gender reassignment' in the provision of goods and services (including health services). The **Equality Act 2010** reinforced this prohibition, and added a legal duty for public sector bodies in England, Wales and Scotland to eliminate discrimination, harassment and victimisation on the grounds of gender reassignment. As of 2010, an individual 'has the protected characteristic of gender reassignment if the person is proposing to undergo, is undergoing or has undergone a process (or part of a process) for the purpose of reassigning the person's sex by changing physiological or other attributes of sex' (Equality Act 2010: Chapter 1, Section 7). Importantly, while this definition conflates 'sex' with 'gender', and has been widely interpreted as relevant only to 'binary' (that is, female or male) trans people, it does leave space for the 'reassignment' of 'sex' to take place along non-binary lines (Whittle, 2016). Moreover, there is no requirement for ongoing medical supervision for an individual to have the protected characteristic. These documents and legislative Acts therefore provide an environment in which public health providers have (in theory) some information on trans issues available to them, healthcare managers are charged with taking action to ensure that trans people do not face discrimination and healthcare providers can (again, in theory) face legal proceedings if discrimination *does* occur.

While many trans people have good experiences of both general and specialist services, the continuing prevalence of ignorance and prejudice show that NHS guidance and legal protections are not sufficient to fully overcome institutional cisgenderism and transphobia within healthcare settings. Trans patients (and patient advocates) still face the problem of challenging cisgenderism and transphobia due to the entrenched nature of these problems on an institutional level, and the adversarial nature of the formal channels by which individual acts of malpractice might be addressed. Nevertheless, there has still been something of a shift in power from service providers to patients; patients now have stronger grounds to oppose inappropriate conduct. In Chapter Six, I explore how these guidelines and laws helped to provide trans patients with a sense that they *deserved* better and could challenge the power of healthcare professionals and institutions alike.

Gender identity services: the patient journey

I now describe how trans patients typically navigate the UK's specialist NHS gender identity services. These services are generally provided through organisations that often referred by patients and practitioners alike as 'gender identity clinics', or GICs; however, in this book I generally refer to them as **gender clinics** for ease of reading.

I begin with a look at the diagnostic criteria that shape this patient journey, and explain how these criteria empower gender identity specialists as gatekeepers, controlling access to treatment such as hormone therapy and surgeries. I then examine the treatment pathway that NHS patients can expect to follow, before briefly describing how political changes have impacted on this pathway since 2012.

Diagnostic criteria

In the UK, access both to gender identity services and to legal recognition through the GRA is typically predicated on a diagnosis 'of or relating to Gender Dysphoria', provided by mental health professionals working at a gender clinic (Ahmad et al, 2013: 176). Relevant diagnoses for adults and adolescents include 'Gender Dysphoria' in DSM-5, and 'Transsexualism' in ICD-10.

> **Gender Dysphoria in Adolescents and Adults**
> A. A marked incongruence between one's experienced/ expressed gender and assigned gender, of at least 6 months' duration, as manifested by at least two of the following:
> 1. A marked incongruence between one's experienced/ expressed gender and primary and/or secondary sex characteristics (or in young adolescents, the anticipated secondary sex characteristics).

2. A strong desire to be rid of one's primary and/or secondary sex characteristics because of a marked incongruence with one's experienced/expressed gender …

3. A strong desire for the primary and/or secondary sex characteristics of the other gender.

4. A strong desire to be treated as the other gender (or some alternative gender different from one's assigned gender).

5. A strong conviction that one has the typical feelings and the reactions of the other gender (or some alternative gender different from one's assigned gender).

B. The condition is associated with clinically significant distress or impairment in social, occupational, or other important areas of functioning.

(American Psychiatric Association, 2013: 302.85)

Transsexualism

A desire to live and be accepted as a member of the opposite sex, usually accompanied by a sense of discomfort with, or inappropriateness of, one's anatomic sex, and a wish to have surgery and hormonal treatment to make one's body as congruent as possible with one's preferred sex. (World Health Organization, 1992: F64.0)

The ICD-11 diagnosis further requires that the 'transsexual identity [is] present persistently for at least two years', and that it is 'not a symptom of another mental disorder or a chromosomal abnormality'. Other gender-oriented diagnoses available to participants in this project have included 'Dual-role transvestitism' and 'Fetishistic transvestitism' in ICD-10, 'Gender Identity Disorder' and Transvestic Fetishism' in DSM-IV (until 2013). From 2018, the ICD-11 diagnostic category of Gender Incongruence is likely to gradually replace the ICD-10's Transsexualism.

Assessment procedures for these diagnoses have historically been built upon a prescriptive assumption that transitions can and should take place within the gender binary, with the only imaginable and desirable outcomes being a permanent transition from male to female, or vice versa (Davy, 2011; Ellis et al, 2015). This assumption has been encoded into the **binarist** language of the ICD-10 – which relies upon binary concepts such as 'opposite sex' (for Transsexualism, which generally allows for physical transition) and 'dual role' (for Dual-role transvestism, which generally does not) – and the DSM-5, which centres an idea of *the* 'other gender' (Davy, 2015). Some health professionals, such as James Barrett (2007), argue that appropriate patient behaviour involves aiming to be 'read' by others as (cis) male or (cis) female. In this way, gender specialists' power to diagnose can effectively reinforce a binary model of gender (NHS England, 2015b). Consequently, many patients withhold 'any level of ambivalence or uncertainty about their gender' from practitioners (Ellis et al, 2015: 12).

In the previous chapter I noted that while gender identity specialists 'rarely relish the exercise of power, or the role of "gatekeeper"' (Richards et al, 2014: 255), the continuing emphasis on assessment and diagnosis within gender identity services nevertheless works to ensure that they *do* play this gatekeeping role, thereby *exercising power* as 'gender experts'. Transitioning individuals can of course act without guidance from such practitioners; as I described in the opening vignette of this chapter, I myself transitioned socially prior to my first gender clinic appointment. However, gatekeepers within gender identity services effectively control access to forms of treatment such as hormone therapy and surgeries. This means that they have the power to determine what constitutes an appropriate or 'trans enough' patient for the purposes of specialist care. I propose that the operation of this power relies upon two binary distinctions. The first is the not-trans/trans distinction, which relies upon the presupposition that 'trans' is a *conditional* category that can be defined and delineated. The second is the male/female binary, which enables health professionals to conceptualise treatment in terms of a transition from one gender to its 'opposite'.

NHS gender identity services: a linear pathway?

Thousands of trans people in the UK access diagnosis and treatment through NHS gender clinics. Treatment regimens can vary considerably between the individual clinics, but are typically based upon a somewhat conservative interpretation of the WPATH *Standards of Care*. It is important to note that the *Standards of Care* do not necessarily require that medical supervision for transitioning individuals be managed through one of these centralised institutions: indeed, treatment can in theory be provided by a family doctor. However, the *Standards* do state that a range of expert knowledges are required to oversee various aspects of transition. These must include a mental health assessment and/or screening from a mental health professional (typically a psychologist or psychiatrist, but this can also be a suitably qualified counsellor or therapist), and can also include hormone management by an endocrinologist and/or relevant operations undertaken by a surgeon. While some countries (such as Canada) offer decentralised, collaborative approaches in which multiple individuals or organisations work together to provide gender identity services (Goldberg, 2006), in the UK there is typically a clustering of expertise within the institution of the gender clinic (Barrett, 2007). This institutional approach is often seen as preferable by UK gender identity specialists; as I shall show in Chapter Six, alternative approaches to treatment can face professional censure, backed by practitioners based at gender clinics.

Gender identity services provided through the NHS have historically been provided according to a linear pathway. Patients following this pathway typically take the following steps:

1. a. Direct referral to gender clinic from GP,
   b. Referral to local mental health service from GP, followed by assessment and referral to gender clinic from a mental health practitioner.
2. Initial assessment at gender clinic, including 'Real Life Experience' (RLE).
3. Hormone therapy and other interventions such as speech therapy or hair removal.
4. Surgical assessment at gender clinic.
5. Surgery/surgeries.

This pathway is generally subdivided into two parallel routes: a 'masculinising' route (involving treatments such as testosterone supplements and chest reconstruction) and a 'feminising' route (involving treatments such as oestrogen supplements and facial hair removal) (NHS England, 2015c). In this way, even treatment for non-binary and genderqueer patients (where provided) is conceptualised in binary terms.

Any given individual might 'finish' their transition after taking only a given number of these steps: for example, a patient might choose not to have surgery, or alternatively they might be refused hormone therapy by practitioners who felt that they did not adequately follow the requirements for RLE. In cases where an individual is denied a referral, funding and/or treatment and still seeks to transition through the NHS, they typically have to begin their journey again from the beginning of the pathway.

In recent years this pathway has become somewhat more flexible. For instance, in some cases gender identity specialists will allow their patients to have certain surgeries without having to first undergo hormone therapy, or to begin hormone therapy without first undergoing RLE. This has followed the implementation of a new national protocol for Scotland in 2012, coupled with legal changes in England and Wales that were implemented in 2013. I discuss these changes later in the chapter.

Referral and waiting

At the time of writing there are 12 NHS gender clinics for adults in the UK and 2 for children and adolescents; the number fluctuated somewhat during fieldwork as some clinics closed and others opened. A majority of these are based in England.

The clinic with the largest capacity by a considerable margin is London's Tavistock and Portman Gender Identity Clinic (formerly the West London Mental Health Trust Gender Identity Clinic), which is the largest service of its kind in Europe. This clinic is more commonly known among patients and clinicians alike as 'Charing Cross', due to its proximity to and historic links with London's Charing Cross Hospital. Charing Cross patients number in the thousands; by comparison, patients registered at the UK's other gender clinics typically number in the dozens or the hundreds (UK Trans Info, 2016). Other notably large clinics include the Nottingham Centre for Transgender Health (formerly the Nottingham Centre for Gender Dysphoria) and Glasgow's Sandyford Clinic.

The NHS has a legal requirement to provide patients with an initial appointment within a maximum of 18 weeks from referral to a service.[1] However, the relevance of this to gender clinics has long been ambiguous and contested. In reality, waiting list lengths for gender identity services are considerable. In 2015, the average wait was 42 weeks for adult services, or 21 weeks for child and adolescent services (UK Trans Info, 2016). In 2017, an NHS report stated that waiting times were 'in many cases over 52 weeks for a first appointment' (NHS England, 2017a). One of the longest waiting lists encountered during fieldwork was for the (now defunct) York gender clinic, which had a waiting time of four-and-a-half years in 2010; as of 2015, the average wait for a first appointment at Leeds Gender Identity Service was four years (UK Trans Info, 2016).

These long waits are due in part to 'financial uncertainties' (including issues with funding) as well as retirements and clinic closures (Combs et al, 2008: 1–2). However, they have also been shaped by the changing landscape of trans possibility following the emergence of the trans movement in the 1990s. Growing public awareness, coupled with some decrease in the stigmatisation of trans people (as now codified in law) has arguably made it 'easier' to be trans. This has resulted in an exponential increase in the visible trans population, leading in turn to an enormous growth in patient numbers (Reed et al, 2009; Davies et al, 2013). In 2008, Ryan Combs and colleagues stated that Charing Cross's maximum capacity was 2,500. By October 2015, 3,645 patients were on the books at Charing Cross, with an additional 1,728 people waiting for their first appointment (UK Trans Info, 2016).

Prior to 2013, patients in England required two referrals to be placed on a gender clinic waiting list: the first being a referral from a GP to a local mental health practitioner, and the second being a referral from the local mental health practitioner to the gender clinic. Some patients were also referred back-and-forth between local services before finally being sent to a gender clinic. In each instance, patients had to wait (sometimes for weeks or months) for a referral letter to arrive, before being placed on a formal waiting list for the requested service. The situation differed somewhat in Scotland, where some patients could self-refer to a gender clinic. Since 2013, trans patients in England have also had the right to be referred directly to a gender clinic by their GP, but in practice many continue to first be referred to local mental health services. Patients may also be directly referred by a GP in Northern Ireland. Patients in Wales still require a second referral from local mental health services, although this is likely to change in the near future.

According to Charing Cross lead clinician James Barrett (2007: 9), the role of local mental health practitioners is *not* to offer (or refuse) a diagnosis of or related to transsexualism, but instead to screen out individuals for whom an appointment at a gender clinic might be inappropriate, such as 'bemused but otherwise contented transvestites, lesbians, gay men and acutely psychotic people'. However, many local practitioners take it on themselves to assess patients, sometimes refusing a gender clinic referral to individuals with an avowed trans identity. To this day, patients may also find that referrals are refused or delayed by GPs or local mental health providers (Barrett, 2016). In this way – and contrary to the stated intentions of specialists such as Barrett – even *non-specialist practitioners* have the power to block access to treatment.

In the recent past, many patients have also found themselves unable to access services due to geographic and/or funding issues. Funding for English and Welsh patients wishing to attend a gender clinic was acquired through their local Primary Care Trust (PCT), NHS Board or Trust prior to 2013. While these bodies were required by law to fund medical transition from 1999, some refused to do so, or placed caps on patient numbers (McNeil et al, 2012). This situation was particularly severe for Welsh patients. Historically, Wales has not had a gender clinic; Welsh patients have instead typically been referred to Charing Cross in London. A blanket ban on funding for gender identity services in Wales – imposed by commissioners in order to save money – prevented many people from transitioning through the NHS in the late 2000s. This caused a considerable patient backlog of Welsh referrals to Charing Cross for some years after the ban was lifted (Combs et al, 2008).

Waits within the system: assessment, diagnosis and RLE

Further waits are encountered once a patient is registered at an NHS gender clinic. There are a number of waiting periods built into the WPATH *Standards of Care*. For example, it is recommended that patients are assessed for gender dysphoria and any coexisting mental health conditions and provided with relevant information prior to hormone therapy, and that they 'engage in 12 continuous months of living in a gender role that is congruent with their gender identity' prior to any genital surgeries (Coleman et al, 2012: 202).

These waits are compounded by UK-specific clinical pathway requirements. Transitioning patients in the UK are typically required to obtain a diagnosis from at least two gender identity specialists and to undergo **Real Life Experience** (RLE) – also known as the 'Real Life Test' – in order to access surgeries, and sometimes also before they can access treatments such as hormone therapy, speech therapy and facial hair removal.[2] The diagnoses are made following assessments undertaken on two or more separate occasions, usually several weeks or months apart. Some gender clinics, such as the Nottingham Centre for Transgender Health, Belfast's Brackenburn Clinic and Exeter's 'The Laurels', require patients to attend three or more initial assessment appointments prior to diagnosis.

Assessments typically involve interviews of 30–90 minutes, in which the patient is asked about their gendered feelings, past and present experiences of gender presentation, their relationship with their body and (often) sexual fantasies and experiences (Barrett, 2007; Speer, 2013; NHS England, 2015c). Sometimes additional requirements are made of patients as part of the assessment process. For instance, research participants attending the Nottingham Centre for Transgender Health reported being asked to keep a diary of their gendered experiences, and required to bring a friend or member of their family to one of their appointments. Specialists working at Nottingham argue that these measures help to assess the level of support that transitioning patients will receive from people close to them (NHS England, 2015c); however, several participants in this study stated that the family/friend appointment in particular was used by health professionals to 'corroborate' their account (I unpack this in Chapter Five). Following an initial diagnosis, patients at Nottingham stated that they were then required to sit before a clinical panel who decide whether or not to offer hormone therapy.

Some patients undergo assessment for several months or years before receiving a diagnosis. In many cases, this reflects their desire to explore their gender identity in depth and be sure that they are making the correct decision (NHS England, 2015c). In other instances, patients argue that this extended period of assessment is the result of their refusing or being unable to meet the expectations of clinicians (Davy, 2011; Ellis et al, 2015). Adolescent patients are typically expected to have demonstrated a clear and consistent desire for physical transition for several years before being offered hormone blockers or (on rare occasions, and only if they are aged 16 or over) hormone therapy.

RLE requires the patient to spend a period of time living in their new gender role: presenting socially in their preferred gender, changing their name and identification documents, coming out to friends, family and work colleagues. Evidence of this must typically be provided to practitioners (Arcelus et al, 2017). This shows 'whether [or not] the patient has demonstrated a satisfactory adjustment to a new gender role in a real-life setting' (Barrett, 2007: 71). 'Success' in RLE tends to be judged in terms of 'occupational, sexual, relationship and psychological stability' (Barrett, 2007: 72–73), with patients being treated as a member of their preferred gender category by others on a *full-time basis*. A number of gender identity specialists regard it as essential that patients have an occupation as part of this process: that is, a job, government training scheme or education course. Barrett (2007: 72) argues that some occupations are 'unacceptable' for the purposes of RLE, including 'work in a purely transvestite or transsexual environment' and 'prostitution'. His logic is that these occupations enable individuals to work *as transsexuals*, meaning that they cannot demonstrate their ability to move through the world as if they were cis. In this way, the power of the gender identity specialist can effectively extend beyond the management of gendered presentation alone.

A requirement for RLE to be undertaken prior to hormone therapy was removed from the *Standards of Care* in 2011, with the publication of Version 7. RLE is, however, always required prior to surgery (Coleman et al, 2012). At gender clinics such as Nottingham, patients may still be expected to undertake RLE before hormone therapy can be offered (Arcelus et al, 2017). This means that during the assessment period, trans patients must attempt to move through the world in their preferred gender role *without* the benefits of physical transition. This can impact on their physical safety (through a limited opportunity to pass as cis) and mental well-being (Namaste, 2000; McNeil et al, 2012).

Policies on diagnosis, RLE and the provision of treatment can therefore vary considerably between (and within) gender clinics (NHS England, 2015c). This is due largely to their historical development as independent entities, with national protocols only very recently implemented in Scotland and England (NHS Scotland, 2012; NHS England, 2013a). However, a feature common to all UK gender clinics is the positioning of health professionals as qualified to *decide whether or not a patient is trans* (enough). The common requirement for at least two diagnoses demonstrates that these assessments are not simply a matter of screening for troublesome co-morbidities, creating a care plan and ensuring that patients provide informed consent in line with the *Standards of Care*. Instead, the assessment procedure is one in which practitioners exercise their *judgement* as to whether or not a patient should receive treatment, with the second (or third) opinion in place to ensure that the 'wrong decision' is not made (Barrett, 2007: 4). The severity of this approach is underpinned by the notion that trans experience is a definable condition, and that transition *necessarily* represents a *permanent* move from one gender to another. Health professionals working in gender clinics frequently highlight the importance of their role in reducing the *risk* of an inappropriate transition, which could result in regret over irreversible physical changes as well as social consequences such as the loss of friends, family and/ or work (Barrett, 2007; Richards et al, 2014).

In 2011, a patient satisfaction survey was undertaken at the Charing Cross and Nottingham gender clinics (Davies et al, 2013). A considerable majority of respondents reported satisfaction with their gender clinic experience. However, in other research many trans people have also described their experience of stringent assessment procedures as demeaning, invasive and disempowering (Ellis et al, 2015; NHS England, 2015a; Women and Equalities Committee, 2016). Participants in a recent NHS consultation argued that mental health professionals 'have too much power around decisions of people within the trans community, both medically and legally' (NHS England, 2015a). A patient quoted by Sonja Ellis and colleagues (2015: 11) describes how questions asked during their assessment 'were overly irrelevant, prying and sexual', leading them to feel 'utterly powerless and infantilised in my dealings with them'.

In this way, the power held by health professionals within gender clinics is reflected in a *lack of power* experienced by patients with regard to the management of their own identity and health. This, too, has its risks: Ellis et al (2015: 13) note that '[a] number of participants … reported feeling that they had been pressured into doing things they did not want to do in order to "prove" their gender to professionals in GICs', such as conforming to a particularly masculine or feminine gender role. Moreover, over half of the respondents in their study 'reported having felt emotionally distressed or worried about their mental health while attending a GIC' (Ellis et al, 2015: 14), and did not feel able to discuss this with practitioners.

Hormones and surgery

If hormone therapy is approved, the gender identity specialist writes to their patient's GP with prescription instructions. The wait for this letter is typically several weeks, but can sometimes amount to several months due to administrative issues at gender clinics. Upon receipt of instructions, the patient's GP is expected to regularly prescribe appropriate hormone supplements and/or hormone blockers. Patients are asked to undergo blood tests at their GP practice at regular intervals to monitor this treatment, with endocrinologists at the gender clinic recommending continued or changed dosages as appropriate. Usually dosage is increased gradually over time, meaning that the resulting physical changes occur more rapidly the longer an individual has been undergoing hormone therapy. Trans women may also be offered vocal training or hair removal treatment (through laser or electrolysis), although prior to 2013 these were usually not funded by the NHS outside of Scotland. Some patients engaged in lengthy administrative battles for access to these services, with mixed levels of success.

Adolescent patients at NHS clinics are not offered hormone therapy prior to the age of 16 at the earliest, although at the time of writing practitioners are debating lowering this to 15. Some adolescents may be offered hormone blockers at an earlier age. Hormone blockers temporarily halt puberty, therefore providing the individual with time to reflect on whether they want to undergo hormone therapy when they are older, without irreversible physical changes happening to their body in the meantime. A handful of young adult participants in this project had recently accessed child and adolescent services; they described a struggle to persuade cautious practitioners that they qualified for hormones and blockers, particularly if their parents did not support them through RLE.

Adult patients can be referred for surgeries (such as chest surgeries, genital reconstruction surgeries, vocal feminisation surgery) following RLE. Barrett explains that the RLE period can vary from patient to patient:

> suitability for gender reassignment surgery is not determined solely by the length of time the patient has attended a gender identity clinic – although a certain minimum time must apply. Rather, it depends on whether the patient has been seen to be or has become a *suitable candidate* in the time that they have attended. (Barrett, 2007: 71, emphasis mine)

For genital reconstruction surgery, the *Standards of Care* recommend a minimum time of one year in a congruent gender role prior to a referral (Coleman et al, 2012: 202); UK gender clinics typically require patients to wait for 12–14 months (NHS Scotland, 2012; NHS England, 2013a). Two mental health professionals are needed to formally approve a referral for genital surgeries.

These requirements once again demonstrate the power of clinical oversight and judgement held by NHS gender identity specialists. Moreover, they show how trans patients are treated differently to cis patients: for instance, cis patients requesting reconstructive surgery for either medical or cosmetic purposes are not expected to demonstrate a consistent commitment to the treatment through means such as RLE. Drawing upon the example of orchidectomy (removal of the testicles), Walter Bouman and colleagues (2014: 380) note that 'a cisgender male with chronic scrotal pain does not require any written psychiatric opinion for an orchidectomy nor does he have to be in pain or distress for a minimum of one year before surgery can take place'; this contrasts with a trans woman seeking the same intervention. Therefore, while some aspects of patient management (such as regular blood tests) are necessary to ensure that treatment goes smoothly and that transitioning individuals are safe, other aspects are based upon the ideological and moral assumption that health professionals should take full responsibility for ensuring that transitioning patients are making the 'right' decisions.

Legal recognition

The professional acknowledgement of trans identity by medical authorities plays an important role in legal recognition due to the design of legislation such as the GRA. This law was ground breaking because it recognised trans genders *without* recipients first having to undergo genital surgeries. However, the Act also remains grounded in conditional, binary medical understandings of trans that do not fully acknowledge transsexual diversities, let alone non-binary or genderqueer genders (Davy, 2011). This can be seen in the Act's recognition of just female and male genders, in line with binary norms, and in the role of health professionals in its enactment.

At the time of writing, trans people must demonstrate *with evidence from medical practitioners* that they have undergone a permanent transition in order to obtain legal gender recognition. This evidence is submitted for approval to the Gender Recognition Panel, whose membership includes practitioners from NHS gender clinics. In practice, several participants in this study described experiencing difficulties in obtaining a Gender Recognition Certificate (GRC) without having first undergone surgical interventions. In one instance, a gender identity specialist who also sat on the Gender Recognition Panel told his patient that they should wait until after surgery before applying for gender recognition. Gender identity specialists therefore play an important role in 'enabling – or disabling – recognition' within both healthcare and legal settings (Hines, 2013: 58).

Reform and austerity

The landscape of public health has changed considerably during the 2010s. This is due in part to wider legal, structural and financial shifts within the NHS. However, there have also been changes made specifically in the provision of gender identity services. In this section, I discuss how these changes have taken place, and note changes to NHS transition pathways.

A Scottish protocol

The Scottish gender clinics have long taken a somewhat less strict approach to assessment, referral and RLE in comparison to much of the rest of the UK. In July 2012 this was extended and codified in a formal Gender Reassignment Protocol for NHS Scotland (NHS Scotland, 2012), which also reflected changes between Versions 6 and 7 of the

WPATH *Standards of Care*, and wider shifts towards patient-centred care within the NHS. Key features of the Protocol include only one assessment being required for hormone therapy, speech therapy, hair removal and 'female-to-male' chest surgeries; no requirement for RLE prior to these treatments; and only one year of RLE being needed prior to genital reconstruction surgeries. Moreover, a less linear approach to treatment was instituted, in which treatment pathways can more flexibly meet the stated needs and desires of patients. For instance, it is now possible for masculinising chest surgery to take place without patients having first undergone hormone therapy.

All change in England and Wales

The **Health and Social Care Act 2012** transformed the structure of the NHS in England and Wales upon its implementation in April 2013. One of the major changes instituted by the Health and Social Care Act was the abolition of PCTs in England. They were replaced with new, more localised, GP-led commissioning consortia – Clinical Commissioning Groups (CCGs) – as well as a new national body overseeing budgeting, planning and commissioning, known as NHS England.

A number of gains originally made by English and Welsh trans activists in the pre-2013 period were effectively lost with the restructure of the NHS. Numerous documents issued by local bodies such as PCTs were rendered obsolete. This led to the effective removal of localised trans-friendly policies in many parts of the country, such as for changing name and gender on GP records (NIGB, 2011). Similarly, national guidance such as Christine Burns's (2008) *Trans: A practical guide for the NHS* disappeared as old NHS websites were archived.

This new landscape has also had an important impact on gender identity services. Responsibility for commissioning specialist services has shifted from the local level (through the PCTs or Health Boards) to the national. This means that transitioning patients in England and Wales are now far less likely to be denied funding for treatment. Numerous Clinical Reference Groups (CRGs) were also created under the guidance of NHS England in order to develop clinical strategies for specialist services: one of these took explicit responsibility for gender identity services.

In May 2013, the Gender Identity Services CRG wrote a letter to stakeholders announcing that elements of the Scottish Gender Reassignment Protocol would be adopted for England and Wales (I explore the political background to this decision in Chapter Six). This represented a shift towards a less strict and less rigid management of transitioning, as well as an increased oversight of gender clinic policies on the part of NHS England. An official NHS England Interim Gender Protocol followed. This protocol instituted several important changes in England regarding access to gender identity services. For instance, GPs can now refer patients directly to gender clinics, and (limited) access to hair removal services including laser and electrolysis is now available, funded nationally through NHS England, rather than locally (NHS England, 2013a).

Additionally, gender clinics have started to permit 'non-binary' transitions in recent years, and practitioners such as Christina Richards and colleagues (2017) have begun to publish clinical literature on the care of non-binary and genderqueer patients. While non-binary and genderqueer patients have in fact gained access to gender identity services through the NHS for decades, this has historically tended to involve misrepresenting their gender identity to clinicians in order to negotiate the assessment procedure. Today, non-binary and genderqueer patients are formally permitted to transition openly through the NHS, although clinics such as Charing Cross may require that they participate in studies on the long-term impact of intervention as a condition of treatment.

These changes have not been uniform. Several gender clinics continued to utilise their old, individual pathways, effectively ignoring elements of the NHS England protocol that didn't fit with their philosophy. For instance, until 2016 the Nottingham gender clinic website stated that its clinicians followed the 'Harry Benjamin Standards of Care' (that is, Version 6), despite these having been superseded by the WPATH *Standards of Care* (Version 7) in 2011. This indicated a continued adherence to a stricter form of oversight for transitioning patients. Other clinics, such as the Northamptonshire Gender Dysphoria Service, explicitly denied treatment to non-binary and genderqueer patients into 2016. Meanwhile, the Welsh protocol continued to require that patients undergo a local mental health assessment prior to any referral to Charing Cross (NHS Wales, 2012). New protocols for England and Wales are being prepared and consulted on at the time of writing, so further changes can be expected in coming years.

The overall shifts that have taken place provide more flexibility for English and Welsh patients undergoing physical transition (albeit not as much as in some areas of Scotland), with greater scope for gendered expression plus fewer waits and referrals built into the system. As in Scotland, these shifts reflect changes that took place between Versions

6 and 7 of the WPATH *Standards of Care*, as well as a wider push for 'patient-centred' care within the NHS. However, they do not change the essential nature of gender identity services, in which clinical judgement remains key in assessing whether or not any given patient is (appropriately) trans.

Waiting times

Ironically, formal waiting lists for many gender identity services increased in length even as waits *within* the system largely decreased. The austerity programme launched by the 2010–15 Conservative/ Liberal Democrat Coalition Government had a significant impact upon funding for public health (Roberts, 2015). This in turn contributed to a financial squeeze on gender identity services, which do not receive funding that reflects the exponential growth in patient numbers (NHS England, 2015c). By late 2015, only two smaller adult gender clinics met the NHS 18-week referral standard: Northamptonshire Gender Dysphoria Service and the Brackenburn Clinic in Belfast (UK Trans Info, 2016).[3] A simultaneous crisis in the provision of feminising genital reconstruction surgeries – triggered by the retirement of a senior surgeon and the lack of training for a suitable replacement – resulted in patients waiting up to two years for surgery following assessment and referral (UK Trans Info, 2015). Since this time, gender identity services have undertaken numerous measures to reduce waiting list times, with mixed success. The shortest reported average waiting time at the time of writing is three months, for the Chalmers clinic in Edinburgh; this is maintained in part because the clinic accepts patients only from the NHS Lothian, Borders and Fife areas.

Private pathways

While a majority of transitioning patients access care through NHS gender clinics, other options do exist. In this section, I discuss the private care options available to those who can afford them, and how transitioning individuals might manage their own hormone therapy through self-medication.

At the time of writing there are three major private gender identity services in the UK: GenderCare in London, England, YourGP in Edinburgh and Aberdeen, Scotland and the more recently established GenderGP clinic in Abergavenny, Wales. A fourth service, Transhealth, which was run by Richard Curtis, closed in 2017 (the background to this is discussed in Chapter Six). Private services offer a faster route to treatment: waiting times are short, patients can self-refer and RLE requirements tend to be less demanding. Moreover, non-binary diversity has historically been more widely recognised among private practitioners. Participants in this study generally feel that the private route offers a great deal more agency to those who could afford it, reflecting Zowie Davy's (2010: 123) finding that 'quality and opportunity of treatment' was more likely to be guaranteed through private treatment.

Self-medication

Another option available to individuals wishing to physically transition is self-medication, with hormones acquired outside of a formal medical context. Like private care, self-medication offers trans people more control over their own transition. Dutch consultant Henk Asscheman (cited in Morgan, 2016: 208) notes that 'self-medication has always existed and is not related to legal restrictions … it is related to waiting lists and difficulties in obtaining treatment'. In addition to highlighting the impact of long waits for treatment, Asscheman's comments suggest that strict approaches to the assessment and management of transitioning patients may lead many to self-medicate if they are denied treatment (or fear being denied treatment) by an NHS gender clinic and cannot afford private care.

Some individuals buy hormones through one of several internet-based pharmacies that exploit loopholes in UK law. It is illegal to *sell* certain drugs (including oestrogen and testosterone supplements) *in* the UK if a patient does not have a doctor's prescription. However, it is not illegal for patients to *buy* these drugs. This means that it is technically legal for UK consumers to buy prescription medication from internet pharmacies based *outside* of the UK without the stated approval of a health professional. Other individuals obtain spare pills, patches, gel or needles from trans friends. Some educate themselves extensively regarding the management of their own hormone regime, drawing on evidence from scientific papers and/or a myriad of trans websites offering (sometimes contradictory) advice on the matter.

Self-medication is a highly contested practice within many trans spaces: some participants in this research advocated for the self-management of transition, while others argued that supervision by trained medical professionals is required for safety. Within the professional literature, it is generally agreed that hormone therapy is safest under clinical supervision, where relevant aspects of patient health such as liver function and blood pressure can be monitored by trained endocrinologists (Coleman et al, 2012; Weinand and Safer, 2015).

There have been no studies looking specifically at self-medication in the UK. However, it is likely that the number of trans people who self-medicate is rising as information on the topic becomes more widely available and waiting lists grow longer in many parts of the country. According to Charing Cross endocrinologist Leighton Seal (cited in Morgan, 2016: 207), about 40% of the clinic's patients are self-medicating upon their arrival at the service. If this proportion is similar across the national patient population, then thousands of trans people must be self-medicating in the UK.

Gaming the system?

A number of patients traverse both public and private health pathways. This is usually done in order to speed up the process of transition as much as possible while minimising the financial impact of doing so. Some individuals seek quick access to hormones through private means while waiting to be seen at an NHS gender clinic. Others ask their GP to provide a *repeat* prescription through the NHS (along with blood monitoring for safety) after they have gained an initial hormone prescription from a private clinic or begun self-medicating. There is some disparity between NHS gender clinics and gender identity specialists in their response to this: while it is increasingly standard practice for gender clinics to allow patients to continue their pre-existing hormone regimes during initial assessments (NHS England, 2015c), some gender identity specialists have been known to write to GPs to insist that patients be taken off hormones until they have met clinical requirements regarding RLE.

A contemporary point of political contention between and within several UK medical professions is the possible provision of **bridging hormones** by GPs while trans patients are waiting to be seen at a gender clinic. WPATH (Coleman et al, 2012), the Royal College of Psychiatrists (2013) and the GMC (2016) all recommend that hormones can be provided directly by GPs prior to a gender clinic appointment if a patient is already self-medicating. This guidance is intended to reduce the possibility of harm to trans patients, as the mental health implications of stopping hormone therapy can be profound. However, it caused concern among GPs, some of whom feel that they do not have the appropriate expertise to provide this care (NHS England, 2017a).

Some trans activists argue that bridging hormones should be provided by GPs regardless of whether a patient is self-medicating. A

2016 petition entitled 'Make bridging hormone prescriptions easier to obtain for transgender people' received almost 2,000 signatures on the UK Government and Parliament petition website. As waiting lists for gender clinics persist, and hormones become increasingly available to trans patients through primary care on the basis of informed consent in countries such as Australia, Canada and the United States, demands for similar access in the UK are likely to grow.

Mistrust of health professionals

Trans patients frequently exhibit a mistrust of health professionals (Sanger, 2010; Davy, 2011; Ellis et al, 2015). This can be linked to the difficulties I have described in both general healthcare settings and specialist gender identity services, in which trans patients may be frustrated by ignorance, prejudice and/or the power that health professionals can wield over their lives.

Stories about transphobia and/or cisgenderism in the provision (or denial) of both general and specialist health services feature prominently in community and activist spheres on the internet. These stories are narrated in – and constructed through – discussion threads where individuals seek support following bad experiences, plus lengthy conversations (and sometimes heated debates) around the relative merits or demerits of different doctors and clinics. Such discussions have long taken place within the relatively hidden realms of forums, mailing lists and private social media groups, but are now increasingly visible on public social media platforms such as Twitter, YouTube and Tumblr. Activist groups – such as those observed on Facebook for this project – typically take a more interventionist approach, with individuals seeking advice on how best to actively address either a personal issue or a more systemic problem in their local area.

In January 2013 a large *public* discussion about trans healthcare in (primarily) the UK took place on the Twitter hashtag **#transdocfail**. This was a spectacular manifestation of the stories that are told about cisgenderism and transphobia. According to hashtag instigator Sarah Brown, #transdocfail was created with the explicit intention of offering a counter-discourse to prevailing medical and media narratives of trans health, which centre on matters such as the management of transition and public expenditure on services.

Tweets to the hashtag encompassed an enormous range of different issues. For example, a number of participants describe institutional problems such as ableism, binarism and unnecessary rigidity, grounded in the care pathways and diagnostic criteria of the gender clinics.

To prove commitment to transitioned life, you usually need an official full time occupation. Unfortunately I was a [full-time] carer. (Phoebe Queen)

Have an appointment with a local GIC next month. Not sure either of us see the point because non-binary treatment isn't funded. (Kat Gupta)

Other participants noted examples of individual transphobia from health professionals. Within these stories, practitioners frequently draw upon factually inaccurate assertions in support of prejudiced claims.

My psychiatrist initially refused to refer me cos 'most people regret transitioning'. (Naith Payton)

Instances in which practitioners focus upon a patient's trans status in an irrelevant context are frequently outlined.

Routine appts about non-trans stuff turned into chats about my gender even when I just wanted help for a hurt back or [whatever]. (Tom Robinson)

Many participants note the commonality of inappropriate language. This sometimes arises from ignorance on the part of health professionals. It can be ignorance without malice if the practitioner in question is unfamiliar with trans issues, but ignorance can also arise from an *active* refusal to engage with requests from trans patients or their advocates.

Talking about me my wife kept correcting nurse from him to her, husband to wife. Nurse still continued to misgender each time. (Judith Jones)

Other participants described more explicitly abusive transphobic language from health professionals.

'You're too tall, too fat, too hairy and too masculine to even pass in public as a female.' (Emma)

The sheer volume of such stories – which numbered in the hundreds on #transdocfail alone – demonstrates that these are not isolated incidents. However, as described earlier, many patients feel unable to complain for fear that this will affect their treatment.

In 2015 evidence was heard from a number of trans individuals and organisations at the House of Commons Women and Equalities Committee 'Transgender Equalities' inquiry; in light of this, the Committee issued a damning statement on public health provisions.

> The NHS is letting down trans people: it is failing in its legal duty under the Equality Act. Trans people encounter significant problems in using general NHS services, due to the attitude of some clinicians and other staff who lack knowledge and understanding – and in some cases are prejudiced. The NHS is failing to ensure zero tolerance of transphobic behaviour. GPs too often lack understanding and in some cases this leads to appropriate care not being provided[.] (Women and Equalities Committee, 2016: 3)

Cumulative narratives of cisgenderism and transphobia have therefore increasingly come to shape public and political discourse on trans health. In turn, these narratives come to shape trans patients' everyday expectations of health services, thereby impacting on even the most mundane engagements with service providers. I analyse these phenomena in detail in Chapters Five and Six.

Notably, many of the *positive* stories about health professionals within my data corpus (including on the very short-lived #transdocfail spin-off #transdocwin) involve health professionals of all backgrounds *providing very basic services that patients are entitled to*. These might include writing a letter, offering a referral, using a patient's correct name or preferred pronouns or changing medical record details.

> My NHS number was changed as soon as I submitted my change of name and whether done by the official process or by my very helpful GP, my gender was changed to female even though I was then more than 2 years pre-op. (Ellie)

> I received the letter telling my doctor which hormones to prescribe me this morning :) #TransDocWIN ★Cries with happiness★. (Sarah Savage)

The implication here is that a large proportion of trans patients do not *expect* to be treated well: rather, they anticipate being treated poorly, and adjust their expectations and views of what might constitute a notably 'positive' experience accordingly. Zowie Davy therefore argues that access to affirmative, supportive treatment is frequently regarded by trans patients as a matter of 'luck', particularly in the case of gender identity services.

> [E]xperiences of accessing body modification technologies can be both positive and negative, experience of which is contingent on whether they were taken seriously or not by the GIC and GPs. Both quality and opportunity of treatment depended on the 'luck of the draw' or a 'postcode lottery' for the participants in this research in relation to both GPs and psychiatrists. 'Luck' was often replaced by agency and respect if the participant was fortunate enough to have the capital to fund their body modifications privately, indicating that trans experiences are situated within a class system. (Davy, 2010: 123)

In this context, private healthcare services offer an alternative to the uncertainty and mistrust most commonly associated with health professionals working for the NHS. However, given the very nature of private healthcare, these services are by no means available to all, leading to an inequality in access along economic lines.

Conclusion: characterising care

The overall picture of trans health in the UK is a complex one. Trans patients tend to value the existence of the public health system and the provision of both trans-specific and more general services; however, challenges must frequently be negotiated.

Within general healthcare services, some practitioners openly discriminate against trans people; many more are ignorant of the best ways to help trans patients even if they have good intentions. Institutional attempts at reform have met with mixed success, a situation complicated by the 2013 NHS restructuring in England and Wales. GP practices often refuse to engage with trans inclusion programmes.

Within gender identity services, specialist practitioners act as gatekeepers and wield a great deal of power over patients. Waiting times are typically long, with patients frequently waiting months or years to access initial appointments, and then many months more in order to access interventions such as hormone therapy and surgery. Assessment procedures – which vary greatly from clinic to clinic – can be seen as unnecessarily demanding by patients. The combination of long waiting times and strict assessment procedures leads many patients to seek private services if they can afford them, while others self-medicate. Recent changes have seen NHS rules and guidelines relaxed somewhat – particularly in Scotland – but the essential nature of the system has not changed.

Trans patients are therefore likely to feel disempowered, and many also come to mistrust practitioners. The professional capital of healthcare providers means that it is difficult to challenge practices that are experienced by patients as unfair, inappropriate or discriminatory. I understand this as a power differential between practitioners and patients, which works to shape patient expectations and perspectives on trans health. In the following chapters of this book, I explore the impact of this power differential – as well as waiting times and binary logics of definition – upon discourses of trans health. I also examine how trans activists have drawn upon legal and clinical frameworks such as the Equality Act 2010 and WPATH *Standards of Care*, Version 7 to push for change.

Notes

[1] For many years most NHS bodies (including a number of gender clinics) claimed that the 18-week waiting list limit was not applicable to gender identity services. However, following a campaign by trans organisation UK Trans Info, a letter from NHS England's Director of Commissioning Specialised Services to Healthwatch England's Chief Executive in January 2015 confirmed that the 18-week requirement *is* in fact applicable in this case. Since this time, some efforts have been made (with mixed success) to reduce gender clinic waiting lists.

[2] Versions 6 and 7 of the *Standards of Care* require the approval of just one mental health professional for the provision of hormone therapy and/or chest surgeries. This standard is followed in Scottish guidelines (NHS Scotland, 2012).

[3] Ironically, the publication of these waiting times by UK Trans Info led to an enormous increase in referrals to the Northamptonshire service from across England. By 2017, this clinic had the longest average waiting times in the country. By contrast, the number of referrals to Brackenburn is limited by the comparatively small population of Northern Ireland.

Part Two
Navigating health services

FOUR

(Re)defining trans

> One might wonder what use 'opening up possibilities' finally is, but no one who has understood what it is like to live in the social world as 'impossible,' illegible, unrealizable, unreal and illegitimate is likely to pose that question. (Judith Butler, 1999)

'Coming out' ... as what, or who?

When I first began coming to terms with being trans, I faced two major challenges.

The *second* of these was coming out to other people. How could I describe this ... *thing* ... that might appear so alien and irrational to many? How could I explain that I, who was known to all as a boy, felt myself to be a girl, and wanted and *needed* to move through the world as such?

Should I appeal to science and medicine, noting that 'transsexualism' is an internationally recognised condition, for which treatments have been carefully developed? Should I describe how dysphoria around gender and the sexed body can be deeply experienced, and explain the depth and perseverance of my feelings? Should I explain that I was one of many, part of a long history of gender-variant people who have collectively worked to find new ways in which we can live and prosper? Which of these approaches might be best for talking to my friends, my parents, my school – and my doctor, from whom I would seek both everyday healthcare services and a referral to the gender clinic?

The *first* challenge, however, was coming out to myself; recognising my trans experience as real. Like many trans people, coming to terms with the reality of my gendered identity involved finding a language to account for my feelings and experiences. At first, the only resource I had available to me were the limited images of trans possibility found in the mainstream media of the early 2000s. Guided by vicious tabloid headlines and popular TV comedies such as *Little Britain*, I believed that I must be mentally ill, that there was something 'wrong' with me that couldn't be cured, that I perhaps deserved to be the subject of cruel jokes, that perhaps I *was* a joke. This belief was only compounded by the everyday sexism and homophobia of the playground and my journey to and from school, in which any deviation from norms of masculine behaviour in children coercively assigned a male gender at birth was mocked and punished. I felt that my experience was somehow invalid or unreal, and any expression of it would certainly be socially unacceptable. I therefore repressed my feelings for many years, avoiding any acknowledgement of what felt like an awful impossibility.

Later, I encountered the languages of transsexualism and transvestism. Neither initially made much sense to me. Being a transsexual seemed to require a particular kind of suffering – a deep mental health crisis that I couldn't immediately recognise in myself – along with a strongly sexed/gendered sense of self as (in my case) female. I wasn't sure if I really 'fitted' into this category. While I was certainly depressed about my gender, I'd had a pretty happy childhood, and while I might like to wear make-up and paint my nails, I also enjoyed dressing casually in jeans and heavy metal T-shirts. I wasn't sure that it was *possible* for someone like me to be trans. I inevitably faced similar issues with describing myself as a transvestite or cross-dresser.

It was only when I encountered a diversity of gendered experiences within transgender communities that my feelings really began to make sense. I met trans people who had come to terms with their dysphoria at a far younger or older age than I, trans people who were happy in their own skins as well as those who were deeply troubled, butch trans women and effeminate trans men, genderqueer and non-binary people, trans punks and trans politicians. I came to see how *I* could be transgender, how this could account for both the complexity and individuality of my own experience, my relationship with my body and my connection to a great range of other people.

However, this growing sense of trans possibility – of trans possibili*ties* – still didn't necessarily give me the tools to communicate my feelings and experiences to others. So while I eventually came out and *defined myself* as trans or transgender, I also came out to others first as a cross-dresser, then as a transsexual, drawing strategically upon the narratives that I felt were available to me in order to communicate the reality of my experiences to others.

Cisgenderism, reality and the bounds of possibility

In this chapter, I look at the difficulties of language and definition in a range of healthcare settings, exploring how trans possibilities are defined, redefined and reified through differing processes of recognition in healthcare and community settings. I draw upon three loose models in order to describe how this can happen. These include the discursive repertoires of trans as condition and trans as movement, outlined in the first two chapters of this book. The third model is that of cisgenderism, which I first mentioned in Chapter Two but expand upon here.

In this discussion, I refer to the social construction of reality, through which our ideas about what is 'real' are linked to social recognition as well as the operation of power. In doing so, I draw upon Deborah Lynn Steinberg's description of reality

> as a filter, as a *field of intelligibility* that reciprocally imbricates what is *material* (our senses, our experiences, our mutual publics composed of laws, institutions and place) with what is *understood* – as much a projection as it is a consequence of fact. Thus, what is real is both consequential *to* and a consequence *of* what is seen, and not only that, but what is *sought*. (Steinberg, 2015a: 153, emphasis in original)

This is not to say that reality is a completely subjective matter. Rather, I mean to emphasise how what *seems* real can be shaped as much by shared, social notions of the possible as by material fact.

The historic *un*reality and *im*possibility of trans identity and experience is grounded in cultural and professional cisgenderist norms. Cisgenderism 'represents a systemic erasure and problematising of trans people, [and] an essentialising of gender as binary, biologically determined, fixed at birth, immutable, natural and externally imposed on the individual' (Kennedy, 2013: 4). Within a cisgenderist context, trans lives and bodies represent an impossible deviation from the seemingly necessary alignment of assigned gender, social gender role, gender identity and sexed body as male or female: an alignment described by Butler (1999) as the 'heterosexual matrix'.

Natacha Kennedy (2013) describes **cultural cisgenderism** as a phenomenon with 'low discursive saturation'; by this she means that it is predominantly held and communicated in a tacit or implicit manner. Kennedy draws upon the example of gender-nonconforming children to illustrate this. She notes that: '[t]rans children, like other children, understand that it is usually likely to be socially unacceptable to adopt certain behaviour[s], preferences or appearance[s], particularly those that are outside the social norms of their gendered community of practice' (Kennedy, 2013: 7). Such children therefore typically learn to conceal or suppress their gendered feelings (Kennedy and Hellen, 2010), understanding them to be *impossible* within the context of cultural cisgenderism. This process can also be seen in the personal experiences I outlined in the vignette that opens this chapter.

Kennedy contrasts cultural cisgenderism with **professional cisgenderism**. Drawing upon the work of Y Gavriel Ansara and Peter Hegarty, she argues that this form of cisgenderism exhibits a high discursive saturation; that is, it can be seen explicitly expressed in professional discourse. It is 'a prejudicial *ideology* ... that is systematic, multi-level and reflected in authoritative cultural discourses' (Ansara and Hegarty, 2012: 141, emphasis in original). Ansara and Hegarty illustrate the impact of professional cisgenderism with reference to academic literature from an 'invisible college' within the field of psychology. Cisgenderist language – such as misgendering, which actively ignores the self-ascribed gender of patients – is employed by members of the invisible college in accordance with their ideological views on gendered possibility. This language works to 'dehumanise, silence and erase' all of those who fail to meet normative gender expectations (Ansara and Hegarty, 2012: 152).

Both cultural and professional cisgenderism therefore work to deny the *possibility* of gender variance by delineating the bounds of the real. The children described by Kennedy (2013) learn from the discursive saturation of binary gender norms that it is not *really* possible to be gender variant. They thus hide or amend their behaviour in a manner that serves to reinforce this social reality by keeping alternative possibilities out of sight. The psychologists described by Ansara and Hegarty render trans genders unreal and impossible in a professional setting through actively refusing to acknowledge them, thereby implying that individuals who hold these identities are somehow deluded.

Within cisgenderist discourses, only normative, binary, 'cis' gender identities and experiences are real and possible. It is for this reason that the traditional transsexual narrative offers gender-variant people an opportunity to effectively *become* socially cis through an erasure of their transness.

Consequently, both trans patients and gender clinics have historically faced significant challenges in establishing trans identities, experiences and bodies as possible and real within the UK's public health system. For example, patient access to gender identity services through the NHS became an entitlement only following a legal ruling in 1999.[1] Numerous commissioning bodies attempted to circumvent this in the decade that followed, often due to concerns about being 'publicly seen to be supporting or "advocating" gender reassignment'; this resulted in a number of de facto local bans on gender identity services (Combs et al, 2008: 19). More recently, Bailey and McNeil (2013) showed how GP practices in the North West of England were disinclined to put up freely provided, NHS-branded posters promoting trans health and/or record the number of registered trans patients. One practice manager told the researchers that their project was irrelevant, stating that '[t]here aren't many around here in Cumbria because they'd stick out like a sore thumb' (Bailey and McNeil, 2013: 22). This comment provides evidence of assumptions about how trans people might look or be perceived, but also actively works to deny the *possibility* of trans patients at the practice.

The following pages of this chapter examine how both health professionals and patients have therefore sought to (re)define trans identities and experiences as possible and real, through drawing upon discourses of trans as condition and/or movement. I examine the interplay and intersection of these discursive repertoires, looking at how they can variously work to counter or reinforce cisgenderist norms and assumptions. Drawing on material from across all three spheres of my data corpus, I illustrate points of similarity, difference and influence, looking particularly at how various understandings and definitions of trans possibility might shape expectations of treatment among practitioners and patients alike.

I begin with a brief re-examination of the traditional transsexual narrative, showing how it emerged to reflect the cultural and ideological investments of trans patients as well as medical practitioners. I then turn to my research findings to look at how discourses of trans as condition can shape medical practice and trans perceptions of self. In particular, I show how understandings of trans as transition can limit the availability of information on trans health, and how gatekeeping processes work to define the scope of trans/gendered possibility. This is followed by a discussion of discourses of trans as movement, in which I show how they can provide discursive alternatives to trans as condition within the realms of both personal identity and gender-pluralist trans community. Finally, I explore the difficult consequences of discursive clashes within healthcare settings, in which cisgenderist norms and differing understandings of trans as condition or movement have separately shaped the respective perspectives of practitioners and patients.

Transsexual histories and posttranssexual possibilities

In Chapter Two I described Stone's (1991) account of 'posttranssexual' possibilities. In contrast to the traditional transsexual, the posttranssexual would 'read oneself aloud' and 'write oneself into the [medical, feminist, transsexual] discourses by which one has been written' (Stone, 1991: 232). Stone's account recognises the social and historical contingency of transsexual identity and experience, created through patients' interactions with medical literatures and health institutions.

This does not mean that transsexual people were (or are) without agency, nor does it mean that they were (or are) necessarily dupes of the medical establishment. As Stone (1991: 228) herself notes, transsexual patients historically took the seemingly necessary steps required to access treatment; for instance, through describing an experience of 'being in the "wrong" body', in line with Harry Benjamin Association (later WPATH) *Standards of Care*. Joanne Meyerowitz (2002) argues that patient demands for treatment were a key factor in the emergence of the transsexual medical model in the first place. Such demands could involve active efforts to educate health professionals. Patients sought to explain themselves through drawing emotively upon personal accounts and discursively upon the authoritative languages of psychology, biology and religion. For example, many patients 'portrayed themselves as intersex, hoping perhaps, as one psychiatrist phrased it, to "substantiate a biological basis for their condition["]' (Meyerowitz, 2002: 140).[2]

The discourse of transsexualism offered more than access to hormones or surgery; it also provided an identity, and an explanation for otherwise inexplicable feelings of dysphoria. Rubin argues:

> As much as these claims [to transsexual identity] substantiate the logic of treatment and provide a rhetorical justification for treatments, they also represent [transsexuals'] attempts to theorize the circumstances that confront them, to put their enigmatic existence into words, and to relieve themselves of the constant queries about who and what they are. (Rubin, 2003: 498)

Transsexual identities can therefore be understood as constructed in *collaboration* between trans people and health professionals (Ekins and King, 2006). The traditional transsexual narrative represented a move by gender-variant people to write themselves into the available condition-oriented discourses of gendered possibility. Coming out as transsexual offered people the opportunity to counter cultural cisgenderism by explaining their existence to themselves *and* to the health professionals who might be able to help them transition. However, this was not the only vision of gender-variant possibility that emerged during the 20th century. In Chapter Two I also showed how discourses of transgender or *trans* identity and embodiment offered a vision of posttranssexual possibility from the 1990s onward, with writers such as Leslie Feinberg envisaging trans as a broad *movement* of gender-diverse minority groups uniting around shared oppressions. I further conceptualised the growing range of non-binary or genderqueer identities – which emphasise fluidity, complexity and the multiplication of possibilities – as inherently bound up in discourses of trans as movement.

The fragile alliance of disparate groups under a trans umbrella has resulted in numerous discursive conflicts over language and the boundaries of identity, but has also worked to create more space for diversity and difference *within* as well as between constituent identity categories. Shifts in language and community, shaped by the growing possibilities of trans as movement, have broken down the monolith of (restricted) transsexual possibility described by Stone. In the 21st century, a 'transsexual' might transition socially but not physically; they may choose to undergo some medical procedures but not others; or they may seek to transition into a non-binary role instead of endeavouring to live as a woman or as a man.

These days, a desire for physical transition does not necessarily entail a transsexual identity. Transitioning individuals increasingly understand themselves as (for example) genderqueer, transgender or simply trans. Some trans people continue to 'fade into the "normal" population' (Stone, 1991: 230) by passing as cis, a course of action known as 'going stealth'. However, the increasing ubiquity of internet communities and growth in the number of localised trans groups means that it is now possible to go stealth while retaining contact with trans communities. In this way, new understandings of physical transition allow for *both* the expansion of existing female and male categories *and* movements beyond the gender binary altogether (Monro, 2007). These possibilities represent a complex interaction between the discursive repertoires of trans as condition and trans as movement, in which trans people draw upon a range of ideas to understand and explain themselves: to write themselves into the discourses by which they have been written.

Conditional possibilities in trans healthcare

Discourses of trans as condition may be utilised by both trans patients and health professionals to a range of ends. In this section I explore several of these, unpacking how different discourses can be utilised in order to explain and justify modes of treatment as well as the bounds of gendered possibility.

A considerable majority of research participants from the activist and community spheres draw in some way upon discourses of trans as condition in describing their gendered identities and/or interactions with healthcare services. This is particularly the case among individuals who are undergoing, have undergone or intend to undergo a physical transition. Similarly, all but a small number of the materials sampled within the practitioner sphere conceptualise trans as condition. These materials focus upon matters of gatekeeping, diagnosis and the treatment of gender disorders or dysphoria, representing professional engagement with trans possibilities in a manner that prioritises medically mediated transition. I shall show that condition-oriented definitions of trans within all three spheres of the field can also limit the scope of trans possibilities, thereby rendering trans *conditional*.

I begin with a look at modes of possibility within the practitioner sphere. A range of positions are apparent in the materials from this area of the data corpus. However, two patterns were observed. Firstly, an overwhelming majority of sources focus on issues of diagnosis and treatment for transitioning patients, to the extent that other issues concerning trans health remain largely unaddressed; this derives from and feeds into an understanding of **trans as transition**. Secondly, accounts of specialist diagnosis and treatment position health professionals as gatekeepers in relation to trans healthcare provision, with the power and responsibility to shape notions of what appropriate trans lives, trans bodies and transitions might look like. Having examined these patterns, I then draw upon data from the activist and community spheres to show how discourses of trans as condition can be used by transitioning patients to rationalise personal experiences of dysphoria and explain trans issues to the wider cisgenderist world.

Trans as transition

With the transition process almost unique to trans people,[3] it is inevitable that discussions around 'trans health' will frequently centre upon gender identity services. Nevertheless, there is a disproportionate dearth of services and public documentation addressing wider issues of trans health. I attribute this to a pervasive understanding of trans *as transition*, which works to erase wider conceptualisations of trans health.

Very few of the materials sampled from the practitioner sphere specifically address trans health issues other than gender dysphoria and transition. The majority of those that do were acquired from websites belonging to trans-specific sexual health services, such as cliniQ in London. The cliniQ website provides a range of health information for trans patients, plus links to guides on trans sexual health created by cliniQ and/or in collaboration with external bodies such as HIV/

AIDS charity the Terrence Higgins Trust and youth group Gendered Intelligence. Aside from these materials, and occasional documents with basic information on trans people produced for GPs and other non-specialists, I found only three other publications which explicitly focused on trans health issues other than physical transition within the practitioner sphere during the main period of fieldwork. Two of these were administrative documents outlining a process by which trans patients can change their name and gender marker on NHS health records. The other was a guide for trans victims of domestic violence published by NHS Barking and Dagenham. This compares to a great number of consultation documents, formal letters, guidance for health professionals and patients, position papers, protocols, meeting minutes, blogs and websites produced by, for and about gender identity services in the UK.

The lack of information on wider issues of trans health arises in part from a paucity of formal evidence on the matter (Meads et al, 2009). The difficulty of generating an evidence base within the realm of primary health is also powerfully illustrated by Bailey and McNeil (2013) in their description of barriers to engagement among GP practices. However, the little evidence that does exist strongly indicates that trans people have specific health needs and concerns beyond dysphoria and transition that require particular attention. With reference to a handful of large US studies and a small UK action research project, Julie Fish (2007: 4) argues that trans people are at particular risk of experiencing alcohol and substance abuse, depression, suicide, self-harm, violence and HIV; similar findings are reported by Sari Reisner and colleagues (2016) in their review of international evidence. Whittle and colleagues (2007) and McNeil and colleagues (2012) report on the disproportionate prevalence of mental health issues, suicide ideation and suicide attempts among trans people in the UK. Furthermore, recent research indicates a significantly higher apparent prevalence of autistic spectrum conditions among trans people than within the general population (Van Der Miesen et al, 2016); this is perhaps particularly the case among non-binary and genderqueer people (Kristensen and Broome, 2015; Valentine, 2016).[4]

I previously noted that concrete engagement with the issues outlined above is almost entirely absent within the practitioner sphere. This has wider consequences for the provision of public information around trans health. For example, at the time of writing, the NHS Choices web page 'Transgender health' – part of the 'Live Well' series on healthy living – provides little information on trans health issues beyond those related to transition. Most of the resources linked to from the page provide personal accounts of transition from the perspective of trans individuals, as well as from the perspective of trans people's partners and parents. These stories all rely in some sense on binary logic, with the narratives present on the page all drawing on the language and imagery of (exclusively white) masculine or feminine possibilities for gendered expression.[5] Information on gender dysphoria and NHS gender clinics is also provided. This singular focus contrasts notably with other pages dedicated to minority health within the 'Live Well' series, such as the 'Gay health' page (which provides extensive information on sexual health, mental health, reproductive health and access to services) and the 'Black health' page (which offers information on diabetes, sickle cell anaemia, prostate cancer, blood pressure, skin lightening and mental health).

Wider issues of trans health are therefore effectively erased within the practitioner sphere through a focus on transition. This has some basis in the paucity of available research on wider issues of trans health in the UK; however, the information that *does* exist is often not reflected in available resources. A consequence of this is the perpetuation of a discourse of trans *as* (binary, white) transition, in which gender-variant identity and experience is necessarily linked to a very particular, conditional form of trans possibility. In this way, the dearth of information on wider issues of trans health does not simply mean that vital information regarding trans well-being is not publicised; it also limits the discursive possibilities available to trans people seeking to write themselves into being.

Gatekeeping: the gender experts

Health providers play a further role in defining trans possibility through controlling access to treatment for people who seek to transition. In Chapter Three I showed how gatekeeping operates through assessment and diagnosis as well as through processes of long-term management such as RLE. In assessing patients for diagnosis and managing their treatment, healthcare professionals may draw on and promulgate certain ideas regarding behaviours and bodies that might be considered appropriate (or 'trans enough', in the words of some participants) for transition.

The gatekeeping process relies upon an understanding of health professionals as *experts*. Their expertise is grounded in a learned knowledge of assessment processes and available treatments, tied to diagnostic criteria and institutional protocols. This knowledge is typically framed within the practitioner sphere as authoritative and unbiased, as can be seen in the following excerpt from a draft clinical commissioning policy for the NHS England Gender Identity CRG.

> [I]t should be remembered that the overarching aim of treatment for gender dysphoria is 'to enable affected persons to achieve lasting personal comfort with their gendered selves, in order to maximize their overall health, psychological well-being, and self-fulfilment.' The range of interventions described in this commissioning policy … are recommended as components of a comprehensive, need-related package of care in all relevant, *authoritative* clinical guidelines. All these interventions must be available to all patients within the care pathway, on the basis of their *individual clinical need* (but *not their personal social preference*), as assessed by [gender identity service] clinicians[.] (NHS England, 2015d, emphasis mine)

The language of the draft clinical commissioning policy works to underline the *authority* of gender specialists' expertise. This is set against an implied *lack* of authoritative expertise from two groups: detractors within the NHS, and trans patients themselves.

The first group is implicitly present within the document. Gender identity services have historically had an 'image problem' within the NHS, reflecting cultural cisgenderist norms and transphobic prejudices within wider society (Combs et al, 2008). Physical transition can be seen as the unnecessary disruption of a 'healthy body' by health professionals who lack the relevant expertise. From this perspective, trans accounts of dysphoria are unreal, arising from delusion rather than medical need. This perception is reinforced by media accounts of transition as a waste of public money, which only compounds the ideological, financial and resource pressures upon gender identity services and NHS commissioners (Combs et al, 2008). The draft clinical commissioning policy responds to these concerns with a review of medical literature that demonstrates the benefits of gender identity services for transitioning patients. The 'definitions' section of the document opens with a quote from the ICD-10 section on 'Transsexualism', thereby tying the policy's authority to international clinical consensus. The document's authors take care to employ language that reinforces the medical rigour of gender identity services, as seen in the contextual use of terms such as 'need' and 'authority' in the quoted passage.

This language has consequences for the second group with an implied lack of expertise, who are more explicitly present within the document: transitioning patients themselves. Gender identity specialists have the authority to oversee transitioning patients' 'personal comfort with their gendered selves ... overall health, psychological well-being, and self-fulfilment'; this is clearly prioritised over patients' 'personal social preference[s]'.

A stated respect for this authority can often be seen within trans spaces, particularly within the community sphere. An example can be found in the following comment from a community forum, which was made in response to a post by someone seeking to better understand their gendered feelings and explore the possibility of defining as trans.

> Have you had any appointments with gender specialists, psychiatrists or at the Gender Identity Clinic? Their job is to help us question the way we feel and *decide what's right for us objectively*, so maybe they'd have better advice than anything I can offer. (Aiden, emphasis mine)

In this way, the authority of professional knowledge leads Aiden to invest in their expertise, and encourage other trans people to do so also. I return to this theme shortly.

In managing their patients' transitions, gender specialists frequently go beyond simply making a medical judgement on the basis of diagnostic criteria. Through their interpretation of guidelines (from WPATH, the NHS and/or the individual gender clinics) these practitioners hold the power to determine what constitutes an acceptable form of gendered behaviour and embodiment for the purposes of transition. Until 2016, this was explicitly acknowledged on the Nottingham Centre for Transgender Health 'What we do' web page, which described practitioners' role in overseeing RLE. The page stated that patients need to provide appropriate evidence of their participation in RLE, adding that: '[t]he *gender experts* at the clinic will need to make sure that you are out and about in your new gender role' (emphasis mine). At the Nottingham clinic, this can occur prior to treatment such as hormone therapy being offered: '[i]n order for an individual to be accepted for treatment, they need to socially transition first, which includes not only living as their experienced gender but also changing their name and most legal documents' (Arcelus et al, 2017: 22). It is therefore up to these 'gender experts' to decide what constitutes appropriate conformity to the patient's preferred gender role. Patients who do not appropriately conform to these requirements may face censure.

> Gave GIC evidence for RLE for a year stating I was presenting as male despite also having a gender neutral title (on 3 items). Told I had to change to Mr or be discharged. (TransDocFailAnon)

In the above example from the #transdocfail hashtag on Twitter, an anonymous contributor highlights how conformity to the gender binary was demanded by a gender clinic (GIC) as a condition of continued treatment. As Stone (1991: 228) comments in her description of treatment criteria for transsexual people: '*at the site of their enactment we can locate an actual instance of the apparatus of production of gender*' (emphasis in original). This form of gatekeeping can be understood as a 'border patrol' (Steinberg et al, 1997) that polices the boundaries of the possible. Steinberg (1997) describes how the notion of a 'fit family' can be used to police the borders of heterosexuality in the realm of reproductive health, thereby upholding heterosexist norms. Similarly, the gender experts' 'objective' judgements of appropriate behaviour work to police the borders of gender. Within local mental health settings and in gender clinics, this border patrol is a form of professional cisgenderism, which explicitly prioritises the expertise of a (largely cis) profession over the lived experiences of patients.

A second example of this can be seen in the below quote from a practitioner who is concerned about trans patients who decide not to 'fully' transition. His comment was made during a meeting of gender identity specialists from several different UK clinics.

> [Dr Deenesh Khoosal] spoke to the group about the issue of unintentionally creating 'she-men': patients who have breasts and are on hormones but don't have final surgery as they don't want to go any further. These patients continue to live full time as female but with male genitalia. Many of the services present at the meeting had examples of this happening. (G3 – Gender Governance Group, 2009)

The reference to Dr Khoosal's *intentions* highlights his role in overseeing and controlling gendered embodiment in his patients' respective transitions. The fact that he raises an *un*intentional consequence of treatment with the group in order to ask for advice on the matter, along with his use of the derogatory term 'she-men', strongly suggests that he is concerned about this outcome, as it runs contrary to his *intentions*.

There are two important binary discourses implicit within Khoosal's stated concerns, which I shall unpack with reference to Monro's (2007) terminology of gender diversity. Firstly, he refers disapprovingly to what is effectively an expansion of the 'female' category. A number of his patients 'live full time as female', exhibiting various secondary sexual characteristics normatively regarded as 'female' (such as breasts) even as they retain a body part that is normatively regarded as 'male' (the penis). They therefore effectively threaten to redefine what it *means* to be 'female' through living contentedly as women with penises. Secondly, Khoosal's concerns are relevant to the possibility of movements beyond the gender binary altogether: while some of the patients he describes will see themselves as women, others might understand themselves in non-binary terms. In describing the expansion of gendered categories and potential movements beyond the gender binary as 'unintentional', Khoosal appeals to cisgenderist boundaries of appropriate sexed embodiment, and centres his own professional authority controlling these boundaries. He is not simply acting as gatekeeper for treatment, but is also patrolling the borders of sex and gender.

Khoosal's approach to gatekeeping is by no means universal within the practitioner sphere. My findings provided evidence of a wide range of attitudes towards gender and trans possibility among health professionals, with many individuals considerably more committed to meeting the stated desires of their transitioning patients. Furthermore, there were significant changes in professional discourse over time, with the aforementioned 2015 draft clinical commissioning policy explicitly stating that patients with gender dysphoria might seek some medical interventions but not others, and/or undergo a non-binary transition (I explore the background to this, along with more recent developments, in Chapter Six). Nevertheless, the cisgenderist status of practitioner as 'gender expert' and border patrol within a professional context effectively remains. The role of gender identity specialist continues to entail a pronouncement on the trans status of any given patient, with UK professional consensus providing an authoritative, conditional basis for medical definitions of trans/gendered possibility.

Reifying identity through medical discourse

I now examine how trans people themselves may understand trans as condition. Many participants in this project appealed to discourses of condition in conceptualising their relationship to gender and their sexed body. Discourses of condition are most often used to rationalise personal experiences of dysphoria, but can also be employed strategically in justifying trans identity and experience to friends, family members and work colleagues, and in attempting to gain access to services. In all such instances, there is an agential claim being made about the *reality* of trans experience in response to cultural cisgenderism, with transness rendered possible through medical discourse.

A number of participants describe their trans experience as a 'medical condition'. These accounts implicitly reference the diagnoses present within classificatory systems such as the ICD and DSM. In making such connections, the participants in question draw upon the *authority* of clinical consensus in a similar manner to the aforementioned draft NHS England policy. Descriptions of trans as condition therefore serve to imbue trans experiences with a sense of authoritative weight and seriousness. Two examples follow:

> An individual … posted about troubles she is having changing her name and pronoun with her GP surgery …[.] The author of this post states that [the practice's inaction] breaches her right to privacy in regards to people knowing about her 'medical condition'. (Fieldwork diary: 14 May 2013, quotation marks indicate terminology used by the post author)

> We have a condition that we were born with, that causes sufficient distress/ dis ease for a large number of us to try to take our own lives. (Shannon)

Both of these accounts represent a move to explain and validate trans experience. In the first instance, the author sets the discursive weight of 'medical condition' against the dismissive actions of her GP practice, thereby portraying the practice as failing in duty of care *in its own terms*. In the second instance, Shannon draws upon the high prevalence of poor mental health and suicide within the trans population to reinforce the seriousness of the dysphoric 'condition'. In this way, trans experiences can be interpellated as *real* through claims to discursive authority in medicalised language.

Within the above examples it does not really matter *what* the 'condition' is, only that the individual in question has it; however, other participants sought to provide a more grounded medicalised account of being. For instance, some people sought personal validation through a specific diagnosis of transsexualism or gender dysphoria. Like the broader notion of a 'medical condition', the specific conditions spelled out in the ICD and DSM provide an alternative to the internalisation of cultural cisgenderist discourses that render trans unreal. An example of this can be found in the account of Chris, who writes about a forthcoming assessment appointment.

> I'm going to know whether I have [gender identity disorder] or not on friday when I go to see the psych [to find out] if I do have it and I suspect that I do. (Chris)

This post positions the 'psych' as an expert who can effectively determine whether or not Chris is trans. Chris 'suspects' that this is the case, but seeks external confirmation. A second forum user replies to argue that it is not the role of the medical practitioner to determine anyone's gender. Chris offers an ambivalent response:

> I know that it's not dependant on the shrink, it's just I'd like a name to put on why I'm feeling the way I do if that makes sense. (Chris)

Chris's perspective demonstrates the powerful validating potential of medical diagnosis. He is in touch with his gendered feelings and doesn't feel that the practitioner has an absolute say on the matter, but nevertheless hopes for a diagnosis. A medical 'name' for Chris's feelings would provide an authoritative claim to an experience that might otherwise be concealed or suppressed (Kennedy and Hellen, 2010), if not regarded as somehow unreal or impossible. This demonstrates an *agential* engagement with medical expertise by Chris, who – like the trans patients described by Meyerowitz (2002) and Rubin (2003) – is actively seeking to define himself with reference to an established authority on the matter.

Medical discourse can also be used to persuade *others* that transness is real and possible. For example, several younger participants refer to the benefit of professional support in persuading parents and/or schools to take trans feelings seriously. In the below examples, Brian and Aiden offer advice to other young trans people.

> It might be useful to have the backing of a person in the medical profession when talking to your parents because they will be more inclined to take you seriously[.] (Brian)

> I don't know the formal route for this mate but I'd recommend getting your doctor to write you a note [for school] about having gender dysphoria (have you been to see a psych who has 'officially' confirmed this?) (Aiden)

Similarly, Ellie describes drawing upon medical discourse to explain her existence to people who question her gender.

> Although my voice is better I still get read [as trans] on the phone at least 4 times out of 5. If I get any trouble for this, I just tell the truth – I was born male and am an MTF transsexual in the care of Charing Cross[.] (Ellie)

In the three above instances, participants recommend that others employ the authoritative weight of professional acknowledgement to persuade others that their gender is real and valid, thereby countering cultural cisgenderism. This can be regarded as a strategic move, rather than one grounded in any actual special knowledge held by practitioners rather than trans patients. For example, Aiden's use of quotation marks around the word 'officially', indicates the contingency of the 'official' position (this also reflects a shift in Aiden's personal perspective on medical authority, which occurred over time as he encountered cisgenderism in gender clinics).

Regardless, the value of diagnosis is that practitioners are more likely to be seen as 'experts' than ordinary trans people, due to their professional standing as well as wider cultural cisgenderist attitudes towards trans authenticity. This means that an appeal to medical expertise is effectively an appeal to a higher discursive authority. The prioritisation of professional expertise is therefore self-perpetuating: as trans people take advantage of this socially legitimated expertise, they work to reinforce that legitimisation through prioritising the informed opinion of health professionals over their own experiences.

One consequence of health practitioners' authority with regard to trans issues is that they are called upon to support trans people's legal claims to gendered identity and civil rights in a range of contexts. Sometimes this is legally required: for example, a doctor's letter is necessary for a change of gender marker on a passport. Similarly, the GRA requires the support of a gender identity specialist for an application to the Gender Recognition Panel. On other occasions, participants noted that the support of a health professional could be beneficial even when not technically required, such as in applying for a change of name at a GP practice or in the workplace. The specific perceived expertise of the professional in question is also of relevance.

> [S]ome new comments on the long [Facebook] thread about changing gender/titles with GPs. An individual draws upon passport name change guidance to recommend that people

get a psychiatrist's letter confirming that their gender change will be permanent ('this will be a permanent change') in order to update their passport (passports were mentioned in passing by an individual on an earlier occasion). She also states that her PCT stopped using [inappropriately] gendered pronouns and that they now use the right name and pronouns for her. (Fieldwork diary: 3 June 2013)

The above quote from my fieldwork diary highlights how getting a letter specifically from a *mental health* specialist can help trans people more efficiently change name and gender in a variety of contexts, even though in some cases (such as for passports) any medical practitioner will do, while in other cases (such as for NHS records) no medical approval is required. This shows the existence of a perceived hierarchy of gender expertise, with psychiatrists and psychologists prioritised in a range of social contexts.

In contrast to quests for personal and social validation through mental health diagnosis, some participants instead regard dysphoric feelings as a condition of the body. This reflects Meyerowitz's (2002) observation that many trans people have historically sought a biological basis for their experience, effectively positioning transsexualism as a form of intersex. For instance, in the following extract from a post addressed to a cis man, Alex refers to neuroscience research to argue that trans/gendered feelings are innate.

If you had an accident tomorrow and you lost your penis would you want to then go shopping for female clothes and shoes? No you would likely want that rebuilt. As you are not a female. As trans men prove having a penis does not make you a man – it's a brain sex issue. (Alex)

Alex included a link to a research paper in her post, thereby using medical research to provide an explanation for trans experiences. In the linked article, the authors draw upon an initial comparative analysis of neurons within trans and cis brains to argue that trans women's brains might more closely resemble those of cis women than cis men (Kruijver et al, 2000). This account offers a particular take on the 'wrong body' narrative of transsexual possibility, in which individuals desire transition because they are 'born in the wrong body'.[6] Alex grounds her *justification* for being trans in both mind/body dualism and 'scientific' discourse: the gender dysphoric person's 'body' is 'wrong' because it is at odds with their brain. A related account is provided by Serano

(2007), who argues that gender-dysphoric individuals experience a conflict between their sexed body and the 'subconscious sex' of their mind. As with Chris's appeal to diagnosis, these conceptualisations are important in offering a counter-discourse to cultural cisgenderist norms, thereby rendering trans possible and intelligible. This is seen most clearly in participant accounts that describe the process of physical transition and the changes that can take place, highlighting the comfort of transitioned individuals in their changed bodies. For instance, Ellie provides an overview of the MTF transition process, describing at length the satisfying physical, emotional and sexual changes that accompany hormone therapy and surgeries. She adds:

> A transsexual isn't a guy pretending sometimes, she is someone who was ALWAYS female inside. A transsexual changes sex and drops a pretence of being a guy that she was forced to learn by pressure from parents and society, based on the birth-defect between her legs … So – we aren't men-who-got-their-body-changed – we ARE women, apart from perhaps being a bit big and angular … We make a change because it's who-we-are. (Ellie)

Trans patients may therefore seek an explanation for being trans grounded in medical practice and/or medical science, as part of a quest for personal and social understanding. In this way trans identities and experiences can become possible, reified as real and intelligible. These efforts frequently represent an appeal to the specific professional expertise of gender identity specialists, as well as to wider cultural investments in the 'truth' of scientific language (Steinberg, 2015a). While trans might be understood as *conditional* in these terms – something that requires that conditions are met, or something specific that is 'wrong' with the mind or body – it can nevertheless be defined and constructed as *real*.

This is not simply a matter of trans patients being 'passive or culturally determined by coercive forces': instead, it represents a 'situational' engagement with available discourses (Davy, 2011: 107). For those such as Ellie who seek to change their bodies, the very act of physical transition on the NHS pathway serves to reify her identity by offering an alternative to cultural cisgenderism, even as this possibility continues to be shaped by the professional cisgenderism of gatekeepers and clinical pathways. In this way, trans patients' own accounts of trans as condition 'have both agentic and subjugating elements to them' (Davy, 2011: 107).

The possibility of movement

I have shown that discourses of trans as condition play a key role in shaping both clinical practice and patient approaches to trans identity, experience and embodiment. However, these conceptualisations typically intersect with understandings drawn from the discursive repertoire of trans as movement, particularly within trans community and activist spaces. I therefore turn now to examine how discourses of trans as movement complement and/or provide an alternative to discourses of trans as condition, while also challenging cisgenderism.

Alternatives to the transsexual narrative

Feinberg's (1992) account of *collective* trans movement incorporates a wide range of identities that, unlike 'transsexual', are not so typically associated with medical mediation or discourses of trans as condition. Historically, this includes 'drag queens and drag kings, cross-dressers, bull-daggers, stone butches, androgynes, diesel dykes', among others (Feinberg, 1992: 206); more recent movement-oriented possibilities include non-binary and genderqueer identities. All offer a fluid range of *individual* movement-oriented possibilities for identification and social belonging to those who do not want to transition as well as to those who cannot do so because of medical conditions, social circumstances and/or gatekeeping practices.

One non-transsexual identity that *can* be linked to discourses of trans as condition is 'transvestite'. The term originates from medical literatures; however, in contrast to transsexualism, transvestism is no longer strongly associated with discourses of condition, in part because there are no medical gatekeeping processes associated with access to cross-dressing. Notably, none of the participants in this project who identified as transvestites or cross-dressers expressed a desire to seek confirmation or validation of their gender identity through medical diagnosis; this was similarly the case with individuals who held a non-binary or genderqueer identity.

Alternatives to transsexualism offer new modes by which physical transition can be conceptualised by those who do desire to undergo such processes. Movement-oriented identities provide a means by which trans people can expand traditional gender categories or otherwise conceptualise gendered possibility beyond the binary bounds of male/female. This is coupled with a sense of belonging and validation grounded in shared experience and community. In this way, trans identities of movement offer a counter-discourse to cultural *and* professional forms of cisgenderism. In this context, gendered knowledge and expertise resides within the individual and with trans communities, rather than with health professionals. This has consequences for all transitioning individuals, including those who continue to describe themselves as transsexual.

Embracing diversity? Building trans communities

Community spaces both online and offline offer trans people the opportunity to come together with others who share similar or comparable experiences. These spaces often constitute a 'community of care', in which members offer mutual emotional support and practical advice that is not necessarily available within the predominantly cisgenderist spaces of the wider world (Hines, 2007). For instance, trans communities of care can provide some of the wider information on trans health that is missing from the practitioner sphere. They also offer members an opportunity to explore and experiment with gender in relative safety, which can feed into the emergence of new language and modes of possibility, such as non-binary identities.

This is not to say that trans community spaces are without conflict. One common basis for quite severe disagreements is identity. Many trans communities retain either an explicit or implicit identity-oriented focus, which works to include some and exclude others. Sometimes, this focus can be relatively narrow, as seen in social groups and online forums based around specific categorical identities such as MTF cross-dressers, or transsexual men. There is a long history of 'border' politics associated with such spaces (Bornstein, 1994; Elliot, 2009). Nael Bhanji (2013: 515) argues that '[i]n many trans communities, the pressure to pass, to blend into the mainstream, can be intense. The push from pre-op to post-op, from transitioning to transitioned, from transgressed to trans*fixed* results in the transsexual forever rushing onward to find the space beyond.'

Community members may work to delineate the boundaries of their identity category through strategies of social inclusion and exclusion, or they can seek to validate their chosen identity category as 'real' through undermining related but alternative modes of identification. For instance, Jack Halberstam (1998: 287) describes how the borders of transmasculinity can be contested between butches and transsexual men: 'Some butches consider FTMs to be butches who "believe in anatomy," and some FTMs consider butches to be FTMs who are too afraid to transition.' I read Halberstam's (1998) account as illustrative of how an identity category rooted in a discourse of condition (FTM transsexualism) can be set against an identity category rooted in discourses of lesbian and/or trans movement (butch). The result is a form of sociocultural border patrol, with members of both categorical camps acting as an alternative form of 'gender expert'.

However, many trans spaces are more inclusive. The very concepts of 'trans' and 'transgender' in their widest sense are of relevance here. A strategic employment of either term in the title or description of an activist or community group often signals a certain malleability of categorical borders (Pearce and Lohman, 2018). There are a growing number of trans spaces that aim (with varying levels of success) to be inclusive of all trans people, regardless of gendered (or intersectional) identity. In these contexts, '[i]t is not that there is an absence of divergence; it is that the divergences are framed in a non-conflictual way' (Richardson and Monro, 2010: 104). One of the two forums from the community sphere visited for this research – which I refer to as 'Forum 1' – was an example of this. Other spaces focus on a particular part of the trans spectrum while taking care to be inclusive of diversity *within* that area: examples include non-binary spaces that encompass a range of identities such as genderqueer, genderfluid, agender and non-gendered, and some transmasculine spaces which are inclusive of non-binary individuals, butches, drag kings and FTM cross-dressers as well as trans men. One instance of the latter is the other forum from the community sphere, which I refer to as 'Forum 2'. This forum is for individuals on the 'female to male spectrum'. The existence of these more diverse spaces reflects the discursive reach of Feinberg's (1992) conceptualisation of trans as movement, enabling gender pluralism (Monro, 2005). In this way, inclusive trans spaces can work to unite people from a range of gender-diverse backgrounds on the basis of perceived shared experiences and interests, in contrast to more exclusive spaces that divide on the basis of perceived difference.

Discourses of trans as movement and spaces that prioritise diversity create room for individuals who are exploring their gender but are not sure where they might fit in. For example, in the following quote trans journalist Juliet Jacques explains how the term 'transgender' offered her a conceptual space in which she could name her feelings, thereby enabling her to explore her gender without having to adapt to meet the criteria of a more rigid form of categorisation.

> Gradually, I came to define as 'transgender'. I understood that transgender could include cross-dressers, transvestites, male-to-female (MtF) and female-to-male (FtM) transsexuals, and anyone else who considered themselves beyond the

traditional gender binary. Having found a suitable term for myself, which allowed space for me to explore my gender, I wanted to find places where I could express myself and meet like-minded people. (Jacques, 2010)

When she was first coming out, Jacques did not yet know how she might fit into the trans spectrum. She was not entirely sure how to describe her gender, whether she desired to transition or what interventions she might seek if she *were* to transition. In defining herself as 'transgender', she found a category that encompassed and described her experience, while retaining space for fluidity and uncertainty. For Jacques, 'transgender' enables affiliation and belonging without border control, within a category that is relatively wide and has fluid boundaries. This enables her to seek a 'trans counter-culture' without first meeting a strict set of criteria.

Spaces such as Forums 1 and 2 and accounts such as Jacques's demonstrate a gender-pluralist understanding of trans/transgender. They unite identities such as transsexualism – more likely to be associated with discourses of essentialism and/or condition – with more fluid and postmodern non-binary possibilities *and* room for uncertainty. In this way, belonging and definition as 'transgender' need not be confirmed by external experts, be they adherents to the traditional transsexual narrative, practitioners who subscribe to professional cisgenderist norms or movement-oriented border patrols.

The sense of possible trans unity across categories of gendered understanding and identification has given rise to an 'imagined community' of trans people (Anderson, 1991; Bhanji, 2013): that is, a group (supposedly) bound by a sense of community affiliation and shared experience. This imagined community is frequently referred to as '*the* trans community', conjuring up the impression of a single grand social unit to which all trans people might belong (Valentine, 2007). An example can be seen in the following quote from an article about #transdocfail by trans journalist Jane Fae:

[I]f you have been following the news over the last few days, you may have noticed something odd. The trans community, notoriously fissiparous, disunited and eternally at loggerheads with itself turned with one accord and sent forth a shaft of pure anger in the direction of the medical establishment ... Never have I seen the community so united: never so angry. (Fae, 2013)

Fae invokes *the* trans community in describing the high level of interest and participation in #transdocfail among trans groups online. Her account acknowledges divisions and the border politics of identity, but suggests that these differences can be overcome in the name of shared interests and concerns, such as with tackling transphobia and cisgenderism in healthcare. In this sense *the* trans community becomes *the* movement, united through both anger and political action.

In this book, however, I intentionally refer to 'trans communit*ies*' in the plural. In conflating the complexity and diversity of intersectional trans experiences into a single entity in the form of the one 'community', there is a risk that more marginal voices become lost. As Bhanji (2013: 522) notes in his account of implicit racial exclusion within the overwhelmingly white, Western trans imaginary, a singular approach 'effectively ignores the dynamics of power, or the continued hegemony of the center over the margins'. *The* trans community in its singular form is most often invoked by those trans people who are already most visible in the popular imaginary: white, binary-identified trans women such as Jacques and Fae. Similarly, while #transdocfail included contributions from a genuinely diverse range of trans people, many of whom described how factors such as ableism, classism and racism intersected with transphobia and cisgenderism in medical environments, media accounts of the phenomenon were written largely by white, middle-class trans women and men. The unacknowledged privilege of these accounts informed a flattening of 'the' community, with certain intersectional accounts quietly erased from the mainstream narrative of 'transphobic doctors'.

Both trans communities and 'the trans community' therefore offer means of social affiliation that broadly reflect Feinberg's (1992) conceptualisation of trans as movement. As I have shown, these can be exclusive of condition-oriented and/or intersectional trans identities, but they may also *incorporate* discourses of trans as condition in a gender-pluralist manner. They further offer a posttranssexual alternative to the professional cisgenderism of gender clinic experts, providing a means by which a diverse range of trans people can 'read [themselves] aloud' (Stone, 1991: 232) as part of a community or movement without being bound by the strict medical dictates of trans as transition.

'Be yourself': validation through individual belonging

Through a proliferation of gender-pluralist trans communities, the boundaries of both trans and gendered belonging have become more fluid and less clearly delineated. While there was evidence of continued border patrols within the dataset for this project, exclusionary actions and language were more often opposed and condemned within both the community and activist spheres. This typically creates additional room for gendered complexity and bodily diversity.

In the example that follows, participant Joshua criticises a particularly stringent form of the discourse of trans as transition; one that reflects both the traditional transsexual narrative and Khoosal's concerns regarding the bounds of sexed and gendered possibility. A user of Forum 1 had posted to imply that trans identity should be linked to a desire for surgical intervention; by implication, anyone who does *not* desire surgery is 'not really trans'. Such beliefs can arise from trans patients internalising 'societal beliefs about normality and disdain for those with such a condition' (Dewey, 2008). In response, Joshua argues that it is up to the individual to define the scope of their own identity and transition.

> I don't hold with this 'trannier than you' attitude. Really don't. Not wanting surgery is a common and perfectly understandable choice. I don't know why trans people have to imply that by not wanting the surgery you're somehow not truly trans. (Joshua)

The above quote is drawn from a wider argument put forth by Joshua in which he supports the gender-pluralist idea that a spectrum of gendered options should be available to trans people. He suggests that trans people should feel able to find their own place within this spectrum, rather than be bound by 'trannier than you' hierarchies of appropriate(ly) trans behaviour. Thus, through opposing strict delineations of trans possibility, individuals such as Joshua aim to open the boundaries of trans definition.

I have previously described how some community forum or Facebook group members advise new arrivals to follow the authoritatively 'expert', 'objective' advice of health professionals. However, others, including Joshua, instead tell newcomers seeking answers to 'be yourself'. The implication of this instruction is that the person in question should seek an identity and body they feel comfortable in, instead of working to meet some external criteria for transness. In the following example, Jake responds to a transmasculine individual who is worried about living up to normative ideals of male behaviour.

> Be yourself. Whatever you choose to do with your physical
> appearance, don't force yourself into a gender role if it
> doesn't feel right. (Jake)

In another instance, Ellie – who identifies as transsexual – informs a new
forum member that multiple identity categories and possibilities for
physical transition exist. Her post implies that however the individual
she addresses chooses to describe themselves or plan their transition,
their choice is reasonable and valid.

> If you want a label, 'Genderqueer' could work. If you
> want to present as a woman but keep a male body (Hope
> I got that the right way round!) you could be a transsexual
> (non-operative) ... so – follow your heart, be who you
> want to be. (Ellie)

Advice offered within the community sphere by forum users such as
Joshua, Jake and Ellie stands in stark contrast to the strictly delineated
possibilities for identification and transition seen in the traditional
transsexual narrative, as well as in the gatekeeping activities described by
writers such as Barrett (2007) and Arcelus et al (2017), and evidenced in
Khoosal's account. Drawing on alternatives to the traditional transsexual
narrative and notions of gender-pluralist trans community, Jake and
Ellie imply that the validity of any given gender identity or body lies in
a personal sense of comfort – what 'feels right' (Jake) – rather than in
professional cisgenderist models of appropriately gendered behaviour
or embodiment. In this way, expertise is located within the individual,
and granted authority through collective community recognition.
This approach provides trans authenticity through the fluid and open
possibilities of a gender-pluralist approach to trans as movement, rather
than the more carefully delineated and managed possibilities of trans
as condition.

Differing understandings of trans health

I have shown that multiple discourses from the respective repertoires
of trans as condition and trans as movement continue to influence
practitioner and patient perspectives in the UK. Seemingly
contradictory discourses can sometimes coexist: for example, within
gender-pluralist trans communities. However, differing definitions and
understandings of trans possibility can also lead to conflict, as border

patrols within both the health professions and trans spaces seek to delineate the bounds of trans possibility.

Discursive conflicts also arise within the context of care. Medical understandings of gendered possibility rooted in cisgenderism and/or discourses of condition increasingly contrast with patient understandings of trans as movement, leading to difficulties in the provision of care. I use three examples to illustrate how this can take place. Firstly, I show that essentialist approaches rooted in cultural cisgenderism can work to erase the gendered reality of trans patients. Secondly, I show how the discourse of trans as transition can inform inappropriate practices. Finally, I look at how gatekeeping practices within mental health and gender identity services can work to deny certain possibilities for individuals hoping to transition.

'Misgendered three times': essentialising gender, erasing trans realities

Numerous participants referred to instances in which health professionals working outside of gender clinics denied the very possibility of their being trans. In some cases, this was due to narrow ideas about how trans people could possibly look or behave: an extreme version of the discourse of trans as transition. However, on many occasions the reported behaviour of non-specialist practitioners would seem to indicate a denial of trans reality altogether. This reflects the findings of Bailey and McNeil (2013), who found that some GP practices refused to acknowledge the possibility of trans patients being registered there, and Combs et al (2008), who were told by gender clinic specialists that health professionals from outside their discipline would often baulk at disrupting a 'healthy body' through hormonal or surgical intervention. Such perspectives arise from a cultural cisgenderism (Kennedy, 2013).

In the following example from my fieldwork diary, a trans patient seeks help from other members of an activist Facebook group in preparing a complaint.

> An individual posts about poor treatment they have received at a local hospital after going in to see a doctor about a recurrent bladder problem, saying they are thinking about making a complaint. They were misgendered three times and asked what genitals they had in spite of the doctor having their gender history available to him. (Fieldwork diary: 18 April 2013)

The patient in question feels distressed because their gender identity has not been respected. This perspective arises from the notion that trans people can and should determine their own gendered identity: as participant Ellie argues in asserting her womanhood, 'we aren't men-who-got-their-body-changed – we ARE women'. As I have shown, this perspective can be grounded both in discourses of trans as condition and in discourses of trans as movement.

The hospital consultant's failure to acknowledge the patient's gender could be described as transphobic, in that it is an example of individual, inappropriate behaviour towards a trans person that was experienced as disrespectful and prejudiced. However, it is entirely possible that this doctor did not intend to harm his patient. Instead, his behaviour could be linked to the wider, unspoken cultural processes of cultural cisgenderism, through which trans genders are rendered impossible and unreal. This was not, after all, an isolated incident (Whittle et al, 2007; McNeil et al, 2012; NHS England 2015b). Indeed, other members of the same Facebook group responded with their own stories of misgendering in hospitals, such as in the following case.

> She ... relates a story about how she was assigned to a male
> ward with a male name on her ward file when she was last
> in hospital, in spite of transitioning 25 years ago and having
> a GRC. (Fieldwork diary: 24 April 2013)

The pervasiveness of misgendering in hospitals points to the wider influence of cultural cisgenderism on medical practice. Kennedy (2013: 4) explains that cultural cisgenderism is 'predominantly tacitly held and communicated'. In the instances described above, there are no hospital policies that intentionally discriminate against trans people; there are instead tacit assumptions on the part of health practitioners and administrators that gender is 'binary, biologically determined, fixed at birth' (Kennedy, 2013: 4). This can be seen in the repeated misgendering of the trans patients, in placing a woman on a male ward, and in having only female or male wards available. Such occurrences betray a cisgenderist failure to acknowledge trans genders as real, in line with normative, essentialist discourses of gendered possibility. They hence work to erase transness within medical institutions (Bauer et al, 2009). For the trans patients in question, addressing these issues was frequently described as a matter of basic respect; however, the very possibility of 'respect' in this instance must be linked to a recognition of trans possibilities. To meet the needs of these patients, it is therefore necessary to recognise trans genders as real, through subscribing to discourses of (diverse) trans possibility.

'Trans Broken Arm Syndrome': transition as definition

A weaker form of cultural cisgenderism can be seen in the behaviour of health professionals who recognise trans lives as real, but then associate all trans patient health needs with that patient's trans status in an extreme understanding of trans *as transition*. This phenomenon is referred to by many participants as 'Trans Broken Arm Syndrome'.

> Then there's the phenomenon known as Trans Broken Arm Syndrome. It's when healthcare providers assume that all medical issues are a result of a person being trans. Everything – from mental health problems to, yes, broken arms. (Payton, 2015)

I have previously noted that the discourse of trans as transition works to reduce the scope of information available on trans health. With Trans Broken Arm Syndrome, we see how this limited understanding of trans possibility can extend beyond information services and into everyday healthcare practices. In understanding 'trans health' *in terms of* transition, practitioners may fail to take trans patients' *other* health concerns seriously.

Trans Broken Arm Syndrome appears to be most common among mental health service providers, many of whom appear to regard trans people's mental health as relevant only in terms of or in relation to transition. This means that support for mental health issues unrelated to transition may be difficult for patients to access.

> Secondary care refuse to treat my mental health problems because I'm attending a GIC. The GIC won't treat them either. (TransDocFailAnon)

Some participants who did successfully access mental health services found that counsellors and therapists would unnecessarily raise their trans identity as an issue. This reflects the findings of Jane Hunt (2014: 293–294), who observed that 43% of participants in a survey of counselling clients 'indicated their counsellor wanted to explore transgender issues in therapy with them even when this wasn't the reason they had sought help'.

However, the flawed logic of Trans Broken Arm Syndrome can be applied to almost any health issue.

> Go to GP about non-trans related issues: 'Have you seen the GIC about that?' Reduced down to my trans status everytime. (TransDocFailAnon)

> One trans person, J, gave a long list of physical injuries, including a sprained ankle, a dislocated shoulder, broken ribs, and, of course, even a broken arm where their trans status and HRT [hormone replacement therapy] were discussed unnecessarily, and at length. (Payton, 2015)

In these accounts, the discourse of trans as transition leads many healthcare professionals to conceptualise trans patients entirely in terms of their access to gender identity services. This is a form of cisgenderism, in that it problematises trans patients and can mean they are treated differently to cis patients, who are implicitly regarded as 'normal'. While trans possibilities are therefore not completely erased by Trans Broken Arm Syndrome, the phenomenon represents a tendency to define trans patients' reality *entirely* in terms of their trans status, as well as through the trans-specific medical process of physical transition.

The situation is somewhat complicated by the fact that some health conditions *can* be affected by transition, including (ironically) the eponymous 'broken arm'. For instance, changes to an individual's hormone regime may have implications for their bone density and risk of osteoporosis (Weinand and Safer, 2015). However, the high prevalence of *unnecessary* incidents of Trans Broken Arm Syndrome – plus invasive questions that go beyond discussing relevant matters of (for instance) hormone regime – mean that health professionals who *are* asking relevant, sensitive questions about a patient's transition might not be trusted by patients.[7] In this way, the example of Trans Broken Arm Syndrome shows how some conditional discourses of trans possibility can put patients directly at risk.

'My name change was too ambiguous': authoritative expertise vs personal identity

I have previously discussed how gatekeeping practices can limit the bounds of gendered expression. As with essentialising discourses and Trans Broken Arm Syndrome, the cisgenderist assumptions that frequently underpin gatekeeping practices can lead to clashes between health professionals and trans patients; clashes that are rooted in differing understandings of trans possibility. However, while the tacit assumptions of cultural cisgenderism are relevant to gatekeeping practices, I have also shown that the professional cisgenderism described by Ansara and Hegarty (2012) is particularly present within authoritative discourses of trans as condition. This is manifested through policy, practice, and in professional writings. I now show how misunderstandings and practitioner–patient conflict can arise when the professional cisgenderism of conditional gatekeeping practices clashes with patient self-definitions rooted in discourses of trans as movement.

There is a notable difference between participants in this project who respectively report positive or negative experiences with gatekeeping. Participants who report positive experiences tend to meet normative, binary expectations of gendered behaviour and presentation. This did not necessarily mean that they embodied the bluntest gender stereotypes. Barrett (2007: 73) states that '[i]t is not the function of a gender identity clinic to operate as some kind of style council concerning what does and does not constitute feminine or masculine dress'. However, gatekeeping processes often emphasise 'passing' and encourage patients to adopt a consistent gender presentation. This can be seen, for instance, in the use of RLE by gender clinics such as Nottingham that more closely manage their patients' transitions. It can also be seen in Barrett's account: despite his determination to avoid being part of a 'style council', he also emphasises the importance of guiding patients to pass. In his description of the assessment process, he recommends examining 'the physical composition that nature has provided the patient with ... how well the patient manages to pass ... mannerisms and demeanour' (Barrett, 2007: 15). He further passes judgement on the sartorial choices of his patients, describing how some 'state that every item of their clothing is appropriate to their new gender' when 'the final combination that has resulted seems not to be so' (Barrett, 2007: 73). As with Khoosal's concerns regarding patients with a mixture of sex characteristics, Barrett's approach implicitly works to reinforce (binary) norms of gendered presentation. Transitioning patients with desires, expectations and styles that happened to meet these norms – particularly those who seek to reify and validate their identity through diagnosis – are less likely to have trouble with gatekeeping.

Participants who report negative experiences with gatekeeping are more likely to deviate from normative models of gendered possibility. These individuals tend to subscribe to understandings of trans as movement: for example, through describing themselves as genderqueer, androgynous or neutrois, or through incorporating non-binary understandings into a transsexual identity. An instance of this can be seen in Reubs J Walsh's contributions to #transdocfail.

> In my initial consult, the Oxfordshire gatekeeper told me I was a 'dual role transvestite', which isn't true (I'm non-binary). (Reubs J Walsh)

In Walsh's account, we see that practitioner and patient understand the patient's identity quite differently. Walsh draws on a discourse of movement to understand her gender as non-binary: her sense of self does not conform to normative understandings of gender as entirely, straightforwardly female or male. She is 'being herself'. By contrast, the practitioner (in this case working at a local mental health service responsible for referring patients on to a gender clinic) draws upon the ICD-10 diagnostic category of 'dual role transvestism' to describe Walsh. Two key criteria of this diagnosis incorporate a cisgenderist assumption of binary gender, relying upon a notion of 'the opposite sex': 'The individual wears clothes of the opposite sex in order to experience temporary membership in the opposite sex ... The individual has no desire for a permanent change to the opposite sex' (World Health Organization, 1992: F64.1). In using this diagnosis, the practitioner rejects Walsh's non-binary account, instead seeking to make sense of her gender with reference to a binarist clinical discourse of trans as condition. This is an example of professional cisgenderism in that the formal diagnostic categories by which the practitioner attempts to understand Walsh are prioritised over her own, more sophisticated understanding of her gender. Occurrences such as this often lead to patients being delayed in their journey along the treatment pathway, or being denied treatment altogether. Alternatively, patients may mislead health professionals about their gender by withholding information, contributing to the atmosphere of mistrust I outlined in the previous chapter.

Walsh faced further challenges upon eventually attending an appointment at a gender clinic:

> The GIC doc told me my name change was too ambiguous and told me that even though I have a cousin Ruby, I should get that name (Reubs J Walsh)

In this instance a gender identity specialist objects to the name 'Reubs', asserting that Walsh's chosen name is 'too ambiguous'. They instead tell Walsh to adopt the more feminine name 'Ruby'. This requirement reflects Barrett's (2007: 73) concerns regarding patients behaving in a manner that is not 'appropriate to their new gender'. It is also reminiscent of the aforementioned NHS England draft clinical commissioning policy, which prioritised 'clinical need' over 'social preference'. There are two presumptions at work here: firstly, that transitioning patients should define themselves in line with a binary gender category, and secondly, that the category of womanhood cannot expand to incorporate a more ambiguous name. Both presumptions draw upon a professional cisgenderism rooted in discourses of trans as condition, implicitly asserting that the (largely cis) medical profession is in a position to tell patients that they should present their gender(s) in a broadly binary manner. There is also an ethnocentrism in this approach, with binary approaches to naming/gendering reflecting a specifically *white*, Western cultural approach (Ansara, 2010).

A professional cisgenderist approach can therefore be rooted in inflexible discourses that prioritise practitioners' understandings of trans as condition over patient understandings of trans as movement. In this approach it is possible to observe both an 'apparatus of [the] production of gender' (Stone, 1991: 228) and a means by which certain trans identities and experiences are rendered impossible by health professionals. Liam Davidson states on #transdocfail that a greater focus on trans understandings of self is required from gender identity specialists. This would mean '[fewer] nonbinary trans people being coerced into inappropriate binary transition as only option' (Davidson); moreover, a greater range of options for gendered expression would be available to binary-identified transitioning patients.

Conclusion: the (im)possibilities of trans patienthood

'Trans' remains a fluid category. There is not one language of trans possibility, but instead multiple languages and understandings that serve to both challenge and reinforce cisgenderist norms. Different uses of trans language continue to be shaped by the overarching discursive repertoires of trans as condition and trans as movement. In turn, the employment of these discourses within professional and trans patient settings feeds into trans/gendered possibilities of identity, experience and embodiment, and into the practice and perception of healthcare in the UK.

Discourses of trans as condition both enable and constrain the provision of healthcare services in the UK. Variants on the traditional transsexual narrative are grounded in ideals of medical authority and expertise. These offer a means by which trans people might come to understand themselves and seek treatment, and by which practitioners working in gender identity services can justify their practices to other professionals within public health. However, this same notion of medical authority also empowers gatekeepers to determine what constitutes an appropriate form of gendered embodiment. This is a form of professional cisgenderism, in that the expert, professional opinion of practitioners is prioritised over the lived identities, desires and experiences of trans patients in terms of recognising gendered possibilities. That is not to say that all gender identity specialists are as strict as Khoosal: rather, the *operation* of medical practices and gendered discourses continues to empower specialists to impose their view of gendered possibility onto patients.

Discourses of trans as movement offer trans people an alternative to pathologising narratives. Non-binary gender identities, along with other alternatives to (and within) transsexualism, enable identification beyond the cisgenderist constraints of normative gender. While border conflicts may occur, gender-pluralist trans communities offer space for gender-diverse people to find identity and belonging outside of medical definitions and pathways. This can be seen especially in the commonly offered advice to 'be yourself', which locates authentic possibility in individual experience and need rather than clinical definitions.

The respective discursive repertoires of trans as condition and trans as movement are not necessarily contradictory. Many individuals with movement-oriented identities seek or undertake physical transition under medical supervision, while gender-pluralist communities offer space for multiple conceptualisations of trans possibility to coexist. However, different understandings of trans possibility can also lead to conflict: within the health professions and within trans communities, as well as between trans patients and healthcare professionals. The consequences of this are particularly severe when healthcare provision is at stake.

Notes

[1] AD and G v North West Lancashire Health Authority, Court of Appeal, 1999.

[2] Intersex people are born with chromosomes, genitals, gonads and/or hormonal conditions that do not meet the expected binary male/female norms of the sexed body. While intersex and trans communities and activisms are frequently entwined in the global South, they tend to remain somewhat more separate within the

West. This is due to a range of factors, including the different social issues faced by intersex people – such as coercive surgery upon infants – and the common appropriation of intersex issues by trans activists (Clune-Taylor, 2016). As such, discussion of intersex issues is largely beyond the scope of this book.

[3] Many intersex people also have reason to undergo treatments such as HRT, surgeries and hair removal for the purposes of alleviating dysphoria with respect to gender and/or the sexed body.

[4] A range of biological, neurological, psychological and/or psychiatric hypotheses have been proposed to explain the apparent co-morbidity of autism and gender dysphoria. However, there may also be social explanations for this phenomenon. Kennedy (2013) argues that autistic spectrum children might be less likely to acknowledge cisgenderist social norms that limit gender identity and expression. Kristensen and Broome (2015) suggest that binary gender expectations are more likely to be seen as irrational and inconsistent by individuals with a 'systematising' view of the world. Both explanations imply that autism is actually no more common among the trans population than the cis population, but that autistic individuals are *more likely to be visible* as trans.

[5] To my amusement, every time I visit the NHS Choices 'Transgender Health' page for research I encounter a video of myself talking about my experiences of transition. This was filmed in 2008 and is now somewhat dated. Moreover, if I were approached to participate in producing a piece like this today, I would agree only if trans people of colour were also involved. White trans people are over-represented in NHS and media materials; it can therefore be necessary for us to sometimes take a step back so that non-white stories of transition can be seen and heard.

[6] For critiques of the 'wrong body' narrative, see Stone, 1991; Carter, 2013; Catalano, 2015; Lester, 2017.

[7] I would like to thank Dr Rosanna Bevan for advising me in this discussion, particularly regarding what physicians do and don't need to know about trans patients' hormone regimes.

FIVE

Trans temporalities: imagining a future in the time of anticipation

We live in a time of anticipation.

We anticipate misgendering, perplexed looks, ignorance, transphobia. Even when what we anticipate does not occur (yet), we act as if it has, and it becomes an inevitability.

I think it has something to do with waiting lists. My whole life seems to be about waiting lists nowadays (even if I am not on one yet – I am waiting to be on one). We are kept in a constant state of anticipation: waiting for a letter or phonecall from the GIC, a prescription, a surgery date …

We are used to waiting, orientated towards the future like iron filings lining themselves up towards a magnet. We are focussed on the future whether that's the future where we have already had access to healthcare treatment, or the future where the (seemingly inevitable) acts of transphobia have already taken place. Because we are always waiting for this future the present seems compressed somehow, like our lives are in limbo.

But looking to the future can also be positive. Creating change requires us to live in a state of anticipation. It seeks to build a politics of hopefulness rather than of dread, preparedness rather than an anxiousness … the way we think about the future has an impact on the present. (Jess Bradley and Francis Myerscough, 2015)

Living in the time of anticipation

Back in 2015 I began the process of seeking a referral for laser hair removal through the NHS. It was the first time I had sought access to gender identity services since being discharged from Charing Cross gender clinic in early 2009.

I had previously considered my engagement with gender identity services to be long over. According to the traditional pathway narrative, my transition had taken place and ended. I had experienced counselling, negotiated various referrals and waiting lists, undertaken RLE and had been prescribed hormones. This journey culminated in surgery during the summer of 2008, after which I received a handful of final follow-up appointments.

Facial hair removal was absent from this NHS pathway; as was typical for the time, this intervention was not publicly funded in my area. I paid for a small number of private laser hair removal sessions with my savings and the last of my student loan. The introduction of the NHS England Interim Gender Protocol in 2013 changed the situation, however; for the first time, facial hair removal was funded nationally, meaning that it was (in theory) available throughout England.

Unfortunately, it did not seem likely that I would gain a direct referral from my GP. Written into the new pathway was the presumption that patients seeking facial hair removal were doing so under the care of a gender clinic. I – a former patient seeking access to a newly available treatment long after I had originally left the pathway – was an aberration. Would I be able to persuade my GP to refer me anyway, drawing upon old letters from Charing Cross in my medical records? Would I have to obtain a referral to a gender clinic and once again spend months on a waiting list, only to eventually request that a practitioner at said clinic fulfil a simple administrative task on my behalf? Tied up in these concerns were my personal experiences of ignorant, transphobic and cisgenderist behaviour from past GPs, as well as my knowledge of friends' negative experiences. I therefore worried not simply about negotiating the administrative complexities of seeking a referral, but also the possible social and emotional consequences of doing so.

I wrote about these concerns in my fieldwork diary ahead of an initial appointment with my GP. I *hoped* to obtain a direct referral for hair removal and be treated with respect, but *expected* to either obtain a gender clinic referral or otherwise be delayed, while possibly also encountering unhelpful or discriminatory behaviour for my troubles. Drawing on Jess Bradley and Francis Myerscough's (2015) post 'Transitional demands' from the Action For Trans Health blog – an excerpt from which opens this chapter – I reflected on the notion of **anticipation**. 'I feel really *weird* about [my appointment]', I wrote, 'I'm not used to the anticipation any more – the anticipation of being refused treatment, of having to fight … I hate that feeling of powerlessness I associate with being a trans patient on the NHS' (Fieldwork diary: 30 March 2015). Bradley and Myerscough's account spoke cogently to me. I could feel myself 'orient[ing] towards the future', anticipating – if not transphobia – then confusion, ignorance, cisgenderism and the wait: a long, perhaps complicated administrative and emotional process to undergo prior to any eventual access to treatment.

This anticipation of a difficult experience arose not simply from my own past experiences of unhelpful and unpleasant health professionals, but also from community discourse. I found myself reflecting on the stories and perspectives shared among my trans friends, and in numerous spaces online. My feelings were further informed by my ongoing analysis of research data for this project, in which I encountered innumerable stories of inappropriate behaviour from health professionals that ranged from innocent ignorance, to rudeness and prejudice, to dangerous malpractice.

In turn, I saw a similar process of anticipation play out time and time again among the research participants. Every participant who wrote about their experiences of planning for treatment – particularly those seeking access through NHS gender clinics – lived 'in a time of anticipation'. As with my personal experience, there were stories of worries and fears, informed by waits, delays, gatekeeping practices and community discourses of mistreatment and malpractice. However, there were also stories of excitement and hope, informed by the freeing experiences of coming out and seeking authenticity, as well as community discourses of satisfaction and wholeness associated with completing elements of the transition process.

In this chapter, I explore Bradley and Myerscough's 'time of anticipation' as a form of trans temporality. **Temporality** refers to 'the social patterning of experiences and understandings of time' (Amin, 2014: 219). It is not simply about the passing of time, but about how time is felt by individuals and shaped through social circumstance. The time of anticipation, therefore, refers to *emotional* engagements with time and the politics of time. It is grounded in the temporal displacements of transition and cisgenderism, and mediated by community discourse and communal identity. In this sense, it is about the individual's relationship with oneself *and* others, as well as the influence of wider social factors. It emerges through a collective management of uncertainty: oriented towards the future, but shaped by many people's experiences of the past, and experienced as a liminal, never-ending present. I thus understand the past as socially constituted and constructed in a similar manner to the present and future (Glass, 2016).

This chapter shows how an engagement with temporality can help us to better understand discourse around patient experience and the operation of the UK's gender identity services. I begin by outlining several theoretical interventions, including Jack Halberstam's description of 'queer time', Julian Carter's analysis of 'transition time' and Laura Horak's observations on 'hormone time'. I also touch briefly upon accounts of queer and trans futurity and liminality from José Esteban Muñoz and Caterina Nirta. I then contextualise these temporal theories in the context of my research findings, looking at how trans patients negotiate waiting, mistrust, gatekeeping, hope and suicide in the time of anticipation.

In this chapter I primarily explore the time of anticipation in the context of gender identity services, although my discussion of mistrust looks at a phenomenon which is relevant to healthcare provision more widely. I draw mainly on data from the community sphere, where forum users discuss personal experiences in the context of their fears, hopes and plans for the future.

Interrogating trans temporalities

Jack Halberstam (2005: 6) theorises **queer time** in opposition to normative notions of the lifecourse, describing queer temporalities as 'those specific models ... that emerge within postmodernism once one leaves the temporal frames of bourgeois reproduction and family, longevity, risk/safety, and inheritance'. These normative temporal frames – which may be described as 'straight time' (Muñoz, 2007) – prescribe a linear movement through life stages such as childhood, adolescence, employment, marriage, reproduction and death. Straight time defines memory and expectation, past and present. By contrast, the concept of queer time recognises alternative continuities and non-normative temporalities. An example of queer time can be seen in the 'stretched-out adolescence' of childless queers involved in subcultural activities such as punk and hip-hop, who challenge 'the conventional binary formulation of a life narrative divided by a clear break between youth and adulthood' (Halberstam, 2005: 153).

Many individuals discussed in Halberstam's project on queer time and place – particularly those active in queer arts and subcultures – demonstrate agency in actively rejecting the constraints of straight time. For instance, gender-variant artist and model Del LaGrace Volcano counters objectification through the intentional exposure of hen[1] transgender body – defined in the present by the surgical and figurative scars of the past – and through bearing witness to the bodies of others in hen art. Conversely, the queer temporality of other figures is shaped more by circumstance beyond the control of the individual. Brandon Teena – made famous through media representations such as the 1999 film *Boys Don't Cry* – is transformed from individual agent to 'fetish, icon, commodity' (Halberstam 2005: 75) after being raped and murdered at the age of 21. Teena left his rural American hometown – where he was known as a woman – several months prior to his death in December 1993, to create a new life for himself as a man (with a new history to match) in Humbodt, Nebraska. In the wake of his death he quickly became a contested martyr figure for trans and lesbian communities, as well the subject of investigative journalism, fictional prose, documentary and Hollywood film; all had their own investment in de/constructing a transgender history. Through these investments, Teena became a timeless symbol, rather than a temporally located individual.

Queer time is therefore associated with liminality (ambiguity or betweenness) and disruption. This may come about through an intentional, agential rejection of normative temporal movements, as in the case of Volcano's art or Teena's decision to create a new, male history for himself. However, it can also occur through the imposition of external narratives. Teena may have sought a queer temporal rupture in building a new life for himself in Humbodt, but rupture was *imposed* upon his memory when the narrative of this life was rewritten for multiple audiences following his death.

Halberstam's account of queer temporalities – conceptualised as ultimately relevant to *all* who reject the prescriptive progression of straight time, regardless of sexual orientation or gender identity – focuses largely upon the interactions of past and present. At its most optimistic, Halberstam's description of queer time offers the vision of an emotionally and politically liberating, continuously extending ever-present in which the past plays a complex but secondary role. This can perhaps best be seen in queer subcultural production, as epitomised in Volcano's art, and dyke bands such as Le Tigre and Tribe 8 (Halberstam, 2005). However, as Bradley and Myerscough (2015) note, a continuous, liminal present can be experienced as an unpleasant 'limbo' by many trans people; a theme I explore throughout this chapter.

I therefore turn now to explore the accounts of trans temporality that centre **futurity**: a temporal engagement with the future *in* the present. Caterina Nirta (2018: 26) describes futurity as the 'material act of progressing now towards something, of going there, where the going there is fully immersed in the present'. In this way, trans experiences of the present may be mediated by a powerful anticipation of the future. As Nirta puts it: 'We are now, at this moment, going there. Our movement is the dimension of the now'.

Julian Carter's (2013) account of **transitional time** draws on a close reading of choreographer Sean Dorsey's dance work *Lou*, a biographical piece about gay transsexual activist Lou Sullivan. According to Carter (2013: 141), 'Dorsey offers us a vision of transitional time, and transitioning bodies, as dynamic and relational negotiations of wrongness ... Anticipation, retroflexion, and continuity co-exist in the same body, at the same moving moment of space and time.' Transitional time involves movements 'forward, backward, sideways, [and] tangential[ly]' and can be seen in the embodied coexistence of past, present and future, along with physical and social changes that might occur, will occur, have occurred. I read this as futurity without linearity. In an echo of Halberstam's account of Del LaGrace Volcano's work, we can regard the transitioning body as simultaneously rooted in a future through anticipation – or even multiple, differently gendered futures – and in the past through social readings that sex the body's physical frame.

In this way, transitioning individuals might 'anticipate a gender content they generate recursively out of their physical medium's formal potential in relation to the context of its emergence ... transition wraps the body in the folds of social time' (Carter, 2013: 141). Given the emphasis on possibility, fluidity and agency in Carter's account of transitional time, and a lack of focus on the linear, conditional norms of medical transition, we may regard it as a form of queer time, and associate it with discourses of trans as movement.

Transitional time accounts for many of the ways in which trans people can embody and experience temporal markers differently to individuals bound by the strictures of straight time. An example of this is found in how trans people tend to age differently to cis people. Halberstam's (2005: 153) concept of a 'stretched-out adolescence' is as relevant to trans narratives of coming out and transitioning as it is to queer subcultures. Many trans men and otherwise transmasculine individuals look particularly youthful if they do not, or are not yet undergoing hormone therapy; their gendered appearance 'anticipate[s] a [masculinised] gender content' (Carter, 2013: 141). This is inconsistent with normative chronological expectations, but consistent with the embodied coexistence of past, present and future that is a feature of transitional time. Conversely, many trans women and otherwise transfeminine individuals look particularly youthful *after* undergoing hormone therapy and/or 'facial feminisation' surgeries. Furthermore, transition can be understood as a second adolescence, in which transitioning individuals of all genders come to terms with moving through the world in their preferred gender role(s). In this second adolescence, the emotional and interactional changes brought about by social transition may be compounded by the physical and biochemical changes wrought by hormone therapies (Serano, 2007).

A model for understanding the more *linear* possibilities of transition is offered by Horak (2014). Drawing on research with trans vlogs on YouTube, she explains how a range of techniques are used to describe and/or depict the changes that come with physical transition. For instance, transition vlogs frequently depict many months' or years' worth of change within a matter of minutes. Horak utilises these manipulations of time to describe the phenomenon of **hormone time**. Hormone time is positioned as distinct from both queer time and straight time. It is 'linear and teleological, directed toward the end of living full time in the desired gender'; in this sense it is utopic, pointing to an anticipated harmony of gender identity, gender presentation and physical body (Horak, 2014: 580). This enables trans people to 'imagine' (or indeed, anticipate) a positive future. Hormone time thereby 'appropriates' elements of straight time for 'radical ends', pointing to the vital *possibility* of a non-normative future in which the transitioned/transitioning individual doesn't simply exist or survive, but instead experiences life as 'joyful' on their own terms (Horak, 2014: 581).

While Horak's description of hormone time generally offers a more linear account than Carter's conceptualisation of transitional time, it also accounts for trans discourses and experiences that cannot be understood within the normative bounds of straight time. To return to the example of ageing: Horak (2014: 579) notes that according to the logic of hormone time, '[t]ime begins with the first shot of testosterone or HRT pills (hormone replacement therapy) and is measured against that date, even years afterward'. This provides a model for understanding the phenomenon by which trans people's chronological age might contrast with their trans age: that is, an age counted from the moment a person comes out, begins to transition socially and/or begins to transition physically (Pearce, 2018). The difference between chronological age and trans age was seen in the community sphere, where trans people in their 20s or 30s who have been out for many years can often be seen offering advice and guidance to chronologically older individuals (perhaps in their 50s or 60s) who are tentatively moving towards coming out and/or transitioning.

The importance of queer and trans futurities – be they in an asynchronous form as with transitional time, or a more linear form as with hormone time – can be found in the possibility of a life that makes sense beyond the confines of straight time: a possibility that can be *anticipated* by 'younger' trans people. In his discussion of marginalisation in Western societies, Muñoz (2007: 364) notes that '[t]he future is only that of some kids. Racialized kids, queer kids, are not the sovereign princes of futurity'. He argues that, for these kids, queer futurities provide 'not an end but an opening or horizon' (360). This is vital because it offers the 'anticipatory illumination' of a future that might not seem possible within the strictures of straight time. While Horak (2014) acknowledges that hormone time can entail elements of temporal disruption in the manner of transitional time (as seen, for example, in the temporal compression that is an effect of many video-editing techniques), the key difference between hormone time and straight time lies not in temporal disjuncture, but in the differing progression narratives associated with each. The temporal logic of straight time is linked to normative reproduction, capitalist continuity, longevity and risk aversion, taking form in social structures such as the heteronormative (or indeed, homonormative) nuclear family (Halberstam, 2005). By contrast, Horak (2014: 581) links the futurity of hormone time to 'expansive trans subjects and communities': that is, subjects and communities who might defy normative, cisgenderist progression narratives.

Telling anticipatory stories

In his account of 'sexual stories', Ken Plummer (1995: 5) encourages the reader to regard such narratives not (simply) as examples of truth-telling, but as 'issues to be investigated in their own right'. The anticipatory trans narratives I draw upon in this chapter are similarly not simply accounts of experience, but a medium in which both discourses of trans health and temporal phenomena play out. The stories I describe here play an important role in constituting a trans temporality, shaping collective ideas and emotive personal experiences of the possible.

Most conversations around issues of trans health in the community sphere centre anticipation. Forum users frequently begin such discussions with a post about their fears, hopes, concerns and/or desires ahead of a forthcoming appointment with a GP practice, mental health service, gender clinic or hospital. Other forum users then typically respond either with their own anticipatory narrative (if they are also waiting for an appointment) or with comments drawing upon their own experiences or those of others, to offer advice, guidance and/or reassurance. Similar narratives can also be found within Facebook activist groups. Most – but not all – of these conversations focus on transition and gender identity services. They tap into a variety of discourses regarding the provision of trans health, offering an insight into patient perspectives on individual practitioners and clinics as well as the wider available treatment pathways.

The mode of conversation differed for #transdocfail. This reflects the more concise, immediate and public mode of communication on Twitter. #transdocfail operated as a very visible platform for the dissemination of trans community discourses of health, with a majority of contributors describing experiences and views rather than engaging in discussion. However, like the exchanges within community forums and Facebook groups, the stories told within #transdocfail reflect wider anticipatory narratives.

In the discussion of research findings that follows, the time of anticipation is employed as a frame for conceptualising trans patient narratives that emerge and are negotiated in community contexts. I read Bradley and Myerscough's time of anticipation as queer time (Halberstam, 2005), which intersects complexly with other modes of temporality. It links narratives of lived experience from trans patients to the possibility of a better future, in response to a 'compressed', liminal present. It enables a 'dynamic and relational negotiatio[n] of wrongness' (Carter, 2013:141), in which 'wrongness' resides not simply in the body of the individual, but also within limited, conditional discourses of trans possibility, stories of institutional cisgenderism and transphobia, and knowledge of the long waits for treatment. The discursive construction of 'wrongness' therefore takes place in and through *communally mediated* narratives. These typically centre apprehensive, often mistrustful attitudes towards healthcare providers. However, they can also enable patients to imagine post-transition futures, which offer an 'opening or horizon' (Muñoz, 2007: 360) and the possibility of joy (Horak, 2014).

The long wait

A defining feature of the time of anticipation is the wait. I showed in Chapter Three that patients seeking access to gender identity services through the NHS negotiate multiple waits, the average duration of which is influenced by the growth in patient numbers and a lack of proportional investment in gender clinics. Most patients now wait for many months or years for an initial consultation at a gender clinic.

In the time of anticipation, the wait lies at a nexus of uncertainty. Trans patients cannot know exactly how long the wait will be or what will happen at the end of the wait, and may wonder how to organise their lives (in both practical and emotional terms) during this time. In contrast to the more straightforward futurity of hormone time – most typically encountered by UK patients *following* assessment at a gender clinic – the uncertainty of the wait is perhaps best understood in terms of the futurity-without-linearity of transitional time, as well as in the 'compressed' liminality described by Bradley and Myerscough (2015).

A typical forum conversation about waiting begins as follows.

> Finally 6 months after the psych evaluation I get a letter from the GIC saying they have sent a fax to my PCT to request funding. They will schedule an appointment when funding is approved. Is this how it normally happens? I know my referral got sent off in January as I double checked with my GP? Anyone got an idea of how much longer I have to wait for an appointment if all goes smoothly with the PCT? (Warren)

The length of Warren's wait is not particularly unusual; neither is his uncertainty. He is reassured of this by other forum users, who note the length of their own waits and explain that applications for funding can cause delays. There is no way of firmly answering Warren's final question about how much longer he will have to wait for an appointment; this will only become apparent once he has been formally added to the clinic's waiting list and received a letter to confirm this. Furthermore, the length of said waiting list depends on which gender clinic he is going to attend.

Delays caused by funding applications are now less common following the abolition of PCTs, but the uncertainty of waiting time illustrated in Warren's post remains. Transitioning patients still find themselves waiting an uncertain period of time: for their referral to be processed by the gender clinic, for the approval of hormone therapy once they are attending the gender clinic, for surgical or laser or voice therapy appointments once they have met the requirements of RLE and subsequently joined another waiting list. Patients with access to the relevant knowledge and a degree of personal flexibility can ask to be put on a cancellation list, meaning that they may be contacted with the offer of an earlier appointment at short notice. This only contributes to the temporal disjuncture of waiting time, reinforcing the sense of 'dynamic and relational negotiation' (Carter, 2013: 141).

Long waiting times can compound pre-existing mental health issues. Trans patients may feel a lack of agency due to the uncertainty and inevitability of these waits. McNeil and colleagues (2012) indicate that patients frustrated with long waiting times are extremely distressed, with many consequently describing experiences of self-harm. Forum users discuss a range of responses to the severe emotional demands of waiting. Some seek private treatment or self-medicate, while others contemplate ending their lives; these responses are discussed in later sections of this chapter. For most patients, however, the best available option is to remain within the time of anticipation, looking forward to a better post-transition future.

> I try my best to simply laugh at it all and focus on a few years down the road when everything is sorted and I'm able get on with being a 'regular' guy. (Aiden)

> I'm really hoping to be seen by a psych this year, at least things are moving forward and in the right direction too. (Warren)

Bradley and Myerscough (2015) describe trans patients in the time of anticipation as 'orientated towards the future like iron filings lining themselves up towards a magnet'. In the above quotes from Aiden and Warren, it is apparent how this orientation towards the future can operate in a manner comparable to hormone time, with participants constructively anticipating a concrete future in order to cope with the unpredictably continuous pre-treatment present. Aiden positions an acceptable ('regular') mode of life in this future as an apparent certainty (*when* everything is sorted); it is the waiting time ('a few years') that remains unknown.

Some participants regard the waiting time as an opportunity, with the wait for an initial appointment offering temporal space to get one's life affairs in order prior to transition. This can involve: coming out to partners, friends, family and work colleagues; changing name by deed poll or statutory declaration; buying new clothes; starting a university or college course; changing job or school in order to enter a more supportive environment. Patients are generally aware that many of these actions count towards RLE at gender clinics, meaning that they can sometimes be undertaken for the purposes of meeting assumed or known medical standards. The waiting time is also portrayed as an opportunity for self-reflection, a space to decide for certain whether transition is an appropriate step. On occasion, this perspective is recommended to newer forum users with worries about transition.

> You can explore this further. You're not committed until you've been on hormones for a couple of months and if you go through the NHS pathway that point in time is six months away at the very, very soonest so don't frazzle – see

a psych or GP and talk about it and take each step through the pathway if and when you're comfortable with it and you know it's what you want. Go at your own speed, don't be pushed (not that anyone in the medical establishment is going to push you). (Steph)

In recognition of how long waits can be, forum users frequently encourage people thinking about transition to approach their GP for an initial referral sooner rather than later. This is typically portrayed as a good first move even for those uncertain if transition is the right decision for them, with the logic being that the wait itself provides plenty of time for both contemplation and coming out to friends, family and colleagues.

> One thing I would say is that you should set the ball rolling immediately with the NHS. It is really very likely that it will take over a year for you to actually be attending the first of two Evaluation appointments at a GIC. Once you HAVE decided to transition, the long waits between different stages of progress are extremely frustrating, so get things in motion now. You don't have to tell anyone now – it could be a year before you are able to say 'In three months time, I have got an appointment about my gender issues.' If you change your mind in the meantime, you can cancel it. They won't mind. (Ellie)

For those who follow this advice, a shift into the time of anticipation might quite rapidly follow their initial coming out. A patient's 'whole life' might '[seem] to be about waiting lists' (Bradley and Myerscough, 2015), with the fundamentals of transitional experience shaped by the uncertain futurity of waiting time. Moreover, practical advice about the management of waiting time can lead trans patients to think about their gendered experience primarily in terms of the formal medical pathway. In this way, transitioning individuals can find themselves 'living in prognosis' (Jain, 2007) in a similar manner to other patient groups, such as IVF (in-vitro fertilisation) patients (Franklin, 1997) and cancer patients (Steinberg, 2015b).

Parallels can also be drawn to legal challenges that trans people often face in the UK. In her account of the gender recognition process, Nirta (2018) argues that trans people waiting the two years to apply for a new birth certificate can find themselves caught in a '"not-yet" limbo'. Her account highlights how a time of anticipation might be mediated by the operation of power as well as the experience of waiting itself. In this sense, the 'not-yet' limbo 'is not just a question of mere temporality, but encapsulates relations of power and dominance between the vulnerable subject and social practice which manipulate the perception of time itself' (Nirta, 2018: 66).

All the issues I explore throughout the rest of this chapter are shaped by the impact of waiting time. Waiting provides a (frequently frustrating) time to anticipate, with agential narratives echoing hormone time in their vision of a better future constructed through the disempoweringly liminal present of the 'not-yet' limbo. I show that patients also draw from the past during their wait – in and through personal experiences and communal narratives – providing temporal and conceptual space for mistrust, fear, uncertainty, hope and excitement to grow.

Mistrust

A second key theme of the age of anticipation is a fundamental lack of trust in health professionals, as first described in Chapter Three: patients anticipate 'misgendering, perplexed looks, ignorance [and] transphobia' (Bradley and Myerscough, 2015). These narratives of cisgenderism and transphobia – from both public and private providers in *all* areas of healthcare provision – derive from trans patients' past experiences and shape the construction of possible futures. They thereby inform a pervasive attitude of mistrust towards healthcare providers, stemming from an anticipation of being treated poorly.

Fearing mistreatment

Trans patients frequently approach forthcoming appointments with unknown practitioners (and sometimes, known practitioners) with a sense of caution and occasionally fear. They anticipate being treated inappropriately, or possibly even being refused treatment altogether. This mistrust can be tied to personal experience, with many participants talking about how a bad appointment with a particular practitioner increased their mistrust of others working in the same field. However, it can also be linked to the sheer number of communally constructed/ disseminated stories of cisgenderism and transphobia. In this way, the trans patient's emotive anticipatory projection of the future incorporates recurring elements of the past. On occasions, this is not the patient's *own* past, but instead *the real or imagined past of another.* For individuals undergoing or seeking to undergo physical transition, waiting offers more time to encounter and engage with stories of cisgenderism and transphobia (both online and offline), and to contemplate negative personal experiences.

Mistrust is most often discussed in relation to gender identity services. For instance, many participants raise concerns about sharing medical problems past and present – particularly those related to mental health – with the gender clinic, for fear of being denied treatment. An example follows from an individual who contributed anonymously to the submissions–based Twitter account @TransDocFailAnon.

> hiding anxiety and self harm from clinic doctors because
> I don't feel safe telling them about it (TransDocFailAnon)

Trans patients who are not specifically anticipating a transition-related appointment can also exhibit a severe lack of trust in health professionals. In the below instance, a TransDocFailAnon contributor fears being openly trans within everyday medical encounters (which might perhaps entail transphobic incidents or – as outlined in the previous chapter – instances of Trans Broken Arm Syndrome).

> Experience extreme anxiety every time I see a doctor wondering if I'll have to disclose trans status (TransDocFailAnon)

The very presence of the TransDocFailAnon Twitter account is important to this analysis. The account – along with an associated e-mail address and Tumblr page – enabled individuals to contribute to #transdocfail if they did not feel confident sharing stories under their own username. For some, this was a matter of protecting their identity if they had gone stealth, or if they were not out in all areas of their life. Others, however, did not trust their doctors to maintain treatment in the face of criticism.

> I have been afraid to post on #transdocfail in case I'm identified and have access to treatment made even more difficult. (TransDocFailAnon)

Similar concerns were raised by research participants from Twitter and the forums when I contacted them to ask permission for the use of direct quotes in this book. Numerous participants wished to withhold personal, geographic and/or demographic information due to an anticipation of possible harm from healthcare providers. While it is deeply troubling that many trans people have these concerns, their decision to withhold information also represents an exercise in agency and resilience (through active self-care) in the otherwise disempowering context of a projected transphobic future (Nicolazzo, 2017).

Strategic futurities

Less severe forms of mistrust can operate as a form of strategic engagement with possible futures, enabling trans patients to plan their medical appointments: whom to see, how to present information. In these instances, which I refer to as strategic futurities, patients respond agentially to matters that concern them. On the forums, this typically involves participants managing their expectations ahead of appointments and/or finding a way to negate their concerns. For example, some participants ask others for advice on what personal information to share (or not) with health professionals. In the below instance, Aiden wonders if he should tell his GP or psychiatrist that he has been having sleeping problems.

> I know the obvious answer is to go and ask my GP, or wait until [date redacted] and mention it at my psych appointment. To be honest, I'm anxious that it'll imply something negative about my transition. (Aiden)

Mistrust can lead participants to feel it is necessary to strategically manage considerable elements of their own healthcare. Most often, this is due to mundane ignorance or a lack of interest on the part of GPs, or due to the high frequency of administrative problems at some gender clinics (McNeil et al, 2012). Many experienced forum users recommend that others become familiar with treatment pathways and draw upon available evidence in making a case for being referred to a gender clinic: for instance, by utilising NHS guidance documents or the WPATH *Standards of Care*. Operating on the presumption that unknown practitioners cannot necessarily be trusted, some trans patients carefully seek out providers whom they can trust. For example, numerous people post to Forum 2 to ask for advice on where to find GPs with a good track record on treating trans patients. On Facebook, a user of one group asked for advice on finding a trans-friendly endocrinologist. These actions represent an attempt to manage and address the uncertainties that characterise the time of anticipation.

Sometimes, community or activist groups make systematic efforts to tackle the intersection of uncertainty and mistrust: for instance, several websites host lists of trans-friendly GPs. More often, advice is offered on an individual, interpersonal basis. On occasions where an individual has encountered problems with a practitioner or clinic, other patients – particularly those with more experience in navigating medical systems – often recommend looking for alternatives. In the below example, Steph responds to a request for advice from a patient whose GP first offered an inappropriate referral, before later asserting that the patient's trans feelings amounted to a 'phase' that would pass.

> I think in this case it might be worth seeing a different doctor if you can which is something you are perfectly entitled to do. I would have a good read around this forum … make sure you're an 'expert' patient and know exactly what *should* happen. (Steph, emphasis in original)

Similarly, Emma recommends that a worried forum user should check up on a forthcoming appointment at a gender clinic known for its administrative troubles.

> Just keep an eye on things, around a month or so before the appointment give them a call and make sure everything is okay still… it's always best to be prepared in case things go wrong admin wise… (Emma)

Emma's advice is important in the context of waiting times. Following a wait of several months (or more), a further setback could cause the patient's anticipated positive future of a possible transition to recede even further into the imagined temporal distance. A strategic management of possible futures therefore offers a means by which trans patients can maintain an 'opening or horizon' (Muñoz, 2007) within a context where long waits and negative, communally mediated narratives of the past dominate and curtail the possibilities of the present.

Myths of malpractice?

While common, mistrust is not universal within trans spaces. Many trans patients have very positive stories to tell about their own interactions with health professionals. Several participants expressed wariness towards what they perceived as inaccurate or outdated information shared in community spaces. In the below instance, Ben cautions a fellow forum user for making what he feels are unnecessary blanket statements about an entire profession.

> It's one thing to have had a bad experience with a specific psychiatrist, but to say ... that [all] psychiatrists are untrustworthy and should therefore never be believed is unhelpful, untruthful and potentially harmful. (Ben)

Gender identity specialists are usually quite aware of the discourses that circulate within online communities. Christina Richards and colleagues (2014) caution that widespread mistrust can damage the mental health and treatment opportunities for the most vulnerable patients.

> Clients who are very young, or who have a learning disability, or mental health problems, frequently present to clinics extremely distressed about things that they have heard ... which are simply not true. Such people often report that they were thinking of settling for sub-standard services, or risky self-managed treatment, rather than approaching reputable clinics. Worryingly, especially given the rates of mental distress and suicide amongst trans people who are not provided with services, there are others who are completely put off by the myths circulating about trans-specific healthcare, leading to desired and necessary treatment being delayed for years. (Richards et al, 2014: 254)

The risk expressed here is that stories of cisgenderism and transphobia from healthcare providers represent an ungrounded temporality. Patient experiences expressed in contexts such as #transdocfail are often undated, meaning that problems that may have commonly occurred a decade or more ago continue to be communally constructed as possible. Trans community discourse frequently re-enacts and re-reifies multiple pasts *as* possible futures for newcomers, even though those pasts are no longer necessarily reproduced in the present. For example, Richards and colleagues (2014) note that – contrary to some stories that circulate – trans women are no longer required to wear dresses or skirts to gender clinic appointments in the UK, and further argue that gender identity specialists now often subscribe to the position that gender is socially constructed and performed.

However, while my research findings demonstrate that potentially ungrounded communal temporalities *do* complicate the landscape of anticipation and uncertainty, there are several important flaws in the argument presented by Richards and colleagues. Until these are addressed, it seems unreasonable to suggest that stories of transphobia and cisgenderism circulate *primarily* as 'myths', even as this evidently is the case with some such stories.

Firstly, practices vary considerably among GPs, local mental health services and gender clinics (with individual clinical policies and practitioners interpreting the WPATH *Standards of Care* and NHS policies quite differently). These differences underpin patients' anticipatory uncertainty and, with it, their mistrust.

Secondly, even the most recently reported experiences from participants in this project indicate that (for instance) binary notions of gendered possibility continue to be imposed in appointments by gender identity specialists. This reflects Barrett's (2007) proposal that clinicians adjudicate patients on how they dress and pass, as outlined in the previous chapter. It is also indicative of a continued adherence to essentialist models of sex and gender among many.

Finally, there is the matter of the power differential between patients and practitioners. Clinical requirements such as RLE place a burden of proof on patients to demonstrate that they are trans, with specialists effectively sitting in judgement during assessment appointments. I argue that this process is *inherently* stressful for patients, and therefore informs many of the distressing stories that circulate. A powerful example of can be seen in the following extract from Emma Victoria Jewkes's otherwise positive account of her transition at the Nottingham Centre for Transgender Health.

> The initial assessment phase was made up of three appointments. The first two appointments I would be seen by two different doctors with the third appointment being with both of them. ... It was at that appointment where it would be decided whether to recommend me for the Gender Reassignment Program. ... The third appointment was the *scariest* ... I knew I wanted to transition. I'd taken it upon myself to begin that process a month earlier anyway. I'd changed my name and began living full-time as a woman. For me, there was no going back. However, there was still that doubt in my mind. *What if they said that I didn't qualify? What if they said I couldn't access hormone treatment?* I knew that if they said that, my life would be over. I could never and would never go back to a male life. It simply wasn't an option for me anymore. *Thankfully they said yes* and just a month later I received my first prescription of hormone tablets. (Jewkes, 2017: 390, emphasis mine)

In Jewkes's account it is clear that she feared being denied treatment *even though* she had already effectively begun to transition. The practitioners overseeing her treatment had the *power* to deny her access to the 'Gender Reassignment Program', to decide whether or not she might 'qualify'. *This was a decision that Jewkes could not count upon.* She is 'scared' before her final assessment appointment, and 'thankful' that her treatment was approved by the authoritative clinicians.

Bradley and Myerscough (2015) suggest that the time of anticipation can inform 'a politics of hopefulness rather than of dread', of 'preparedness' rather than 'anxiousness'. While a considerable number of trans patients report avoiding healthcare services due to their fears – seen especially in contributions to TransDocFailAnon – many more employ their mistrust in order to anticipate and avoid potential problems. Trans patients can utilise mistrust productively by looking for or offering advice and reassurance within community spaces, raising private issues publicly (such as through #transdocfail and later Twitter hashtags such as #nhsgenderid), and through becoming 'expert patients'. In this way, a strategic 'preparedness' with regard to the future can make 'hopefulness' possible. Thus, while the time of anticipation can close down possibilities through the dissemination of fearful stories, it may also open up possible futures through the strategic negotiation of health services.

'Trans enough' to pass the test: anticipating difficulty in assessments

For trans people who undertake physical transition, assessment appointments are vitally important because they determine if a patient might be able to access the necessary diagnosis. A typical anticipatory narrative on this topic is provided by Aiden.

> One more day to go till my appointment. I'm kind of bricking it re: not cocking up the train journey and having to answer a lot of invasive questions. Exciting too though...
> (Aiden)

In his post, Aiden looks forward to his first appointment at a gender clinic. He is worried ('bricking it') about the train journey due to issues around personal anxiety and physical disability, and, like Jewkes, is also concerned about the anticipated events of the appointment itself. Aiden's concerns regarding 'invasive' questions are not limited to the possibility he might find them embarrassing to answer. Implicit within his narrative is the idea that assessment interviews are a *difficult* experience. This can be linked to a more widespread discourse of difficulty, which arises from a subset of the communally mediated stories of cisgenderism and transphobia that reproduce past hardships as possible futures.

Anticipated difficulty

Some of the difficulties associated with attending initial gender clinic appointments are largely external to the medical process. For instance, participants sometimes express emotional difficulty in talking about being trans, because of internalised shame and/or unpleasant reactions from the general public. Similarly, many participants describe a fearful anticipation of negative responses to transition from partners, friends and family members. Others are concerned that the major life changes associated with transition might not be right for them.

However, many anticipated difficulties relate to the assessment process itself. For instance, patients may worry about intrusive questions addressing intimate activities such as sex and masturbation, which are common in assessments at many UK gender clinics (Speer, 2013; Nieder et al, 2016). They might also be concerned about other sensitive issues frequently raised by gender identity specialists, such as mental health diagnoses, education, work and family life (Barrett, 2007). It is apparent from Aiden's wider posts on the forum that his concerns are based in part upon an extrapolation from his experiences with a local mental health professional; however, he is also aware of typical assessment interview content due to past conversations with other forum users.

Encompassing the above issues is the difficulty of the *assessment process itself* as a gatekeeping procedure. Numerous participants describe being 'nervous', 'scared' or 'stressed' about past or forthcoming assessments.

> I recall how stressed I was ahead of the Assessment interviews and that is quite understandable because they are a gateway to further progress, as well as hormones and eventual surgery, if that's your aim. (Ellie)

The above quote is from a post where Ellie aims to reassure other forum users that the care pathway is navigable. However, in the quoted passage she draws attention to the imagined possibility of failure. This is where the difficulty lies, from which stress, fear and nervousness arise: the possibility of failure, thereby foreclosing the desired possible future of transition. Notably, a number of forum users describe the gatekeeping process as a kind of *test*, comparing it to (for instance), a job interview or school exam. It is here, also, that a key difficulty of the 'invasive questions' feared by Aiden lies. His concern is not simply that the appointment will be awkward: it is that in attempting to field the practitioner's questions, he might fail the test, possibly 'cocking it up' in a similar manner to the train journey. Numerous participants describe this common concern as a fear that they will not be seen as 'trans enough' by health professionals.

Preparing for the test

Aiden does seem reasonably sure that he will pass the test: hence his 'excitement', which is unpacked later in this chapter. However, he hasn't left the matter to chance. In a later post, he lists the documents he brought to his first appointment. These include his provisional driver's licence, bank card, bank statement, utility bills, NHS card and letters from the local council. They are intended to provide evidence of his commitment to a new ('trans enough') life as a man through the adoption of a male name in all areas of his life. Such evidence is usually explicitly requested by gender clinics: '[m]ore than in any other aspect of psychiatry … gender identity disorders require collateral history and confirmation' (Barrett, 2007: 14). Aiden also asks other forum users waiting for an appointment at the same gender clinic what documentation they intend to bring with them. This is a form of shared preparedness among community members who *collectively* engage with possible futures.

Advice on preparation is also frequently offered by experienced patients. An example of this is advice on how best to respond to assessment questions. The general feeling within the community sphere is that it is usually best to at first be honest and open with practitioners, with gender-pluralist advice to 'be yourself' applied beyond the realm of personal identity.

> As ever 'just be yourself'; answer the questions honestly and don't try to second-guess the answers. Is [your appointment] at Charing Cross or a local mental health practice? Good luck! (Steph)

> Just keep your mind focused on what you want and be as truthful as you feel you can be. (Felix)

This kind of advice – to 'be yourself', be 'truthful' and be 'honest' – is often offered to individuals anticipating their first assessment appointment. This demonstrates an inclination towards hope and a positive view of the future within the time of anticipation, despite mistrust, reflecting Horak's (2014) analysis of hormone time. Such advice is grounded in *positive* past experiences of trans patients, many of whom do return from appointments with accounts of helpful, kindly practitioners. In this way, communally mediated anticipation can work to negate negative stories and instead construct a more hopeful vision of the future. Indeed, numerous participants question the worries of new patients: many acknowledge that gender clinic policies have changed since the 'bad old days' of the 1990s and early 2000s, while others argue that activities such as 'Charing Cross bashing' are based upon outdated information.

The advice given to new patients within community spaces is liable to change, however, if the recipients of this guidance express grounded concerns about their own ability to prove themselves 'trans enough'. These concerns might arise from patients' non-binary gender presentations, subcultural lifestyles or actual difficulties encountered in a first appointment. In such instances, forum users often switch to recommending alternative tactics for passing the test, in another instance of strategic futurity. For example, Ellie responds to concerns from a trans woman who likes to dress androgynously with the following advice:

> If you have unambiguously female clothes – whatever they are – that you are comfortable in then wear them for the appointment. If you turn up just in a plain T-shirt, plain jeans and white trainers with no make-up or jewellery, there isn't much clue to your gender is there? A girl absolutely has the right to wear what she wants, but at the appointment the objective is to make sure that they see the female inside that XY body so my personal view is that one should make it easy for them to do that from the second they set eyes on you. Why make it harder on some dumbass principle? As soon as you get home, wear what you like! (Ellie)

While more nuanced than advice simply to 'wear a dress', this suggestion would appear to run contrary to some of the guidance from gender clinics themselves. In exploring this matter, I return to the notion of gender clinic 'myths'.

Failing the test?

In 2010 a list of 'myths' about Charing Cross was shared in several trans forums, based on a presentation by a consultant psychiatrist from the clinic. Items on this list of supposedly inaccurate patient expectations included: 'you have to wear a skirt to the GIC', 'you can't admit to doubt', 'they deliberately play Good Cop/Bad Cop', and 'you will have to give a standard trans narrative'. Until 2017, a list of statements counteracting these 'myths' could also be found on the Charing Cross website. Other gender clinics continue to share similar assurances.

> [T]here are no rules or expectations from the service as to how you are expected to dress or to express your gender identity. There are many different modes of dress and it is most important that you wear something that you are comfortable in. (Belfast Health and Social Care Trust, nd)

In this way, reassuring accounts from the gender clinics themselves can join the stories that circulate within community spaces, thereby potentially feeding into the construction of possible positive futures within the time of anticipation.

However, many trans patients do feel it necessary to follow Ellie's recommendations. Certainly, the guidance offered to patients by gender clinics such as Charing Cross and Brackenburn – and the stories of many who attend or have attended these clinics – indicate that the health professionals who work there no longer rely upon the bluntest of gender stereotypes. However, even the most recent accounts from participants indicated that some practitioners in UK gender clinics (including at Charing Cross) still try to ensure that patients 'fit' relatively rigid models of trans as condition. For instance, Joshua describes how a gender identity specialist was perturbed by his interest in fertility. Joshua reported having penetrative intercourse with a cis male partner, and asked the specialist in question about how he might best plan for a family.

> I wasn't taken seriously when I asked about being fertile … the questions I was faced with at the gender clinic just for saying that I have sex with a male was like 'omg you can't be trans!' (Joshua)

Such complaints are most frequently voiced by participants experiencing intersecting forms of marginalisation. This includes gay, bisexual or queer individuals like Joshua, as well as non-binary or genderqueer people, disabled individuals, carers and/or people of colour.

One neutrois forum user described a very negative reaction to their gender presentation during an assessment at a gender clinic. The practitioner repeatedly described their androgynous appearance as too 'gay' and advised them to adopt a more masculine name. The forum user later posited that their (non-Western) name was seen as gender ambiguous by the (white, British) practitioner. Being 'trans enough' to pass the assessment 'test' is therefore not necessarily simply a matter of gender identification or presentation. As discussed in the previous chapter, it can sometimes remain a matter of proving conformity to the practitioner or gender clinic's conditional approach to trans possibility, an approach that may also be shaped by the intersection of gender with other social categories such as race. In this instance, the practitioner's cisgenderism is also shaped by heterosexism, white cultural norms and racism. As Sara Ahmed (2016: 23) notes, 'gender norms so often remain predicated on an unremarkable whiteness'. These findings also reflect Ansara's (2010: 182) account of anti-Black racism from clinical gatekeepers: 'many Black-identified women … complained to me about being denied approval for hormones and surgery by non-Black counsellors of various ethnicities who considered them "too masculine" to be women according to non-Black cultural norms'.

At the Nottingham Centre for Transgender Health, the gatekeeping test is taken two steps further. Patients at the clinic may be asked to write a piece of prose exploring their gendered history for one assessment appointment, and are expected to bring a friend or family member to another. While neither of these requests is necessarily unusual within mental health services (and indeed, several participants described the therapeutic value of writing about their experiences with gender), their presence within *assessment* appointments suggests that they are being used as diagnostic tools. Certainly, this is how they were perceived by many Nottingham patients, who described the anxiety of anticipating and preparing for these appointments. According to the gender clinic, the purpose of the meeting with a friend or family member is to 'socialise the transition that the patient is making … [e]nsuring the patient has the support that they will need and that there is a person or people within their circle that knows the treatment that they will go through over the coming months' (NHS England, 2015c: 20). However, numerous participants attending appointments at Nottingham described an additional reason for this appointment: the *corroboration* of their account.

> Basically they asked him [a close friend] his thoughts on me.
> How well we know one another, how we met. What does
> he think about my decision. Whether or not he thought it
> was a snap decision or is it something that has always been
> there. (Sam)

The above account is a fairly typical community-sphere description
of assessment at Nottingham. In it, we see how this process exists in
part to assess the level of support a patient will receive within their
social circle, but can also operate as a diagnostic tool, with Sam's
friend asked about the conditions under which Sam might have made
the decision to transition. In this way, gender identity specialists are
also concerned with projecting the patient's perceived past into their
present and possible future, looking for clues as to whether a patient has
historically displayed (the right kind of) trans identity. The gatekeepers'
reading of this past – as socially mediated by patients' friends or family
members, in the case of Nottingham – can ultimately determine the
patient's future, particularly in instances of inconsistent pasts. Several
participants described having hormone therapy substantially delayed
after meetings where the person accompanying them was unsure or
offered an account that differed from that of the patient.

I draw out these examples to show how trans community discourses
of difficulty in the gatekeeping context are shaped by the temporal
interventions of the gatekeepers themselves. In some instances, clinics
seek to counter discourses of mistrust by providing an alternative,
reassuring vision of the future. However, the anticipation of potential
difficulty is still also mediated by *continuing* narratives of difficulty
from new patients, which can work to counter these reassurances. It
is important to note also that stories arising from a patient's encounter
with a particular practitioner or clinic can influence *wider* anticipatory
engagements with treatment. For instance, while Joshua's difficulties are
probably due to the individual prejudices of the specialist who oversaw
his appointment, his story feeds into the wider communal narratives of
anticipation that can shape a more general tendency towards mistrust.
In this way, poor practice at one clinic can influence perceptions of
other clinics. Moreover, in the example of Nottingham's insistence
that friends or family members attend an appointment, it is apparent
that gatekeepers may also draw upon multiple narratives of the past to
model an individual patient's future.

It is for these reasons that some patients attempt to meet the perceived
expectations of gender identity specialists by following advice such as
that provided by Ellie, refusing to take the risk of prolonging the waiting

time. My findings here build upon observations from Schonfield and Gardner (2008), and Ellis and colleagues (2015), who observe that a large proportion of UK patients lie or withhold information from gender identity specialists.

Therefore, while UK gender clinics have changed many of their policies and practices since the late 1990s, many individual practitioners and some clinical policies continue to frame '"transgender" as "the effect to be explained"' (Ansara and Hegarty, 2012: 141). Consequently, treatment cannot simply be expected by patients: instead, they feel that they must make a case for care. It is from this that the discourse of difficulty arises, as a form of strategic futurity through which patients draw on communally mediated narratives of the past to plan a swifter transition to their desired future. This is also why the discourse of difficulty arises *in spite of* positive experiences, as well as the common hope of accessing care (as seen in Aiden's excitement). The discourse of difficulty perpetuates fear and concern among patients early in the transition process, but also enables them to prepare. As a trans temporality – an emotional and material engagement with intersecting pasts, presents and futures – the time of anticipation sees trans patients engage with multiple possible futures and past/present narratives simultaneously. In this way, patient perspectives on the probability of accessing treatment intersect with grounded worries about passing the 'trans enough' test.

The possibility of joy: a discourse of hope

I now return to the post written by Aiden ahead of his first appointment with the gender clinic. As previously noted, he is not simply 'bricking it'; he is also looking forward to the appointment:

'Exciting too though … ' (Aiden)

Similarly, Jewkes (2017: 390) describes how obtaining a gender clinic appointment 'felt good and exciting because I knew my dream of living as and being a woman was inching closer'.

For trans patients seeking to transition physically, this excitement is another important element of the time of anticipation. With transition being such an important step for these trans patients, the treatment pathway is tied to a discourse of hope. This defines the waiting period as much as mistrust and difficulty, as a part of the waiting time's wider field of uncertainty. In looking forward with hope, trans patients anticipate a future in which they are transitioning, as well as a 'joyful' future in which they have transitioned (Horak, 2014); a future that becomes possible through positive narratives about the treatment pathway as much as more strategic approaches.

The anticipatory element of the discourse of hope is a community-mediated affair in a similar manner to mistrust and the discourse of difficulty. For example, Aiden's post ahead of his first appointment is just one part of a substantial forum thread themed around experiences at a particular gender clinic. Aiden joins others not just in gathering resources and sharing information that will help with their assessments, but also in sharing accounts of hopeful anticipation. Together they discuss plans for their respective journeys to the clinic and talk about which practitioners they will see. In conversations such as this, participants use words such as 'thrilled' and 'happy' as well as 'excited' to describe how they are looking forward to their appointment.

The hope evidenced within such conversations can also be linked to the prospect of moving beyond the 'not-yet' limbo. In one thread, Aiden swaps appointment dates with another forum user, commenting, 'Yay us'. In this expression of joy, we see the anticipated end of waiting time, with its transitional uncertainties to be replaced with the more linear temporal progress of hormone time. Horak (2014: 579) ties the beginning of hormone time to the 'first shot of testosterone or HRT pills': this can be compared to the implicit countdown *towards* that first shot in Aiden's conversation as the anticipated day of diagnosis draws closer.

In Forum 1 some users embed countdown timers into signatures that append their posts. These timers take the form of images that change every day (and in some cases, every hour or minute) to count down towards a set time, such as a gender clinic appointment or surgery date. This serves to emphasise that point in time as a temporal linch-pin, a focus for the user's time of anticipation. It positions the appointment time as concrete, firm, a point of fixity within a temporal realm of uncertainty and disjuncture: something an individual can look forward to without the doubt or concern that attends other aspects of transition. Notably, no such countdown timers are ever used for the day on which patients begin HRT. This date is usually unknown, due to the commonality of administrative delays in arranging a prescription.

Many participants acquired hope over time as a possible future became a viable conceptual reality for them through community support. Upon joining community forums, individuals who want to physically transition may lament the difficulty of their situation. They often ask more established forum users if their trans feelings are valid, if they can access treatment and how this might happen. New arrivals are often particularly distressed, and write about the intense emotional pain that accompanies their uncertainty. If they remain active within community spaces, these individuals become more familiar with the structure of the available treatment pathway(s) and orient themselves towards a future framed around this. Some more confident new arrivals have already reached this latter stage, and typically include an explanation regarding where they are on the pathway (awaiting an initial appointment, undergoing assessment, just starting hormones, awaiting surgery) when introducing themselves.

Similarly, participants typically gain confidence in themselves and in the concreteness of their projected 'better' future as transition progresses and possibility turns into reality. Entering hormone time is a significant aspect of this, as the uncertain transitional futurity of waiting and anticipation is replaced with the grounded certainty of a physical transition that is definitely underway. For instance, during his initial assessment appointments, Sam demonstrates a similar sense of hope to Aiden's, tempered with concerns about passing the 'test' of diagnosis.

> [The practitioner at the gender clinic] asked how sure I was I wanted treatment – but didn't actually offer it I noted! He said it's mostly down to me as to how I wanted it to play it. Do I really have to 'beg' for this treatment? (Sam)

A few months later, he describes his delight after receiving his first testosterone shot.

> Feeling a lot more confident in myself and a lot happier!! (Sam)

Sam's joy is grounded not simply in the initial physical changes and biochemical rush of hormone administration, but also in the certainty of hormone time. The shift in Sam's posts – away from a discourse of difficulty, towards a discourse of hope – provides a sense of possibility to other community members. Sam's story provides evidence that waiting does not necessarily last for ever, that some practitioners can be trusted to (eventually) provide treatment and that difficulty can be overcome.

As Hines (2007) notes, many trans people remain active in community spaces after their own journey along the transition pathway is over. This enables them to more actively counter concerns about the transition process with positive stories. For instance, in response to the aforementioned 'Charing Cross myth' that practitioners play 'Good Cop/Bad Cop', Alan states:

> As a patient at Charing Cross, I can confirm that many of these are of course myths. The two gentlemen I have had appointments with played a game of *Good Cop/Good Cop* in my opinion. (Alan, emphasis mine)

On another occasion, Ellie details how sad she is to bid farewell to the staff at the gender clinic she attended, stating how grateful she is for their support. She concludes:

> It's been an amazing journey and I'm so happy that I made it. (Ellie)

These accounts work to counteract some of the narratives of mistrust and difficulty that are very much present within the same spaces, demonstrating a different means by which collective pasts and overlapping presents can be used to construct an individual's possible future. They offer a basis for the kind of excitement, thrill and happiness expressed by individuals such as Aiden in anticipating assessment appointments as an 'opening or horizon' (Muñoz, 2007) through which patients can see themselves accessing treatment and being treated well by practitioners. Moreover, these accounts provide a model by which transitioning patients can foresee that they will not be caught forever within the temporally mediated emotional uncertainty of transitional time and the long wait. It is through these means, as well as through strategic futurities and the collective action I describe in the next chapter, that the time of anticipation can be used to 'build a politics of hopefulness' (Bradley and Myerscough, 2015).

Circumventing the time of anticipation: private treatment and self-medication

For some transitioning participants, the discourse of hope was not sufficient to assuage their mistrust of gender clinics or the emotional demands of waiting. There are two alternatives to the public health pathway: private clinics, and self-medication. Those who access these alternative resources seek to escape at least some of the temporal disjuncture and uncertainty associated with NHS services.

Forum participants contemplating transition are often recommended to 'go private' if they can afford it. While explicit praise for the NHS as an institution is common within these spaces, the private route is typically portrayed as easier, faster and more flexible. This perspective is summarised powerfully within a document produced for the NHS by young trans people working with the charity group Gendered Intelligence. In a table comparing the respective 'pros and cons' of NHS and private treatment, the following 'pros' were offered for each category:

NHS
- It's free.

Private
- Will not have to wait long for the treatment.
- You have more choice over timescales and treatment options.
- You have a choice of surgeon if you choose to have surgery.
- You will be treated with respect.

(NHS and Department of Health, 2007)

The document quoted above is now over a decade old, and not entirely accurate (most NHS gender clinics provide patients with multiple surgery options), but it is important in that it codifies a discourse common within many trans spaces to this day. The only 'pro' specific to transitioning on the NHS is that it is free at point of use: in all other ways, private treatment is regarded as superior. Most notably, '[w]ill not have to wait long' and '[y]ou will be treated with respect' are portrayed as a *specific* property of private providers.

In the below narrative, Ben offers a typical rationale for taking the private route.

> From my reading of the web plus various NHS websites and other people's experiences on the forums it looked like there would be a minimum wait of around a year (if you were fortunate with your GP) ... then to be told that I had to have changed my name and done RLE and then come back 3 months later (minimum) before [testosterone] would even be prescribed made me feel anxious and also (if I am honest) resentful that someone else could make all these decisions for me. It was these worries that made me opt for the private route. (Ben)

In Ben's account, we see anticipatory concerns regarding the *time* it takes to prepare for transition (incorporating RLE as well as the various

148

referrals and waiting lists), alongside a mistrust of health professionals (being 'lucky with your GP' to gain a referral) and a rejection of conditional models of trans possibility ('resentful that someone else could make all these decisions for me'). In a separate post, Ben also invokes the discourse of difficulty, stating that he was 'worried' about being assessed through the NHS 'in case I wasn't "trans enough"'. Notably, Ben is *himself* a medical doctor, and frequently states that he is proud to work for the NHS. His mistrust is rooted in community discourses of *trans* health, and specific concerns regarding the operation of gender identity services.

The sense that private services are faster, more flexible and more focused on 'respect' than NHS gender clinics persists within the community and activist spheres. This is the case even as two of the three available private clinics – Gender Care in London, and Gender Dysphoria Clinic and Treatments Edinburgh – are run by individuals who also work or have worked as gender identity specialists in the public sector. This suggests that the 'respect' patients seek can be found in the private *pathway* process at least as much as in the attitude of individual practitioners, with these pathways offering an alternative to some of the institutional issues and anticipatory uncertainties associated with NHS clinics. While all private practitioners claim to operate within the bounds of the WPATH *Standards of Care* with their built-in waiting times, patients can at least expect to know when they will be seen, and can generally also anticipate accessing hormones more quickly. The private pathways therefore offer a more predictable route, characterised less by temporal disjuncture and more by the linear futurity of hormone time.

While Gender Care in particular was discussed relatively often and generally spoken of positively within the community and activist spheres, the most popular private provider among research participants during the early 2010s was Transhealth, run by Richard Curtis. The name 'Dr Curtis' was widely associated with a more liberal form of care that centres informed consent rather than placing the burden of proof upon trans patients, a factor that was sometimes linked by participants to Curtis' own background as a trans man. Transhealth patients such as Ben felt more confident that the possible future of transition would eventually manifest, and within a predictable time frame too. They were less worried about encountering cisgenderism or transphobia from Curtis, or having to prove themselves 'trans enough'. When Curtis faced investigation from the GMC in 2011–15 (see Chapter Six), a considerable number of participants expressed concern about the future for his model of treatment, which provided an alternative *philosophy* of care as much as a competing service.

Of course, private services are not available to all (although various participants from low-income backgrounds described going to great lengths to afford appointments at Gender Care or Transhealth). Some individuals therefore self-medicate with the help of friends, or through online purchases from overseas pharmacies. The legality and safety of self-medication is contested within trans spaces; promoting the practice is considered bad form in Forum 1, and explicitly banned in Forum 2. However, this did not prevent some participants in both forums from discussing their decision to self-medicate, usually out of self-professed 'frustration' or 'desperation'. These individuals see self-medication as an opportunity to take matters into their own hands, gaining some sense of control over the time of anticipation through invoking the more linear temporality of hormone time, while avoiding the need to prove themselves 'trans enough' to an external authority.

Both private clinics and self-medication are frequently regarded as options to take *alongside* the NHS route, rather than as an alternative to it.

> Many of us do start things off by self medding – I did because when I looked at the report from my 2nd Assessment I thought Charing Cross were about to start dithering. (Ellie)

Participants such as Ellie seek to circumvent the emotional and temporal uncertainty of NHS treatment by starting on hormones without the prior approval of a gatekeeper. They are not committed to permanently undertaking private or 'DIY' treatment, and instead prefer to access public healthcare services; however, the financial costs of private treatment and/or the possible risk of self-medication are typically regarded as preferable to the uncertainty of waiting.

The private treatment route and self-medication therefore offer transitioning individuals an alternative means to manage the time of anticipation. Patients taking these approaches can still expect to wait: for the physical and mental changes that accompany hormone therapy, for additional services such as surgeries and even for an NHS diagnosis that enables them to shift from one means of managing transition to another. However, the additional certainty granted through greater personal management over the timing of hormone therapy makes people feel considerably more in control over their lives, enabling them to thrive within the more predictable context of hormone time.

Suicide, and the collapse of possible futures

Private treatment and self-medication offer one form of escape from uncertainty and the liminality of the 'not-yet' limbo. Both approaches offer maintenance of hope, and the continued 'opening' of future possibility. But what of individuals who do not have the financial or social capital to access private care or self-medication, who see no opening, no way forward?

The shadow of suicide lies heavy across trans communities. A majority of trans people in the UK have considered killing themselves, with approximately one in three having attempted suicide at least once (Whittle et al, 2007; McNeil et al, 2012). Similarly high figures have been reported in studies across the world (Adams, Hitomi et al, 2017).

Numerous participants from across the community and activist spheres indicated that they had considered and/or attempted suicide, or that their friends had killed themselves or attempted to do so. It is not within the scope of this book to unpack the many social and individual causes of trans suicide. Instead, this analysis links some instances of suicide ideation to the collapse of trans futurities in the time of anticipation. While I continue to draw on data from the two forums visited during fieldwork, I do not quote directly from the community sphere, due to the sensitivity of conversations I observed there.

Several participants describe a 'choice' between transition and suicide. Such accounts link suicidal feelings to the hopelessness of life in the participants' assigned genders. They feel constrained and unable to express themselves, and imagine that these desperate and frustrating feelings will continue for the rest of their lives. This is a future without a future, bereft of fulfilment and happiness. By contrast, transition offers a way out: an 'opening or horizon' (Muñoz, 2007). Participants who describe the choice to transition in terms of a move *away* from suicide typically narrate an emotional journey in which the decision to transition offers them a new-found resolve and sense of purpose: a meaningful futurity. In this way, transition provides the possibility of a fulfilling, happy future that can be imagined as *attainable*. Narratives such as this informed numerous media articles written by trans people in the wake of #transdocfail, as can be seen in the below example from a piece in *The New Statesman*.

> [Trans] people consider transitioning well worth [doing] because in some cases the alternative is suicide. (Hallam, 2013)

This idea of a 'choice' between transition and suicide is also indicated by McNeil and colleagues (2012: 59), who state that a majority of survey respondents were 'thinking about or attempting suicide more before they transitioned' than after. This indicates a link between transition and suicide reduction, reflecting the authors' wider findings on the benefits of transition for the mental health of trans patients. Conversely, delays and problems *during* transition can be linked to increased suicide ideation and suicide attempts. McNeil and colleagues describe a 7% *rise* in suicide ideation and attempts during transition, even as suicide attempt rates fall post-transition, in comparison to pre-transition levels. Belcher (2014) noted that two of her survey respondents attempted suicide because of how they were treated by health professionals.

Participants in this project most frequently describe suicidal feelings on encountering obstacles to transition. These include waits of an uncertain length, health professionals who delay or refuse treatment and gender clinic appointments where requirements made of patients are opaque, confusing or otherwise difficult. There was also one case in which a very distressed patient expressed suicidal feelings immediately following surgery, upon experiencing bad results compounded by poor follow-up care. In each instance, the obstacle in the pathway works to disrupt the trans patient's passage from past to future, and to erode their sense of agency. In the below narrative from two merged #transdocfail tweets, a patient describes how they became suicidal after being refused a referral for gender identity services by their GP on multiple occasions over a three-year period.

> I went to my GP and asked to be referred. Waited a few months and asked again told they were looking into it. Repeat. Three years later was told it was not available. Became suicidal and was told others are much worse off than you. (TransDocFailAnon)

This story shows how waiting times can be extended over an indeterminate and unpredictable period, with transition becoming a future that is never quite realised, in a temporal space that stretches ever wider. In this way, the joyful future of hormone time becomes unattainable as the patient is instead caught – seemingly forever, as there is no apparent end to the delay – within the 'not-yet' limbo of anticipation.

The future can appear similarly unattainable to participants who do not at first 'pass the test' set by gatekeepers at the gender clinic. For participants in this project, reasons for being (initially) denied hormones included: concurrent mental health problems, a failure to conform to binarist or Eurocentric gender norms, failure to hold down work or a volunteering position and/or failure to inform family members of their intention to transition (in one instance, a patient in his late 40s was chastised by a gatekeeper for not yet having come out to his mother). This can lead to suicide ideation among the most vulnerable. McNeil and colleagues report similar findings. One of their participants states, 'if they had refused me hormones and surgery, I would probably have committed suicide', while another reports that 'NHS refusals [led] to failed suicide' (McNeil et al, 2012: 34/55). In these examples, an anticipated future has effectively been denied, and there is typically no indication of when the continued waiting time might end. I have previously quoted Bradley and Myerscough's (2015) poetic description of trans subjectivities within the time of anticipation as 'orientated towards the future like iron filings lining themselves up towards a magnet'; in an extension of this metaphor, suicide can be understood as a reaction to the removal of that magnet, leaving no focal point for the projection of an optimistic trans futurity.

Participant experiences of suicide ideation further demonstrate the importance of anticipation to trans patients and their communities. For participants who consider suicide, the possibility of a transitioned future can offer an alternative.

> Former GP told me to pull myself together and stop wasting his time[.] Wasted ten years of my life in and out of depression. Became suicidal. Went to Dr Curtis. (Christabel Edwards)

The time of anticipation might be frustrating and difficult, but within this temporal frame a possible future is always invoked. Participants such as Christabel who find a way to re-enter the time of anticipation (such as through private care with a trusted practitioner) may move out from the shadow of suicide. This is, however, a fragile futurity: one that can be shattered through the repeated denial of treatment, or through waits that stretch into a seemingly infinite temporal distance.

In which I continue to wait (a contingent conclusion)

At the time of writing – over two years after my initial attempt to access treatment – I am still waiting to receive laser hair removal. I do not know how long I will be waiting; only that an approval for funding has (now, finally) been sought by the laser clinic. My new GP appeared exceptionally helpful, as did the gatekeeper at the gender clinic to which I was eventually referred. However, even after being bounced from waiting list to waiting list, from appointment to appointment, my future remains deeply uncertain.

Some of the concerns I held in advance of seeking a referral for hair removal – concerns shaped by the overlapping pasts and presents of others as well as myself – are reflected in my current circumstances. My access to treatment was delayed enormously by the inflexibility that resulted in my referral to the gender clinic, rather than directly to a laser clinic. My experience as a trans patient is inherently bound up in the temporal and emotional disjuncture of waiting time, oriented towards a future that I hope will come, but I am not sure *when*. I remain caught within the 'not-yet' limbo (Nirta, 2018). Even as a devout believer in the importance of state-funded health services, I would be tempted by the prospect of paying for hair removal privately, if I could but afford it. Like the research participants, I anticipate, but do not know when the time of anticipation will end. This is not (yet) a linear path equivalent to Horak's hormone time, a futurity fixed through appointment and prescription: instead my experience of seeking hair removal can be understood within the frame of Carter's transitional time, moving backwards, sideways and tangentially even as I progress. Halberstam (2005) and Carter (2013) regard the movement-oriented fluidity of, respectively, queer time and transitional time, as potentially liberating. This liberation comes only with agency: but agency is limited within the time of anticipation. For this reason, the more predictable temporality of hormone time feels – to me – greatly preferable in this instance.

Other concerns I held in advance of my referral for hair removal are *not* reflected in my current circumstances. While my GP was broadly ignorant of trans health issues and the current treatment pathway, she was kind, considerate and supportive. My mistrust ahead of meeting her arose not from any bad experiences at the practice where I am now registered, but from an anticipatory mistrust rooted both in my own negative experiences with my former GP and in wider community discourse. I *know* that transphobia and cisgenderism are common; some level of mistrust feels like a rational, strategic response that enables me to manage my expectations for the future and reduce uncertainty.

Nevertheless, I look forward to the time I will no longer experience the dysphoria of 'male'-pattern facial hair and the associated heightened risk of street harassment or violence. The technological possibility of hair removal and the delivery of this service through NHS commissioning imbue me with a sense of possibility. This is not the all-encompassing hopeful futurity of those who anticipate transition, but it is a future that redefines my emotional experience of the present. It offers 'not an end but an opening or horizon' (Muñoz, 2007: 364), thereby rendering my embodied transness more bearable and the wait less frustrating.

The purpose of this vignette is not to collapse the many stories present within this chapter into one easy narrative. There are some key elements missing from my story, such as the discourse of difficulty and the shadow of suicide. There is, after all, not one trans healthcare system or one trans patient experience in the UK, but instead a myriad of possibilities shaped by geographical location, gatekeeper attitudes, medical institutions, community narratives and individual subjectivity. My own account therefore offers just one more example of trans experience in the time of anticipation.

The time of anticipation is a queer time, defined by disjuncture, liminality and futurity. This temporal frame sits at the nexus of agency and dis/empowerment, offering trans patients a range of discourses to understand and manage their interactions with medical systems and health professionals. 'Time' in this sense is not an object but a context, mediated communally through the queer interaction of multiple pasts, presents and possible futures. Halberstam (2005) and Carter (2013) celebrate the disruptions of queer temporalities, but most participants in this project instead seek some form of stability and predictability through which an escape from the time of anticipation might be imagined. In my own example, as in the examples of project participants throughout this chapter, possible futures come to define the present and past alike, with projected futures offering a means by which we can better cope with the demands of the present.

Note

[1] 'Hen' is a first-person gender neutral pronoun, originating from the Swedish language and used by Volcano.

Part Three
Changing trans health

SIX

The politics of trans health: negotiating credible knowledge

> As a spatial marker of possibility, the prefix, *trans-* does not just signify movement beyond or across a schism. Instead, it is also evocative of the *transgressions*, *transmogrifications*, and *transmutations* of established norms. (Nael Bhanji, 2013, emphasis in original)

A Trip To The Clinic

> Okay, well it tells me here that you have a complaint about your arm. Why don't you tell me about yourself?

You seek help for an injury at the fracture clinic. Unfortunately, the doctor isn't interested in your arm. He wants to know a lot more, asking in an increasingly disparaging manner for irrelevant details from your childhood, and probing your emotional response to the accident. At one point, he insists that you tell him about your sex life. It seems that the burden of proof is on you to demonstrate not simply that you have indeed broken your arm, but that you are also in a great deal of pain and therefore require treatment.

> I feel I should tell you now that, in your notes, I've been writing 'pain' in inverted commas. I'm not yet convinced that you have actually experienced any pain.

This narrative can be found in the short 'choose your own adventure' text-based browser game *A Trip To The Clinic*. It was released for free on the internet by indie game creator Wojit in January 2013, in the immediate wake of #transdocfail.[1] The game, which was shared widely on trans and feminist blogs and social media spaces, is a transparent satire of gender clinic appointments. To 'win', thereby gaining access to treatment, the player must present the correct narrative to the doctor, and respond in a deferential manner to his requests. This can be done by clicking on the 'correct' response to questions where an option is available. A failure to provide enough 'correct' responses may result in the player character waiting longer for treatment, or being denied treatment altogether.

A Trip To The Clinic reflects and feeds into prominent discourses of trans health present within community and activist spaces. Firstly, it addresses the fundamental differences of *definition* and *understanding* that can sometimes exist between practitioner and patient, as discussed in Chapter Four. The game effectively depicts a discursive conflict arising from varying understandings of trans possibility and reality in the context of patient experience and medical practice. Secondly, it both reflects and constitutes an element of the communally mediated temporality of *anticipation* – as discussed in the previous chapter – in reproducing and informing a mistrust of health professionals, through a discourse of difficulty associated with gatekeeping practices.

This chapter examines a third, related aspect of *A Trip To The Clinic*: it aims to communicate and hence reproduce trans knowledges and critiques of the aforementioned issues, thereby challenging the conditions under which these issues arise. I have shown that existing medical policies and practices are often embedded in cisgenderist assumptions and/or discourses of trans as condition. Bringing about change therefore requires an attempted shift in the status of *alternative* trans knowledges – knowledges grounded instead in understandings of trans as movement and/or a gender-pluralist (Monro, 2005) approach – through seeking to render such knowledges *credible*. Here, I follow Stephen Epstein (1996: 3) in using 'credibility' to describe 'the capacity of claim-makers to enrol supporters behind their arguments, legitimate those arguments as authoritative knowledge, and present themselves as the sort of people who can voice the truth'. I shall show that *A Trip To The Clinic* is one node in a great network of interventions by which patient advocates promote trans knowledges and truths through processes of mutual recognition and iterative repetition.

By **trans knowledges**, I refer to discourses of trans possibility constructed in and through trans people's communities, activisms and academic work. Interventions such as *A Trip To The Clinic* represent both an individual act of education and a wider play in the politics of credibility and expertise. Through a myriad of such interventions within social media as well as through traditional media platforms, professional networks and radical activism, trans patient advocates work to *recognise* one another's stories and ideas – thereby reinforcing their claims to knowledge and truth – and *repeat* them through a continued dissemination of evidence. This has the effect of increasing the discursive weight and reach of patient knowledges.

I continue to position the 'reality' of trans health as a social construct, a 'field of intelligibility' (Steinberg, 2015a: 153) linked to the mediation of discourse and the operation of power. As such, discursive clashes on the *macro* level between patient and professional knowledges and understandings – that is, clashes at the level of *collective politics* rather the individual clinical encounters discussed in Chapters Three, Four and Five – must be resolved through gradual negotiation of the respective discourses' status as knowledge claims.

I begin this chapter with a brief look at the **epistemic politics** of trans health. 'Epistemology' is the philosophical study of how knowledge is (and can be) produced: *epistemic* politics therefore describes the struggle to define *who* is capable of producing knowledge, and *how*. Drawing on insights from other patient movements such as AIDS activism, I show how gender identity specialists and the trans patient body might each be collectively understood as an 'epistemic community' (Haas, 1992; Akrich, 2010). In this context, mutual education and the rise of 'activist-experts' (Epstein, 1996) heralds a change 'in the epistemic status of the patient' (Hess, 2004: 697).

I then turn to evidence from the activist sphere to show how trans people have sought to increase the credibility of patient knowledges. Examples in this discussion include personal or individual interventions – such as contributions to #transdocfail – plus forms of journalistic, health-oriented professional and activist intervention. Finally, I look in-depth at how the promotion of patient knowledges can require negotiation between trans knowledges and professional discourse/practice, with reference to a case study: the depathologisation movement.

Establishing credibility: the epistemic politics of trans health

Since the emergence of the trans social movement in the 1990s, patient groups in the UK have sought to change the landscape of healthcare provision, particularly in the context of gender identity services. Persistent concerns have included long waiting times and gatekeeping practices, as well as the continued prevalence of cisgenderism and transphobia. In many ways this has been an isolated struggle, with few formal links existing between trans patient activists in the UK and other patient movements in the UK and beyond. Nevertheless, numerous tactics employed by trans patient advocates resemble those pioneered within other patient movements.

Stephen Epstein's (1996) account of the AIDS movement in the United States shows how a complex and multifaceted range of interventions from various patient groups came to influence both medical science and approaches to treatment. AIDS activists sought to challenge policies, practices and/or the provision of services in a range of contexts, including medical school curricula, clinical trials and the development of potential cures. The aims and tactics of different activist groups varied considerably, but their actions were generally informed by a mistrust of traditional medical experts and shared an urgency that reflected the scale of the epidemic. Many AIDS activists therefore sought to establish *themselves* as credible authorities on matters of medical research and care, leading to a large-scale 'conversion of [people] from disease "victims"' to **activist-experts** (Epstein, 1996: 8).

One of the many issues addressed by early AIDS activism was the perceived paternalism of medical institutions. Numerous individuals and groups argued that traditional medical approaches worked to undermine patient agency.

> Activists ... would exert a demand for greater patient autonomy by challenging medical authority from two directions at once. On one hand, they would insist that patients interested in trying experimental drugs should have the right to assume risks rather than endure the benevolent protection of authorities. On the other hand, they would criticize certain approved and accepted research methods, like trials in which some patients received placebos, characterizing them as unethical for subjecting patients to unfair risks that the patients *did not* want to assume. (Epstein, 1996: 190, emphasis in original)

Many trans people similarly argue that gender clinic policies and practices need to reconsider the role of consent in their interactions with patients. In the below example, Michael Toze – a social researcher based at the University of Lincoln – offers a nuanced assessment of how the gatekeeping system can work to deny patients the opportunity to take responsibility for their own care or provide properly informed consent.

> Assessment procedures in clinics are not transparent and not consistent, and patients are aware of this through informal discussion. For example, Nottingham Gender Identity Clinic recently sent new patients a form asking them what

video games they play. It is not clear why this is relevant to their assessment or care, and if it is relevant, why other clinics are not asking. Some patients suspect this data was collected for a research study, although if so, no informed consent was sought ... Some clinics ask patients highly personal questions about sex; some ask if patients have gay relatives; some have refused treatment for people who are full-time carers and hence unable to work. Other clinics do none of these things. Because clinics control access to treatment, patients do not feel empowered to challenge being asked irrelevant and highly personal questions, or having judgements made about their lives. (Toze, 2015)[2]

The above extract was written in response to the House of Commons Women and Equality Committee's Transgender Equality Inquiry. Toze describes his submission as written 'in a personal capacity'. However, even as he contributes to the inquiry explicitly as a trans man – and hence as a service user, or 'patient' – he draws on an extended and sophisticated knowledge of the UK's medico-legal landscape, and his submission is carefully structured like a formal report. Toze was later quoted and cited repeatedly in the report produced for the inquiry (Women and Equalities Committee, 2016: 37, 44, 48, 61, 62). In this way, he successfully asserts himself as an 'activist-expert' (Epstein, 1996), drawing upon established professional norms of communication to establish his credibility.

In the rise of 'counter-expertise', as exemplified by Toze, David Hess (2004: 697) identifies 'a historic change in the epistemic status of the patient'. Hess argues that this has resulted in wider changes to medical professions and associated research communities. In the context of trans health, this assertion is reflected in the claim that a paradigm shift has taken (or is taking) place among gender identity specialists (Bockting, 2009; Nieder et al, 2016). Cristoph Hanssmann (2016: 124–125) argues that ideological changes *within* gender identity services are being driven by **insider-providers** – practitioners who are themselves trans – as well as '[trans] lawyers, and activists [who] increasingly shape policies and protocols'. Hess (2004: 703) describes interventions by insider-providers as the 'direct form' by which medical science might be shaped. Toze's contribution as a patient and activist is an 'indirect form' of intervention, sitting among 'contributions to the media or to engagement with the policy process and funding decisions' by members of a social movement or advocacy group 'who have developed the appropriate literacy to engage the policy and funding communities' (Hess, 2004: 703).

This chapter looks primarily at the *collective* work of trans people from different backgrounds and within different arenas who engage in both 'direct' and 'indirect' forms of activist-expert intervention. Drawing on Madelein Akrich's (2010) account of health-oriented activist mobilisations on the internet, I regard the diffuse network of trans patients engaging in this kind of activism as an **epistemic community**: that is, a collection of individuals and groups among whom complementary forms of knowledge and expertise circulate. The term epistemic community was originally coined by Peter Haas (1992) to describe specifically *professional* networks who draw upon a shared knowledge base to shape public policy. In this sense, the specialists who work within NHS gender clinics might be said to comprise one such community. Akrich (2010) argues that the extensive epistemic work undertaken by health activists within online communities – through sharing personal stories, collecting and disseminating personal *and* scientific evidence and presenting cases for change to authoritative bodies – means that they are effectively a *lay* body that performs a similar epistemic function to a professional body.

However, it is the professional communities that typically wield authoritative credibility. This means that lay epistemic communities 'have no hegemonic position in the elaboration of public policies. On the contrary, they appear as opposing forces facing professional epistemic communities and reopen the range of possibilities, which professionals tended to limit and keep under their control' (Akrich, 2010: 11.1). Before turning to examine the forms that trans people's activist-expert interventions take, then, I first outline an example of how power can be deployed through discourses of credibility and accusations of misconduct within professional epistemic communities.

Gatekeeping the gatekeepers

In 2006 private practitioner Russell Reid retired, following controversy over his private gender identity service. The following year, a GMC Fitness to Practice Panel found that he had engaged in 'serious professional misconduct' (Bouman et al, 2014). Numerous complaints about Reid had been submitted to the GMC by four Charing Cross practitioners, including James Barrett (Burns, 2006).

Barrett (2007) argues that Reid was not strict enough in managing his patients. He asserts that the GMC findings reflect Reid's failure to follow the (Version 6) WPATH *Standards of Care* (Meyer et al, 2001).

Reid's misconduct included 'administer[ing] hormonal treatment after one consultation in circumstances where patients had neither lived in their desired gender role nor undergone three months of psychotherapy'; 'giv[ing] support for the provision of gender reassignment surgery despite patients not having lived in their desired gender role for what would be regarded as a sufficient length of time'; failing to seek an appropriate second referral for gender reassignment surgery; and making 'no attempt to verify patients' claims' that they had been undertaking RLE (Barrett, 2007: 287). Notably, these complaints describe deviations not just from the Version 6 *Standards of Care* but also from the standard approach taken by NHS gender clinics, including Charing Cross.

Ironically, Reid's approach (as described by Barrett) *does* appear to mostly meet the requirements of the Version 7 *Standards of Care*, published four years later in 2011. These 'flexible clinical guidelines' explicitly acknowledge that experienced practitioners might make an informed decision to depart from the stated criteria; moreover, there is no longer a strict requirement that patients undergo three months of psychotherapy or a period of RLE prior to receiving a hormone prescription (Coleman et al, 2012). As such, many of the complaints against Reid were historically contingent: they reflected an international clinical consensus that has since begun to shift as more practitioners aim to centre patients' informed consent in their approach to trans-specific care.

Following Reid's retirement, his practice was effectively inherited by Richard Curtis, who in turn also become known for a less strict and rigid approach to treatment than that of the NHS gender clinics. As noted in the previous chapter, many research participants held Curtis in high regard; he had a good reputation among the wider patient body as well as among his own clients. However, Curtis was also accused of too easily allowing patients to make the 'wrong' decision about their care. This criticism circulated within some trans community spaces as well as within the practitioner sphere, and – eventually – the mainstream media.

Curtis, too, faced investigation from the GMC following allegations of professional misconduct in 2011. In a January 2013 article for the *Observer*, David Batty described the case against Curtis as follows.

> Commencing hormone treatment in complex cases without referring the patient for a second opinion or before they had undergone counselling, administering hormone treatment at patients' first appointments, and referring patients for

surgery before they had lived in their desired gender role for a year, as international guidelines recommend. One patient allegedly underwent surgery within 12 months of their first appointment. He is also accused of administering hormones to patients aged under 18 without an adequate assessment, and wrongly stating that a patient seeking gender reassignment had changed their name. (Batty, 2013)

Some NHS clinicians again played a role in the case. Research participant JF alleged that his medical notes were provided to the GMC by Charing Cross practitioners without his permission. JF describes the treatment he received from Curtis at the age of 16 – prior to a later adult referral to Charing Cross – as 'a lifeline'. He felt unable to complain while receiving treatment, due to the power differential between patient and practitioner, and did not want to revisit the experience by making a formal complaint afterwards.

> I got a call about [the medical notes] but they said even though I refused they could be used anyway. I mentioned in a follow up consultation with Barrett that I was nonbinary ... he [therefore] felt I had 'detransitioned' and wanted to use my medical records in the case ... I was in the middle of treatment so I didn't want to complain in case I was sanctioned as they already threatened to take away hormones because I was nonbinary. Now I've finished with them I just can't be bothered to complain about the treatment I received. (JF)

The GMC case against Curtis prompted a popular outcry within trans community and activist spaces. One important consequence was the original creation of the #transdocfail hashtag on Twitter, two days after the publication of Batty's article. This saw thousands of contributions from individuals arguing that widespread ignorance, prejudice and malpractice within health services should be the subject of popular scrutiny, rather than any alleged failings on the part of Curtis.

The case was eventually dismissed by the GMC in 2015. In the intervening years, Curtis made several changes to his service so that it involved more extensive gatekeeping, thereby more closely resembling the NHS gender clinics. For example, his patients were required to undergo a second diagnosis from an additional health professional prior to any hormone prescription, and were also asked to provide more comprehensive evidence of their commitment to living full time in their acquired gender role. Curtis also stopped seeing patients under the age of 21. In June 2017, a message was posted to the Transhealth website announcing that Curtis would be closing the clinic by the end of the year, due to 'a number of personal, professional, and business related reasons'.

In 2015 a new private provider emerged: Welsh physician Helen Webberley, of the 'Gender GP' Online Transgender Medical Clinic. Like Reid and Curtis, Webberley has gained a reputation for providing more flexible treatment than the NHS gender clinics. In 2017 she faced restrictions from the GMC, pending an investigation, after NHS gender identity specialists complained about her practice.

In statements to the media, Webberley explained that she had been providing hormone prescriptions to 'a handful' of adolescents under the age of 16 (Rumbelow, 2017). This contrasts with standard practice at NHS child and adolescent gender identity services, but again, does not necessarily contravene the WPATH *Standards of Care*, which allow for a level of flexibility according to individual patient needs (Coleman et al, 2012). Indeed, while hormone therapy is provided no earlier than 16 in most international contexts, a growing number of clinics sometimes depart from this approach in cases where an adolescent's physical and emotional development would seem to warrant an earlier intervention (Spack et al, 2012; Vance et al, 2014; Bonifacio and Rosenthal, 2015; Chen et al, 2016).[3] This is particularly the case with adolescent patients who have been on hormone blockers for a long time due to the early onset of puberty. These individuals may experience severe stress as their peers undergo puberty while they do not, and they are also at greater risk of decreased bone mineral density, which in turn may lead to conditions such as osteoporosis later in life (Delemarre-van de Waal and Cohen-Kettenis, 2006). Webberley has argued that her decision to provide hormones in instances such as this is a matter of harm reduction (Lyons, 2016; Rumbelow, 2017).

Hess (2004: 705) describes how medical 'researchers in ... dominant networks have tended to engage in a wide variety of suppression tactics aimed at activists, clinicians and researchers who have departed from the dominant research programmes'. The GMC cases against Reid, Curtis and Webberley's practices would seem to be instances of this, albeit in the context of medical practice rather than research. This is not to say that these private providers are necessarily innocent of malpractice; in my research, I did not have access to the exact evidence that was provided to the GMC. However, it is notable that these three *specific* individuals have faced censure from their peers for their approach to trans healthcare, whereas numerous individuals working in NHS gender clinics – who are alleged by their patients to have disparaged or mocked them, discriminated against them, or even committed sexual assault – do not seem to have faced disciplinary action.

While Barrett (2007) argues that Reid's approach to treatment constituted a risk to patients, his crime may also be understood as a departure from the dominant paradigm. One effective function of the professional epistemic community of trans health is to police this paradigm. Those who depart from standard UK approaches to gatekeeping face punishment, even for actions that may align with alternative, international standards of best practice. How, then, might patients themselves hope to bring about change?

Recognition and repetition: promoting patient knowledges

Trans patient advocates frequently differ from one another: philosophically, politically and in terms of their tactics for bringing about change. However, a number of goals are quite consistently outlined across the activist sphere. These include: tackling cisgenderism and transphobia within medical settings, reducing waiting times and reforming the adversarial gatekeeping relationship that is satirised in *A Trip To The Clinic* and is so powerfully defended by members of the professional epistemic community. To achieve these goals, trans knowledges must be recognised as credible beyond trans spaces. This can be difficult, given the institutionalised authority of health professionals (Davy, 2011) and the historic silencing of trans people within the professional sphere (Stryker, 2005).

In the face of these challenges, patient advocates promote the credibility of trans knowledges through mutual recognition and iterative repetition. By this I mean: when trans patients explicitly state their opposition to existing inequalities and practices, and propose alternative approaches, the credibility of their position is bolstered if their alternative knowledge of trans health is *seen, acknowledged and reproduced* by others across a range of contexts. I explore four such contexts here: personal or individual discursive interventions, interventions by journalists, interventions by professionals working in the arena of health and interventions by activist groups. Negotiations of knowledge and meaning across these contexts ultimately intersect and influence one another as patient advocates recognise the work of knowledge construction and meaning-making that takes place elsewhere. In addition to drawing on individual examples to illustrate the recognition and repetition of knowledges within these contexts, I use #transdocfail as a running example throughout the discussion.

Personal or individual interventions

There is a long history of trans people drawing on self-knowledge from gendered experience to negotiate access to medical transition (Meyerowitz, 2002; Rubin, 2003; Lester, 2017). These interactions between practitioner and patient typically take place on a 'micro' level: within the private realm of the consultation, or through other discreet means such as letter writing. The data for this project indicated an increasing assertiveness on the part of patients within clinical settings. This can be linked not only to the emergence of new understandings of trans possibility, but also to wider discursive shifts regarding the role of 'the patient' in public health.

In recent years, public health discourse in the UK has shifted away from a prioritisation of medical authority and expertise, and towards more liberal notions of patient 'choice', patient 'rights' and 'putting patients first'. While these ideas were promoted by the New Labour Government of the late 1990s and 2000s, they are perhaps best exemplified in more recent interventions such as the 2010–15 Coalition Government's publication *Equity and Excellence: Liberating the NHS*. This document promised that patients would be involved 'fully in their own care' on an individual level, stating that 'the principle of "shared decision-making"' would 'become the norm' (Department of Health, 2010: 13). The Coalition Government's vision was rapidly undermined by its own extensive cuts to public spending and an extensive reorganisation of the NHS in England and Wales, with a disruptive impact disproportionately felt by the most vulnerable (The Lancet, 2011; UCL Institute of Health Equity, 2012). Mental health services in particular have faced major funding issues (Layard et al, 2012). However, the *ideal* of patients' involvement in their own care has retained considerable discursive capital.

The increasing assertiveness of trans patients can also be linked to contemporaneous legal developments, including the implementation of the Sex Discrimination (Amendment of Legislation) Regulations 2008 and the Equality Act 2010. Research participants discussed appeals to such legislation, as well as to patient 'choice' and 'rights' in contesting health professionals' decisions and power differentials between service providers and patients, with increasing frequency over the seven-year course of the study.

> [A] very long [Facebook] post explores ... removing gendered titles from documentation for non-binary individuals. [The post's author] hope[s] to potentially

make an argument for the removal of gendered titles
with reference to the Equality Act (and are asking others
for advice with this). They ask if the Equality Act, Data
Protection Act (1998) and Human Rights Act (1998) are
useful/relevant to any such attempt. (Fieldwork diary: 15
April 2013)

Within the practitioner sphere, there was occasionally evidence of a
struggle to come to terms with patient demands. The below quote
originates from the minutes of a meeting between representatives
from a number of gender clinics. During the meeting, gender identity
specialists raised issues they had encountered in order to seek help and
advice from fellow professionals. The case of an apparently non-binary
patient who 'knows [they have] rights' was raised in the context of a
discussion about how gender clinics might respond to the requirements
of the Equality Act 2010.

Glasgow currently have a patient who has highly
intellectualised the gender issues, he is biological male and
in between somewhere [sic]. No evidence [base] to treat
it, but knows he [has] rights and how he can be treated.
(G3 – Gender Governance Group, 2010)

The portrayal of non-binary or genderqueer patients as demanding
individuals who have 'highly intellectualised' their gender identity
forms a common trope within some areas of the practitioner sphere.
For instance, Barrett (2007: 43) states that '[p]atients of this sort nearly
all had rather cold, schizoid, personalities. They have tended to lack
humour. Two have been fluent in psychological-sounding jargon[.]'
The Gender Governance Group attendees eventually concluded that
the 'Equality [Act] only mentions the male to female or female to male',
an interpretation that has been contested by trans legal scholars who
argue that the Act's provisions have been written in a manner that is
applicable to trans people of all genders (Whittle, 2016).

The emergence of Web 2.0 social media platforms has enabled
these formerly personal, 'private' narratives to proliferate within *public*
digital spaces (Jenzen and Karl, 2014). In the past, trans community
conversations around health (and related activism) in the UK took place
largely within community groups with restricted memberships, such
as web forums and mailing lists (Whittle, 1998; Hines, 2007; Ekins
and King, 2010). Political demands emerging from these conversations
might then be disseminated by advocacy groups such as Liberty, the

Gender Identity Research and Education Society (GIRES) or Press For Change (Davy, 2011; Burns, 2013). However, in recent years the conversations *themselves* have increasingly taken place more publicly within visible internet spaces such as blogs (Pearce, 2012; Yeadon-Lee, 2016) and on social media platforms such as Facebook, Twitter, Tumblr and YouTube (Horak, 2014; Jenzen and Karl, 2014; Moon, 2018). This means that personal knowledges and trans realities can be more easily asserted in a wider series of public settings. Such '"underground" media-making' can be said to carry 'values and connotations of rebellious authenticity' (Hills, 2009: 115). The key instance of this within my data corpus is #transdocfail.

#transdocfail was not an organised or particularly focused campaign. Instead, the hashtag tapped into a range of (sometimes contradictory) discourses already present within more private trans spaces. For instance, many contributors criticised how understandings of trans as condition can be imposed through gender clinic gatekeeping. Such interventions involved accounts of gender norms being imposed through gatekeeping practices, but also included assertions about how care might be improved.

> Gave GIC evidence for RLE for a year stating I was presenting as male despite also having a gender neutral title (on 3 items). Told I had to change to Mr or be discharged. (TransDocFailAnon)

> [I]f there was less #transdocfail, there'd be less nonbinary trans [people] being coerced into inappropriate binary transition as only option. (Liam Davidson)

Other #transdocfail contributors addressed issues with waiting lists and waiting times.

> I've been in the system for 6 months. Moving to uni has reset the process and I'm not even on a waiting list for a GIC yet. (TransDocFailAnon)

Contributors also discussed wider trans health issues as well as transition-specific care, with users sharing accounts of mistrust and inappropriate treatment, as discussed in previous chapters of this book.

However, a unifying feature across the hashtag's approximately 2,000 tweets is the promotion of personal trans knowledges and experiences as *credible*. This can be seen not simply in the assertive manner of the complaints, but also through retweets and sharing of the hashtag. Patient advocates both trans and cis worked collectively to *recognise* and *repeat* individual stories, thereby imbuing them with a 'rebellious authenticity' (Hills, 2009: 115).

> If you're interested in what the trans* community is up against, get an education and read #transdocfail. (Claire)

> Check out #transdocfail to discover how trans people are still treated by doctors in this day and age #enraged. (Caroline Duffy)

> The #TransDocFail is an object lesson in how stigma, discrimination and poor clinical behaviours can and do go hand in hand. (Christine Burns)

The above examples are just three of a great many tweets directing the users' followers to read patient accounts on #transdocfail. Approximately 100 people shared the hashtag in this manner, sometimes to thousands of followers. Terms such as 'education' and 'lesson' highlight how trans knowledges are positioned as credible through the portrayal of patients as *educators*. The browser game *A Trip To The Clinic* can be understood as a part of this phenomenon. It was produced in the wake of initial interest in #transdocfail and then shared in turn on the hashtag by several people, operating as a sort of educational exercise for cis players, promising an insight into trans perspectives on gatekeeping within gender identity services.

In this way, individual #transdocfail contributors sought to change the way that trans health is publicly discussed by *actively* juxtaposing their experiences of – and perspectives on – trans healthcare services with the accounts of traditional medical and media authorities. #transdocfail provided an important precedent for public displays of trans patient outrage and demands for change on Twitter. This foreshadowed later contributions to the #nhsgenderid hashtag, which is a formal part of ongoing NHS England consultations (NHS England, 2015a). Twitter therefore provides a platform for individual accounts to be collectively and mutually (re)constructed as credible, with these knowledges affirmed through iterative repetition in a public space. However, this sense of credibility does not automatically extend to the professional realm. For that, further interventions are required.

Interventions from journalists

The notion that expert trans knowledge can be drawn from personal experience is similarly asserted by trans *journalists*. I use the term 'journalist' here to refer to all individuals who work for media organisations on a freelance or salaried basis.[4] Media organisations afford journalists a platform from which to provide credible accounts of – or opinions on – current affairs. While the influence of the mainstream media has arguably diminished in the internet age, articles produced by established media organisations retain a high level of authority and plausibility within the popular imagination (Fae, 2015), particularly in contrast to social media and with growing public awareness of 'fake news'. Similarly, journalists retain a position of 'professional power' (Hills, 2009: 115). In writing from trans knowledge in the media, trans journalists are therefore able to imbue the personal expertise drawn upon in social media accounts with an additional *professional* authority.

Until recently, mainstream media articles about issues of interest to trans people were written rarely in the UK, and almost solely by cis journalists (a similar situation in the US is described by Capuzza, 2014). This situation began to change during the late 2000s as newspapers and mainstream news websites increasingly commissioned pieces from freelance writers who were themselves trans. I attribute the growing role of trans journalists to the increasing presence of trans people in public life during the 2000s, which followed the initial emergence of the trans movement in the 1990s and the successes of early UK trans civil rights campaigns.

The emergence of trans journalists as a body of people (as opposed to the occasional isolated individual, such as travel writer Jan Morris) is therefore a relatively new phenomenon. Trans journalists present within fieldwork for this project typically entered public life through activism, often within mainstream party politics or through involvement in campaigning groups such as Trans Media Watch or the National Union of Students. However, there were also a handful of career journalists who came out and/or transitioned 'on the job'; an occurrence that is increasingly likely, given the exponential growth in the visible trans population (Reed et al, 2009; Titman, 2014).

Trans journalists who write about issues of trans health can work to recognise and legitimate trans knowledges as credible in two distinct but interrelated ways. Firstly, trans journalists' connections to the activist and community spheres mean that they are in a good position to amplify the voices of others, thereby extending the reach of trans knowledges on matters of health. This was certainly the case with #transdocfail, for instance: articles written about the hashtag by trans journalists appeared in the *Guardian*, the *Independent* and the *New Statesman*, as well as on prominent LGBT news websites such as *Pink News* and *Gay Star News*.[5] Secondly, the professional power of their role means that journalists' perspectives are imbued with an authoritative weight. In writing as *trans* journalists, these individuals therefore contribute to public discourse on trans health directly in a similar but more authoritative – and thereby credible – manner to trans people who discuss the same issues on social media.

Interventions from health-oriented professionals

A different form of professional authority is held by trans people who have established themselves as activist-experts (Epstein, 1996), taking part in the contemporary production of research, policy and/ or guidance both within the UK's public health setting and on an international stage. While I have noted in previous chapters that a (very) small number of such individuals play a 'direct' part in the epistemic politics of trans health (Hess, 2004) as insider-providers (Hanssmann, 2016), I focus here upon the wider body of trans people who play an *indirect* role through their involvement in other health-oriented professions.

An example of this can be seen in trans people who gain employment as equalities experts, working either directly for the NHS or as private consultants. For instance, Christine Burns developed a career as an equalities specialist after making her name with trans activist group Press For Change. She worked with the Department of Health to commission publications offering advice and guidance for practitioners and patients on the subject of trans health, and was later asked to produce an extensive guide for NHS managers and service commissioners (Burns, 2008). Burns also contributed to formal conversations around renewed clinical protocols and commissioning policies for NHS England following the implementation of the Health and Social Care Act 2012, and wrote extensively about these issues on her blog *Just Plain Sense*. In this way, her connection to the formal structures of the NHS offered an opportunity to pursue evolutionary discursive and policy-oriented change.

Burns played a part in the #transdocfail phenomenon through her equalities role. In addition to posting on the hashtag itself, she wrote several blog posts about #transdocfail, using her position to raise awareness of the hashtag and promote the narratives of trans patients. As with journalistic articles, these interventions represented both a recognition and a repetition of trans knowledges within a wider sphere. In this way, Burns imbued knowledges that emerged from 'ordinary', individual trans people's accounts with a credibility afforded to her professional position.

Another example of the construction of health-oriented professional expertise as credible can be found in trans people who seek to join and change professional bodies from the 'inside'. For instance, at the 'Trans Studies: Reflections and Advances' conference, Stephen Whittle (2016) – a law professor and also a former vice-president of Press For Change – described how a small group of trans activists met in London in 2005 to plan a 'take over' of WPATH. By 2007, Whittle had become the first trans president of the Association. Together with other trans professionals, Whittle played a role in revising the WPATH *Standards of Care*. This ensured the inclusion of concepts associated with trans as movement – such as the possibility of non-binary gender – within Version 7 of the document. In bringing about this change, professionals such as Whittle drew on discourses that had developed over many years within trans spaces online (such as those discussed in Whittle, 1998).

In this way, health-oriented professionals such as Burns and Whittle work to redirect narratives and resources alike, drawing upon ideas that have emerged from lay epistemic communities to push for change within the discursive and material professional landscapes of trans health. While insider-providers may struggle to be heard within their respective fields, their role within the professional realm means that a refusal to fully ascribe to pre-existing norms and expectations around trans health can have profound consequences. Whittle's interventions helped to provide an important groundwork for the depathologisation movement, which I discuss later in this chapter. Whereas the personal and journalistic reproduction of knowledge can be used to produce a somewhat credible *demand* for change, health-oriented professional expertise can occasionally couple this with the authority to more directly *implement* change.

Collective activist interventions

The promotion of trans knowledges through mutual recognition and iterative repetition can also be undertaken by activist groups. Such groups offer a means by which individual interventions might be more coherently harnessed for the purposes of negotiating discursive and material change. Forms of journalistic and health-oriented professional expertise frequently evolve from activist interventions: for example, Trans Media Watch members Helen Belcher and Paris Lees acquired mainstream media platforms as a result of their activist work, while Christine Burns and Stephen Whittle built upon campaigns undertaken with groups such as Press For Change and the FTM Network. However, activist expertise can also be constructed entirely independently of journalistic and health-oriented professional models, as an alternative mode of potentially revolutionary knowledge production. I examine three examples of how activist group interventions can work to construct trans knowledges as credible: undertaking action research, producing guidance and (more extensively) imagining alternative approaches to trans health. Each approach draws on informal community resources in order to establish credibility, although some also utilise authoritative platforms and connections with respectable institutions such as universities.

Action research

Action research enables activist groups to build an evidence base for trans knowledges. For example, Manchester organisation TransForum ran a quantitative survey of trans patient experiences with GP practices (Bishop, 2013). In common with many such studies, the sample size was very small and acquired through snowballing, and findings were not analysed for statistical significance. Nevertheless, the resulting report offered an indicative basis for knowledge claims to be made about the experiences and needs of trans patients, particularly given the dearth of formal research in this area. Studies undertaken by trans activist groups can also be conducted by (or in collaboration with) activist-experts such as trained social researchers. Often, these studies are formally commissioned by public bodies. Examples include Press For Change's *Engendered Penalties* report (Whittle et al, 2007) – commissioned by the Equalities Review – and the Scottish Trans Alliance's *Trans Mental Health Study* (McNeil et al, 2012; Ellis et al, 2015). Both are cited extensively in this book, as well as in NHS and government reports and in the academic literature, reflecting their continuing status as a *credible* basis for (certain) knowledge claims about trans health in the UK. The involvement of trans academics such as Stephen Whittle and Louis Bailey is evidence of an important intersection with health-oriented professional expertise. These reports tend to utilise empirical evidence to call for action against endemic cisgenderism and transphobia, and/ or to promote the incorporation of movement-oriented ideas and understandings into medical policies and practice.

The tradition of action research informed the creation of a qualitative survey to gather information on allegations of abuse and malpractice in the wake of #transdocfail. In a further example of intersecting forms of trans expertise, this was heavily promoted through both media organisation and social media channels. The resulting *TransDocFail: The Findings* report (Belcher, 2014) offered a basis for formal complaints to be raised with the GMC. Findings of the report were disseminated at trans community events, within academic spaces and in the media.

Guidance documents

Guidance produced by trans activist groups can also work to promote trans knowledges as credible, adding to the aforementioned work in this area by professionals such as Burns. A considerable number of documents have been created and distributed by activist groups in recent years. These include guidance for practitioners and/or patients produced by organisations such as the education charity GIRES, community support organisation The Gender Trust, trans youth support group Gendered Intelligence and the Trans Women's Support Group for patients at Glasgow's Sandyford GIC. Such documents are often produced in collaboration with NHS bodies, thereby implicitly reifying the credibility of the contents. As with reports written from action research, guidance documents often call for better treatment of trans patients and/or the integration of movement-oriented perspectives into policy and practice, although this can vary.[6]

Imagining alternative approaches to trans health

This is a considerably larger enterprise than producing research or guidance. Those involve seeking some reform of the existing medical system(s), either through working for improved conditions within the discursive paradigms of trans as condition, or by seeking to build understandings of trans as movement (such as non-binary gender and/ or gender fluidity) into a more gender pluralist medical policy and practice. By contrast, alternative approaches to trans health seek to entirely reimagine how medical provisions for trans people might be conceptualised. Groups who advocate these approaches stand in stark, sometimes proud opposition to normative discourses and authoritative systems.

One alternative approach to trans health was advocated by the Harry Benjamin Syndrome (HBS) movement, which was active during the 2000s and early 2010s. This very loose movement subscribed to a deeply conditional understanding of trans possibility: specifically, its advocates called for a recognition of the titular 'syndrome' as a medical condition. In a manner similar to historical interventions described by Meyerowitz (2002), this approach would position transsexualism as a congenital intersex condition that can be cured through transition. The HBS movement largely regarded gender and sex as binary, referencing Benjamin's (1966) typology of the 'true transsexual' in distinguishing HBS individuals from other gender-diverse people. During the 2000s, at least two HBS *Standards of Care* were produced and disseminated online in an attempt to inform and influence medical practice.[7] In this way, HBS activists sought to reify their experiences with reference to medical discourse while simultaneously advocating a very *particular* means by which trans experience might be understood and cured. By drawing upon medical literature and utilising the pseudoscientific term 'Harry Benjamin Syndrome', HBS activists aimed to establish themselves as experts in a medical realm, with authority over the means by which trans feelings and experiences might be regarded as possible and real.

The HBS movement formed a small but vocal community within the wider Western trans population, with activism generally organised online. However, interest in (and subscription to) HBS knowledges has faded through the 2010s; moreover, the movement never had any significant representation among trans activist groups in the UK. HBS was increasingly seen as prescriptive and exclusive by many trans people (the movement largely centred white trans women with normative gender presentations), while others rejected the conflation of 'trans' with 'intersex'. This demonstrates the importance of a *continual* recognition and repetition of ideas across multiple arenas in order to establish credibility even within community spaces. It also shows how only some trans knowledges achieve a form of hegemony – or transnormativity – within trans groups. As Ekins and King (2010: 26) note, some trans stories are 'unwelcome' within wider community spaces. Therefore, while members of the HBS movement may have recognised *one another* and sometimes worked collectively to promote their ideas, these knowledges fail to gain wider recognition – and hence are marginalised within trans spaces – because they could not speak to a wider breadth of trans experience (as indeed they often worked to explicitly exclude many trans people).

A quite different example of an alternative approach to trans health – rooted in understandings of trans as movement – can be found in Action For Trans Health. This network of activist groups campaigns for a 'democratic trans healthcare system', a concept that draws upon a Marxist philosophy of collective action and public ownership (echoing Feinberg, 1992; 1999; 2006) as well as anarchist ideals of autonomy.

While some members of Action For Trans Health acknowledge the medical expertise of health professionals and others are more critical, they collectively argue that greater authority should be invested in trans patients in both clinical encounters and policy making. This position is coupled with a critique of private healthcare providers, with a 'democratic' approach to trans health requiring ownership *by* trans people in a material as well as a discursive sense.

> Trans people are experts on our own lives and we know more about our health care needs than NHS management (and frequently, the doctors who are treating us). We need trans people at all levels of decision making regarding our healthcare and an end to cis (non-trans) gate-keeping of our lives. We need a health care system which is based on what we need, not on some psychiatrist's outdated idea of what gender should look like. We need an end to the privatisation of health care services, and a massive investment in transition-related care and mental health services which are actually empowering rather than institutionalising. (Action For Trans Health, 2015a)

In this way, Action For Trans Health interpellate trans knowledges as authoritative through the rhetorical device of *demanding* revolutionary change. The intended credibility of their case is constructed through a recognition of trans people's lived experience and forms of self-education: 'we know more about our health care needs than NHS management'. While this approach emphasises 'transition-related care', it also addresses healthcare more widely, particularly services such as mental health provision. Action For Trans Health assert the value of an intersectional approach in a mission statement on their website, acknowledging the differing ways in which trans people from different backgrounds experience marginalisation. In doing so, they locate a *diversity* of trans expertise in a range of socially situated subject positions, each shaped by intersecting experiences of marginalisation and privilege. Moreover, they aim to extend mutual recognition beyond the limits of an explicitly trans activism through coalition building.

> We believe that trans people come from all walks of life: we are working class, we are black, we are disabled, we are LGB, we are women. As such, for trans liberation to be achieved we need to also be actively fight[ing] against all

forms of bigotry and build coalitions with other groups with progressive aims. (Action For Trans Health, nd)

Notably, Action For Trans Health couple their demands with public engagement, as well as extensive knowledge of relevant academic literature and public policy. In particular, they utilise international medical literature on the informed consent model of trans healthcare to promote alternative, non-binary approaches to the existing gatekeeping model. This can be seen, for instance, in their submission to the Transgender Equality Inquiry, which references a range of academic articles and recommends:

1   There is an urgent need for greater training within NHS and private gender identity services on the needs of non-binary patients.
2   That an appropriate treatment pathway for non-binary patients is developed as a matter of priority and will be included within any future incarnations of the protocols governing trans healthcare.
3   That this pathway is treatment focused, operating on an informed consent model which centres the patient's healthcare needs flexibly without gatekeeping treatments based on identity.

(Action For Trans Health, 2015b)

The group (both nationally and through a number of largely autonomous local chapters) are also involved in providing formal advice to both patients and health providers through casework, workshops and conferences. In this way, the overtly radical political stance taken by Action For Trans Health is coupled with an activist-expert approach in which they might seek to establish the credibility of their ideas.

The notion of a democratic trans healthcare system offers a holistic alternative to the existing provision of trans healthcare: one that locates authority in the political demands of trans (social) movement, and credibility in individual patient experience. While Action For Trans Health differ enormously from the HBS movement in terms of ideology and in their more careful reliance on contemporary research literatures, they are similar in seeking to establish their own authoritative expertise *as an activist collective* on the matter of trans health.

Expertise through authority; authority through expertise

I have shown that individual and collective actions are employed by trans patient advocates to reproduce trans knowledges in a range of contexts. These processes frequently intersect and interact. Individual trans knowledges of *self* – identity, embodiment and experience – can be drawn upon to conjure a sense of authority, which can in turn be reinforced and constructed as credible through mutual recognition. When trans knowledges are recognised and repeated by advocates in positions of power (such as platforms within journalism or health-oriented professions) they can also be reified as credible through established channels of authority. In this way there are multiple means by which the *reality* of trans health – its field of intelligibility – can be challenged and reconstructed: 'the fundamental instability of the law's foundation – its fiction – is unmasked and a space for change is opened' (Bunch, 2013: 53). The broad, loose collective of individual and group contributions to this process of challenge and reconstruction can be said to constitute a *lay epistemic community* (Akrich, 2010), in that members of this 'community' collectively provide new means by which knowledge of trans health might be constituted.

I have largely portrayed these complex processes as empowering for trans patients and trans knowledges. However, it is also possible for such processes to erase patient advocates even as their knowledges are reified. An example can be seen in the guidance document *Advice Process for Changing Name and Gender in Primary Care*, produced in 2011 by the National Information Governance Board for Health and Social Care (NIGB, 2011). The document cites a guide previously produced by Press For Change: *Name Changing on Personal Documents: A Guide for Organisations*. In this sense, it does work to interpellate activist group knowledge as credible, and refers to Press For Change as an authoritative source on the matter. However, the NIGB document further draws extensively upon the example of an NHS Coventry policy, also entitled *Advice Process for Changing Name and Gender in Primary Care*. This was produced in 2010 in consultation with local trans patients – including myself – following complaints about misgendering in GP practices. The role of patient advocates in shaping the NHS Coventry policy is not acknowledged on paper, meaning that it is the named author (a cis NHS Coventry employee) who receives credit from the NIGB document, and *not* the trans patients and activists who made the demands that shaped it. The trans people involved in producing the document are effectively erased, with the constructed reality in this case locating credibility primarily in the institution of NHS Coventry.

All of these materials were then removed from NHS websites during the implementation of the Health and Social Care Act 2012.

A similar process sometimes occurs with documents produced *within* trans communities and by trans activist-experts. Many years of discursive work by a myriad of individuals – through street protest and physical meetings as well as the online distribution channels described in this chapter – may be assimilated into a book or report or document with a particular named author or authors. This action of naming can unintentionally eclipse the collective work of knowledge production, even as *ideas* are recognised and reproduced. The work of the most marginalised of trans people – such as trans people of colour – is most likely to be erased and devalued (Raha, 2017; Ware, 2017).

My point here is that the credibility of trans knowledges is negotiated only through the work of mutual recognition: writing, researching, theorising and sharing. This work is necessarily constant, collective and often unrecognised.

Negotiating change: the depathologisation movement

I next look in depth at how knowledges constructed and constituted as credible within the lay epistemic community of patient advocates may *directly challenge* the entrenched power and carefully guarded borders of the professional epistemic community. While UK practitioners such as Reid, Curtis and Webberley continue to face censure for attempting to employ a model of specialist care that centres patients' informed consent, I argue that discursive changes have led to a wider shift towards the depathologisation of gender identity services in the UK. To contextualise this discussion, I first outline some examples of changes that have taken place in recent years.

Discursive shifts: embracing movement?

The professional epistemic community of trans health increasingly recognises gender pluralism and partially incorporates insights from understandings of trans as movement. Trans subjectivities are increasingly regarded as (potentially) fluid and not necessarily diagnosable. This is evidenced in several recent publications from UK health professionals working with trans people in gender clinics and/or mental health settings. For example, Richards and colleagues (2015) and Barrett (2016) argue that being trans is not a psychiatric disorder, while Richards and colleagues (2017) discuss how non-binary identities and experiences might be understood and managed within gender identity services. This approach paves the way towards a context in which a wider range of trans knowledges and identities are affirmed in healthcare settings, thereby challenging current conditions in which many patients experience distress.

Discursive shifts within the practitioner sphere are also evident in the changing language of NHS documents. This can be seen in the following excerpts from equivalent sections in recent draft policies that were circulated for consultation by NHS England, in 2013, 2015 and 2017. Once implemented, the final version of this document is intended to guide the commissioning of NHS gender identity services in England. In this way, it will in theory provide a level of oversight regarding acceptable clinical practice.

> Gender Dysphoria (GD) is a rare condition in which there is a psychological experience of oneself as male or female, which is incongruent with the external sexual characteristics of the body. An individual with profound and persistent GD may need clinical intervention to facilitate a change of status, to live in accordance with his or her core gender identity rather than with the phenotype. This degree of GD is termed transsexualism[.] (NHS England, 2013b)

> Gender dysphoria refers to discomfort or distress that is caused by a discrepancy between a person's gender identity and that person's sex assigned at birth (and the associated gender role and/or primary and secondary sex characteristics). Trans and gender variant people are not necessarily gender dysphoric. There are gradations of gender experience between the binary 'man' or 'woman', some of which cause discomfort and may need medical intervention; others may need little or none. A few people who reject the gender concept altogether, and see themselves as non-gendered, may require gender-neutralising treatments from appropriate clinical services. (NHS England, 2015d)

> The term currently used to describe a discrepancy between birth-assigned sex is gender incongruence; this term is preferable to the formerly-used terms of gender identity disorder and transsexualism. Gender incongruence is frequently, but not universally, accompanied by the symptom of gender dysphoria … a cognitive symptom characterised by persistent concerns, uncertainties, and questions about

gender identity[.] … Gender dysphoria is not, in itself, a mental health condition, reflecting contemporary professional opinion. All individuals referred to a Gender Identity Clinic may exercise full personal autonomy in respect of their gender identity and presentation; and must have equitable access to the range of interventions described in this service specification. (NHS England, 2017b)

Both the first draft commissioning document (from 2013) and the second (from 2015) outline the how the DSM-5 diagnosis 'gender dysphoria' and the ICD-10 diagnosis 'transsexualism' are to be conceptualised for the purposes of the commissioning policy. However, two important discursive differences can be noted.

Firstly, there is a shift away from understanding gender in innate, positivistic and prescriptive terms. Where the 2013 document utilises language such as 'core gender identity' and employs a more traditional understanding of 'transsexualism', the 2015 document draws upon the emergent language used by many contemporary UK trans activists. It acknowledges the possibility of gender as social construct through the use of inverted commas around 'woman' and 'man', and through use of the term 'assigned at birth'. The inverted commas serve to destabilise understandings of womanhood and manhood as natural and given. The term 'assigned at birth' is commonly used within trans spaces, echoing Stryker's (1994: 244) critique of the 'collective assumptions of the naturalized order' manifested in coercively declaring a child to be a boy or a girl at birth. The term can therefore be linked to an understanding of sex and gender as historically contingent and socially constructed.

Secondly, there is a move away from binary language. This represents a shift towards the possibility of *non*-binary treatment; that is, treatment possibilities which encompass the expansion of 'female' and 'male' categories as well as moves beyond these categories altogether (Monro, 2007). Where the 2013 document refers to a 'psychological experience of oneself as male or female', the 2015 document describes gender and sex in non-binary terms: 'a person's gender identity' and 'person's sex assigned at birth'. It also explicitly states that there are 'gradations of gender experience between the binary "man" or "woman"'. This provides space for some trans people to identify into a 'binary' (male or female) and for others to identify with non-binary possibilities in a gender-pluralist manner.

In the third document (from 2017), binary gendered language has been dropped altogether. There is no mention of 'men' or 'women' in the quoted passage; or indeed, in the entire document from which the quote is drawn. Moreover, the document now employs the term 'gender incongruence', which is due to be formally introduced in the 2018 revision of the *International Classification of Diseases*, ICD-11.

In the discursive shift between the three documents, there is a weakening of the gender identity specialist's authoritative power to assess and diagnose *gender*. The 2013 document primarily employs assertive language to denote clinical possibilities; for instance, the phrase '[a]n individual with profound and persistent GD' is indicative of a clinical category that can be firmly defined and assessed by health professionals. By contrast, while the 2015 document utilises similar language in describing 'appropriate clinical services', it states that these services should be available to people who '*see themselves* as non-gendered' (emphasis mine). The 2017 document bluntly states that gender dysphoria 'is not … a mental health condition', raising questions about the role of the DSM-5 diagnosis in clinical settings.

In all three documents this is a complex positioning of authority and knowledge, in which patient accounts are provided greater credibility over time, and expertise is increasingly shared (and potentially contested) between practitioner and patient. As I shall show, the discursive shifts which enabled these substantial changes required extensive epistemic and political negotiation.

Negotiating depathologisation

The trans depathologisation movement exists to '[challenge] the dominant medical understanding of transgender' (Vähäpassi, 2013: 34); that is, the understanding of trans as *psychiatric condition*. This understanding is associated with diagnoses found in the DSM and in the 'mental and behavioural disorders' chapter of ICD-10. In this way, the movement can be understood as primarily concerned with de*psycho*pathologisation: its proponents don't want to remove access to medical interventions for transitioning individuals, but rather aim to see trans health being understood and treated differently.

The depathologisation movement is a loose, multifaceted coalition of campaigning interventions involving both trans activists and health professionals. It operates on an international level, shaped by multinational networks such as Global Action For Trans★ Equality (GATE), but taking on different characteristics in differing countries according to the local socio-political and medico-legal context. Trans activists have organised coordinated international campaigns for depathologisation since the early 1990s, but activity intensified ahead of the publication of DSM-5 in 2013 (Burke, 2011; Vähäpassi, 2013). I shall show that depathologisation activism has contributed significantly to changing discourses of trans possibility both internationally and within the UK's NHS.

Davy (2015: 1166) identifies two central 'arms' of the depathologisation movement. The first arm 'casts trans identities within a biogenetic framework, or as an intersex condition'. Its activists aim to reconceptualise 'trans' as an issue of *physical* condition rather than *mental* health; we can locate the HBS movement within this framework. The second arm of the depathologisation movement 'proposes a self-determination and human rights model', effectively rooted in discourses of trans as (social) movement. This encompasses campaigns for 'complete depathologisation', as well as those that seek diagnostic reform (Davy, 2015: 1173). It is the latter incarnation of the movement's second arm that is most strongly supported within UK trans communities.

On an international level, the second arm of the depathologisation movement has achieved several important successes. These most notably include the aforementioned revision of the WPATH *Standards of Care* to incorporate a more flexible approach to treatment in Version 7, and moves towards de*psycho*pathologised public health pathways for transition in countries such as Argentina and Malta (Davy, 2015). Importantly, while Western figures such as Whittle have played an important role within WPATH, much of the external pressure on the organisation has been led by trans activists from the Majority World, through multinational organisations such as GATE and Southern African groups such as Iranti-org and Gender DynamiX (Cabral et al, 2016; Davy et al, 2018). This runs contrary to parochial notions of Western superiority with regard to trans 'tolerance', or 'progressiveness' within social movements (Aizura, 2012).

In the UK context, debates around depathologisation are primarily shaped by the political realities of NHS funding. Many trans patient advocates, sympathetic academics and gender identity specialists have argued that diagnosis offers an important basis for the funding of gender identity services through the NHS (Davy, 2015; Richards et al, 2015). This has not prevented fierce disagreements around the issue of diagnosis, however, particularly in conjunction with the international 'Stop Trans Pathologization!' campaign in 2012. Opinions on the matter were most divided within the community sphere, where support for the current medical system – often drawing upon the importance of an 'expert' perspective for the purposes of reifying identity – was expressed alongside (and in opposition to) arguments favouring various forms of depathologisation. Within the activist sphere, by contrast, I observed a broad consensus in favour of some form of depathologisation, reflecting Mary Burke's (2011) findings among US trans activists. The evidence of discursive change seen within documents such as the NHS England draft clinical commissioning policies suggests that the depathologisation movement is gaining ground in the UK. I attribute this to two key factors: changes within WPATH, and long-term activism on clinical pathways within the NHS.

Revising the WPATH Standards of Care

The shift in discourse between Version 6 and Version 7 of the WPATH *Standards of Care* is significant. Version 6 centred the role of the health professional in 'guid[ing] treatment and research' on the basis of mental health assessments informed by the DSM and/or ICD (Meyer et al, 2001; Coleman et al, 2012). Version 7 instead 'established a language which mandates a shift in trans healthcare from a gatekeeper to a collaborative model ... stress[ing] that it is important for healthcare professionals to recognize that transpeople's health interventions should be principally based on patients' decisions' (Davy, 2015: 1176). This more collaborative, patient-centred approach marks a move away from understandings of trans as (fixed) condition *and* a move towards a more gender-pluralist affirmation of trans patient knowledges, which includes a tentative recognition of non-binary gender possibilities. Moreover, the publication of Version 7 was pre-empted by a formal statement calling for a wider 'de-psychopathologisation of gender variance'.

> The WPATH Board of Directors strongly urges the de-psychopathologisation of gender variance worldwide. The expression of gender characteristics, including identities, that are not stereotypically associated with one's assigned sex at birth is a common and culturally-diverse human phenomenon which should not be judged as inherently pathological or negative. (Bockting et al, 2010)

While the literature of transgender studies is notably absent from the bibliography of the Version 7 *Standards of Care* and the recommendation of depsychopathologisation, the impact of social scientific and lay epistemic communities is nevertheless felt. As previously noted, Whittle (2016) argues that changes in discourse and policy occurred within WPATH *because* of trans activism. He highlights the importance of an emerging body of evidence from transgender studies – which recognises and repeats everyday trans knowledges even as it interrogates them – as well as interventions from health-oriented professionals. Through obtaining formal recognition in their respective fields, activist-experts such as Whittle (and 2013–16 WPATH president Jamison Green) gained the credibility necessary to enter WPATH *and* the necessary authority to negotiate change within this professional organisation. The recognition of both *personal* and *collective* activist trans knowledges as credible can also be seen in interventions from other members of WPATH. For example, Nicholas Matte and colleagues (2009) and Sam Winter (2009) explicitly drew on an international range of patient knowledges and experiences in recommending that WPATH reconsider its use of pathologising, ethnocentric binary language.

At the time of writing, the *Standards of Care* are once again under revision, with Version 8 due for publication in 2019. The final document will no doubt be the product of substantial contestation and compromise. One of the two co-chairs for the revision process (working alongside long-standing chair Eli Coleman) is Asa Radix, a physician and researcher at the Callen-Lorde Community Health Centre in New York. This clinic has pioneered hormone therapy protocols utilising an informed consent model. The other is Jon Arcelus, a consultant psychiatrist at the Nottingham Centre for Transgender Health, which generally centres gatekeeper authority. Trans activist-experts and insider-providers can be expected to play a more significant role in the process than ever before, with new international group TPATH (the Transgender International Association for Transgender Health, an organisation for health professionals and researchers who are themselves trans) encouraging and supporting members to apply for revision committee places.

Appeals to international authority

The *Standards of Care* have, in turn, been of benefit to trans activists seeking to reform gender identity services in the UK. In providing an authoritative international standard, the Version 7 WPATH guidelines offered a basis from which to negotiate change. For instance, where the *Standards of Care* now coincide with movement-oriented and/or gender-pluralist trans knowledges and perspectives on health, they work to enhance the credibility of activist calls for diagnostic reform.

The role of local activists is important here because the existence of a new version of the *Standards of Care* does not *necessarily* lead to changes within gender identity services. For instance, for several years the gender clinics in Leeds and Nottingham explicitly stated that their respective pathways adhered to the 'Harry Benjamin International Standards of Care' (that is, Version 6 of the *Standards of Care*, published prior to the renaming of WPATH) rather than the more recent Version 7 *Standards*. This approach was attributed to a need for the continued implementation of RLE prior to hormone therapy, so that practitioners could ensure that their patients conformed to a consistent gender identity and presentation.

> [O]ur Care Pathway follows the stages laid down within The Harry Benjamin International Standards of Care (this differs from the WPATH guidance), as we believe that hormone treatment is best undertaken after real life experience has begun to ensure that, possibly irreversible hormone treatment is not undertaken without there being a completely coordinated comprehensive care approach which has the ability to meet the changing needs of our service users flexibly and safely. (Leeds and York Partnership NHS Foundation Trust, 2012)

Both individual and collective action was undertaken by activists to challenge the gender clinics' continued adherence to Version 6 of the *Standards of Care*. An example of this can be seen in the letter quoted above, which was submitted in response to a Freedom of Information request and later circulated within the activist sphere. Trans health advocates subsequently wrote to gender clinic administrators and NHS commissioners to request a change in policy.

These actions, which appealed to the *authority* of the Version 7 *Standards*, were ultimately somewhat successful. At the time of writing, references to the 'Harry Benjamin International Standards of Care' have been removed from the Leeds and Nottingham gender clinic websites and there is some evidence from participants to suggest a slight relaxation of these clinics' particularly stringent assessment procedures. However, the Nottingham clinic continues to require patients to begin RLE prior to hormone therapy (Arcelus et al, 2017).

Appeals to the *Standards of Care* form just one part of a wider use of newly credible trans knowledges in public health reform. Through successfully building recognition of trans knowledges, activists have been in a strong position to benefit somewhat from recent changes in the NHS, both discursive (such as in the shift towards 'choice' and 'patient rights') and material (such as in the structural re-organisation of the NHS in England and Wales). This position is also bolstered by a related move towards 'patient and public involvement at all levels in the governance of science and health services' (Weiner, 2009: 255). The *Gender Reassignment Protocol for Scotland* (NHS Scotland, 2012) was therefore shaped in part by the newly published Version 7 *Standards of Care*, but also by the input of stakeholder groups such as the Scottish Trans Alliance. This document takes steps towards depsychopathologisation, such as through the relaxation of assessment criteria; for instance, only *one* assessment is now formally required for Scottish patients to obtain access to hair removal, speech therapy, hormone treatment and 'masculinising' chest reconstruction surgeries.

Similarly, trans knowledges play an important role in ongoing stakeholder consultations regarding gender identity services under the management of NHS England. The 2013 restructure of the NHS in England and Wales offered new opportunities for trans people to have more of a say in the policies, practices and treatment pathways of NHS gender clinics. CRGs were created to oversee the national development and commissioning of specialist services within NHS England, in contrast to the local commissioning previously undertaken by bodies such as PCTs. The Coalition Government's *Transgender Action Plan* – itself a product of extensive lobbying from trans activists – included a commitment to '[c]ommission and publish a clear and concise guide for health practitioners ... and the transgender community on care pathways and available treatments' by April 2013 (Home Office, 2011: 11). The Gender Identity Services CRG therefore sought to replace the patchwork of existing approaches with a single commissioning policy and a national protocol for treatment. Previous attempts to create a national framework for gender identity services had taken place during the 2000s, but these had stalled due to disagreements between gender clinic representatives and trans patient advocates (Burns, 2013). On this occasion it appeared that change was to be enforced by the newly formed NHS England, in line with external political priorities.

A draft protocol for NHS England was made public in July 2012, just weeks after the publication of the *Protocol for Scotland*. This document had been prepared by representatives of the English gender clinics at the request of the Department of Health. In contrast to the Scottish protocol, the English document relied on a broadly psychopathological understanding of trans possibilities.

> The most recent WPATH guidelines emphasise the *pivotal role* of the qualified Mental Health Practitioner: a mental health professional (eg. psychiatrist or psychologist) who specialises in transsexualism/gender dysphoria and has general clinical competence in diagnosis and treatment

of mental or emotional disorders ... Anyone referred to a Gender Service will be assessed to ensure that there is a confirmed diagnosis relating to Gender Dysphoria. (Department of Health, 2012, emphasis mine)

The supposed adherence to the WPATH guidelines in the creation of this draft protocol was questionable, particularly given WPATH's stated opposition to psychopathologisation. Indeed, like the aforementioned Leeds and Nottingham gender clinic pathways, the protocol appeared to contradict a number of passages in the Version 7 *Standards of Care* that emphasise patient agency and a more movement-oriented understanding of trans possibility.

> The overall goal of the [Standards of Care] is to provide clinical guidance for health professionals to assist transsexual, transgender, and gender-nonconforming people ... This assistance *may* include ... mental health services[.] (Coleman et al, 2012: 166, emphasis mine)

> Health professionals can *assist* gender dysphoric individuals with *affirming their* gender identity, exploring different *options* for expression of that identity, and making decisions about medical treatment options for alleviating gender dysphoria. (Coleman et al, 2012: 171, emphasis mine)

The contrast between the language of the draft English protocol and the *Standards of Care* was not lost on trans activists familiar with the latter document. This was particularly relevant as the Department of Health sought the view of trans stakeholders in an online survey. Numerous trans bloggers sought to encourage participation in the survey, while raising awareness of the psychopathologising language within the draft protocol and its contrasts with the Version 7 *Standards of Care*. My own presence within the field is of importance here. I wrote several popular posts in 2012 and 2013 about the Scottish and English protocols on my personal blog, *Trans Activist Takes On World*. My analysis in these posts was based in part upon work undertaken for this project.

The critical feedback offered by trans groups and individuals in response to the Department of Health survey put the new Gender Identity Services CRG in a difficult position. Reconciling the psychopathologising perspective of many gender clinic representatives with the anti-psychopathologising stance of numerous respondents might require months (if not years) of work. The April 2013 deadline passed without any public action being taken. However, on 16 May 2013 a letter was sent to stakeholders (including trans survey respondents *as well as* gender clinic representatives) by NHS England deputy national medical director Steve Field and newly appointed CRG chair John Dean. They announced that 'the specification and policy for Gender Services did not obtain approval by the Clinical Priorities Advisory Group, largely due to inconclusive feedback through the consultation exercise on specifications and policies'.

The CRG therefore imposed an amended version of the *Protocol for Scotland* upon the English gender clinics. In July 2013 this was replaced with the *NHS England Interim Gender Dysphoria Protocol* (NHS England, 2013a), which was again based largely upon the Scottish protocol. At the time of writing, this interim English protocol is still in place. More formalised consultations hosted by NHS England have followed, with input from trans stakeholders leading to outcomes such as the previously quoted 2017 draft clinical commissioning policy.

Gender recognition

In the tumultuous weeks that followed the UK's 2017 general election, the country's two largest political parties (the Conservative and Labour parties) both committed to a revision of the GRA, possibly as a distraction from the chaos of Brexit. Statements to the press suggested that this might enable a form of self-declaration for trans people wanting to change their legal gender, in contrast to the existing system that requires the extensive approval of gender identity specialists. This would be a form of *legal* depathologisation, following calls for change from activists and academics alike, and the implementation of similar changes in Argentina, Colombia, Ireland and Malta (Davy et al, 2018). As I complete this book, formal proposals from the UK's minority Conservative Government have yet to materialise. However, the devolved Scottish Government, led by the Scottish National Party, has announced a consultation on the reform of gender recognition laws in Scotland. This may include non-binary recognition as well as provisions for self-declaration.

The depathologisation movement has therefore seen several successes in the UK, including shifts away from pathologisation in gender clinic care pathways, somewhat more progressive national protocols for Scotland and England, and possible amendments to legal gender recognition. These changes have been made possible through extensive negotiation both within the UK *and* on an international level. They rely upon a restructuring of macro-level power relations through the establishment of trans knowledges as credible. However, the *delivery* of gender identity services in the UK continues to rely on an extensive process of gatekeeping, which broadly maintains the micro-level power differentials between practitioner and patient.

Conclusion: the epistemic politics of epistemic analysis

In this chapter I have shown that the repetitive recognition of knowledges *within* lay epistemic communities is important for negotiating change. Concepts such as 'Harry Benjamin Syndrome' that do not gain wider purchase as an explanatory basis for trans existence and/or politics remain relevant only to a relatively small group of adherents. By contrast, ideas such as 'non-binary identity' speak to the experiences of a growing number of people, and can therefore eventually gain credibility within a wide range of contexts. This does not just 'happen'; it comes about through collective interventions over time, as ideas are disseminated and discussed and repeated over and over and over again; by individual community members, activist groups and professionals of all kinds, including activist-experts, insider-providers, trans journalists and cis allies. These processes can ultimately work to grant trans knowledges *credibility*, thereby providing a ground upon which they can be drawn on to actively negotiate change within the discursive and material realm of healthcare provision. Shifts in understanding and practice are therefore the outcome of concerted, non-linear collective negotiation involving a multitude of actors, with each newcomer to trans activism building upon, rejecting, and/or reconceptualising the achievements of those who came before them.

Important discursive and material changes *are* taking place within the realm of trans health, albeit at a relatively gradual and uneven rate. The emergence of credible trans experts, coupled with a growing recognition of everyday trans knowledges within authoritative professional bodies, has influenced moves towards depsychopathologisation within WPATH and the NHS, which also entails a growing recognition of non-binary patient experiences. These changes grant increasing prominence to discourses of trans as movement in a gender-pluralist manner, in that they acknowledge a myriad of trans possibilities that can operate beyond traditional boundaries or means of categorisation.

However, these *macro*-level events still fail to immediately impact upon the power differential located in the individual relationship between the transitioning patient and gatekeeper, where trans knowledges continue to compete with the (frequently cisgenderist) knowledge held by gender identity specialists. On this *micro* level of gatekeeping encounters, 'difficult' trans patients face particular challenges in attempting to access treatment, as highlighted and satirised in *A Trip To The Clinic*. Of course, the very presence of the game demonstrates that patients are increasingly asserting themselves in turn. I regard this as an epistemic *clash of credibility*, in which the authority of medical knowledge is questioned in the context of increasingly credible trans patient discourses.

This book too, of course, is an epistemic intervention. Like Michael Toze, I write as an activist-expert. I assert myself as credible through the conduct of social analysis and the production of empirical data, through academic citation and references to the field; simultaneously, I reproduce a range of trans activist and community knowledges *within* this field through the recognition and repetition of their ideas and insights. As such, this book forms another link in a long chain of collective interventions. I do not pretend to be apart from the field because *no* actor, no contributor to this conversation is 'unbiased' or removed. This book is both a product of, and a contribution to, the very phenomena that it seeks to analyse.

Through my research, I have come to believe that changes to medical discourse and practice are necessary and urgent. Issues such as the power differential between practitioner and patient, long waiting times and limited understandings of gendered possibility cause stress, anxiety and depression for a great many individuals, and can lead to treatment being denied to those who don't 'fit' into a very narrow model of gendered reality. This is most likely to impact upon patients who experience a greater number of intersecting marginalisations, such as disabled trans people, trans people of colour, poor trans people and/or trans sex workers. Mistrust of health professionals remains common among trans patients, meaning that many regularly mislead practitioners in medical settings. This is not a productive way to manage the healthcare of a deeply vulnerable population.

While the considerable collective achievements of activists in interpellating trans knowledges as authoritative, expert and *real* are not in doubt, I believe that current reforms do not go far enough in addressing substantial problems in the provision of gender identity services. Unnecessarily strict interpretations of the *Standards of Care* continue to provide a justification for clinical practices that exclude and control. The changes achieved by the depathologisation movements have succeeded in reducing the extensive demands of the assessment procedure (particularly in Scotland), but not in replacing them with a more collaborative model.

Even emerging guidance for the management of non-binary patients within current gender clinics (such as in Richards et al, 2017) may result in a form of 'inclusion' that does not address the wider problem of the micro power differential between individual practitioners and individual patients. As Davy (2015: 1167) argues, 'diagnoses of multiple gender disorders under one overarching [gender identity] diagnosis [maintain] the clinical monopoly on additional forms of permanent or non-permanent gender transitioning practices'. Or as a participant in a 2017 consultation event put it: 'non-binary people have been invited to your table, but they weren't actually there when the table was built'.[8]

In the final chapter of this book, then, I will argue for a shift towards the informed consent model for gender identity services in the UK and beyond.

Notes

[1] You can play *A Trip To The Clinic* here: http://aliendovecote.com/uploads/twine/others/chaosjam/Clinic.html.

[2] Technically speaking, informed consent *was* sought for the Nottingham video game study. However, this comprised a brief information sheet and informed consent form attached to the *end* of a 21-page battery of questionnaires (including one on video gaming) sent to all new patients at the clinic as part of their registration process. Patients were informed that the questionnaires 'are an important part of your assessment', implying that participation was mandatory. Arcelus et al (2017: 23) report that 95.3% of new patients at the clinic 'agreed to participate in the study'. This unusually high participation rate for a clinical survey implies a possible element of coercion. In November 2017 a Nottingham clinician tweeted to ask how people felt about research questionnaires being sent out with appointment letters. Numerous patients replied to state that they felt this approach was unethical, with some of these individuals also disclosing that they responded with the answers they thought would most likely ensure access to treatment.

[3] International guidance recommending provision of hormone therapy only from the age of 16 relies primarily on evidence from extensive studies undertaken at a gender clinic for children and adolescents in the Netherlands. However, transitioning adolescents at this clinic are permitted access to cross-sex hormones from 16 because this is the age of majority in the Netherlands. There is therefore a political rationale underpinning this age limit, rather than a medical rationale (Bonifacio and Massarella, 2017).

[4] Recent years have seen a break-down of the binary division between 'mainstream' and 'alternative' digital medias with the rise of citizen journalism and news/opinion blogs, and as mainstream media platforms increasingly make use of 'amateur' footage and insights in their reporting. An in-depth discussion of these complexities is beyond the scope of this book; therefore, my brief account of trans journalism focuses on individuals who build a living in full or part around working for media organisations.

[5] #transdocfail coincided with a high-profile debate about freedom of speech in mainstream media. This debate originated in objections made on Twitter to

the use of alleged transphobic and racist language by columnist Suzanne Moore following the publication of her article 'Seeing Red' in the *New Statesman*. The heated series of discussions that followed on Twitter inspired a second article by Julie Burchill, writing for the *Observer*. Entitled 'Transsexuals should cut it out', Burchill's piece was written in an overtly inflammatory manner and attracted a considerable number of complaints, resulting in it being withdrawn from the newspaper's website with an apology from the editor. The affair attracted a great deal of commentary from numerous other newspapers, websites and blogs from across the political spectrum. The level of coverage offered to the debate around Moore and Burchill's articles contrasted greatly with that of #transdocfail. Many cis editors and journalists were interested in commissioning and writing articles about how the Moore/Burchill affair spoke to issues of free speech, tolerance and offence; by contrast, #transdocfail was reported on by a relatively small number of trans journalists, working largely for publications with a left-wing reputation. #transdocfail therefore held less interest for cis editors and journalists. Articles on #transdocfail were published due to the particular efforts of trans journalists who sought to raise awareness of the hashtag.

[6] See Davy (2011) for a discussion of how the language used by trans activist groups can sometimes work to reinforce pathologising discourses.

[7] The existence of more than one such document reflected divisions within the HBS movement, such as between groups that were respectively inclusive or exclusive of 'pre-operative' individuals. The original websites that hosted the HBS *Standards of Care* have now been removed from the internet. However, the Internet Archive's Wayback Machine hosts a copy of one such document here: http://web.archive.org/web/20070111194727/http://www.harrybenjaminsyndrome-info.org/soc.html. I would like to thank Freja Sohn Frøkjær-Jensen for providing me with advice and information on writing about this topic.

[8] I heard this comment while attending the Specialised Gender Identity Services for Adults Public Consultation in Leeds on 2 October 2017.

SEVEN

Towards affirmative care

Jess Phillips MP: I think I'd like to go back again to this idea of living in one gender identity: I wonder if you can tell me – clinically – what 'living like a woman' – or alternatively, man – actually means?

Will Huxter (NHS England): I'm not a clinician I can't tell you what that's –

Jess Phillips: Do you think that there is a clinical way to live as a woman? Or a man?

Will Huxter: The point I am making is that we are guided by specialists who work in this area, the clinical consensus among gender identity specialists about how services should operate. We are absolutely open to looking at how that might change, but I'm not in a position to make a change to the way in which those services are commissioned without having gone through a clinical process.

Maria Miller MP: Mr Huxter, sorry, I think we're going to have to press you on that. Is – this is just factual, we have read that people have to 'live like a woman' or 'live like a man', we as a committee have struggled to know what that looks like in a day and age where men and women live in very similar ways. What do you – factually – what does that mean?

(Women and Equalities Committee, 2015)

'Living like a woman': gatekeeping, power, and models of care

In late October of 2015 I took a break from writing an early draft of this book to watch a livestreamed oral evidence session from the UK Parliament's Transgender Equality Inquiry. The House of Commons Women and Equalities Committee had scrutinised written and oral evidence from range of stakeholders – including activists, academics, health service managers and gender identity specialists – on a variety of issues pertaining to trans equality. In this fourth session, members of the committee addressed the issues that had been raised by stakeholders to a number of government ministers, as well as an NHS England representative.

One exchange particularly caught my attention. With reference to assessment procedures such as RLE, committee members Jess Phillips and Maria Miller raised a pointed question about some of the underlying assumptions present in many clinical encounters for trans patients attending gender identity services. As gender roles become less rigid in everyday life, what does it *mean* to 'live like a woman' or 'live like a man'? Surely, 'there cannot be a clinical list of things that a person can be told to do by a doctor in order to tick those boxes?' (Jess Phillips).

These are questions that strike at the heart of the issues discussed in this book. As I have shown, patients who fail to fit with health professionals' understandings of trans and gendered possibility are likely to encounter substantial difficulties in accessing care. This is particularly pertinent in the context of gatekeeping for gender identity services. The intention of gatekeeping is to avoid harm by ensuring that patients do not regret their decision to transition, and that those with significant co-morbid conditions (mental or physical) do not undergo unnecessary and potentially dangerous irreversible treatment (Barrett, 2007; Richards et al, 2014). In practice it would seem that the *impact* of gatekeeping reaches beyond this. Assessment procedures require patients to wait months for treatment even after they have made it past the formal waiting lists, and many individuals also feel coerced into changing how they behave, dress and even think in order to access healthcare. This is a context in which regret and harm proliferate.

Over the summer of 2017, NHS England invited trans patients and advocacy groups to participate in a consultation on new, proposed gender identity service specifications. The documents include numerous clauses that promise to further standardise clinical practice and explicitly ban a number of more questionable practices, including unnecessary genital examinations and requirements for friends and/or family members to attend appointments. As I explained in Chapter Six, they also represent a shift towards non-binary recognition, in their careful evasion of gendered language (although the surgical specification continues to refer to 'feminising' and 'masculinising' procedures). Moreover, the documents explicitly state that a flexible approach to treatment must be discussed collaboratively by practitioner and patient, as an alternative to the more linear historical approach in which patients are required to undertake interventions in a particular order. These interventions can be seen as a response to the emergence of new, non-binary trans knowledges rooted in discourses of movement and to resulting criticisms levelled by MPs during the Transgender Equality Inquiry.

However, the service specifications produced for consultation by NHS England arguably pay lip-service to the wider question of depathologisation. References to 'personal autonomy' and 'shared decision making' are undermined by a continued reliance on psychiatric assessment using the DSM-5, and a continued adherence to the gatekeeping model that I have critiqued in this book.

The NHS pathway of care may be summarised as:

- Referral to a specialist Gender Identity Clinic from primary, secondary or tertiary care
- Assessment for gender dysphoria, and diagnosis
- Individuals who meet the criteria for gender dysphoria related to gender incongruence are accepted on to the NHS care pathway and an individualised treatment plan is agreed
- Therapeutic interventions delivered by the specialist Gender Identity Clinic; and/or referral for interventions with other providers; which may include recommendations for prescribing hormone treatments, and surgical interventions
- Ongoing review and monitoring during and after interventions
- Conclusion of contact: discharge to primary care

(NHS England, 2017b)

We can see from the above passage that the proposed service specification for non-surgical interventions allows for existing approaches to assessment to continue as they always have done. It is this approach that makes clinical requirements such as RLE possible in the first place, resulting in a situation whereby an individual may have to demonstrate that they are capable of 'living like a woman' in order to access treatment.

In concluding this book, I argue that the power invested in – and actively *wielded* by – gender clinic gatekeepers has significant consequences for the possibility of 'trans' subjectivities, as well as for the wider terrain of trans health. To make this argument, I first revisit the original stated aim and questions for my research project.

The project aimed to uncover how both 'trans' and 'trans health' are *understood* in multiple contexts, in order to grasp the social processes at play in encounters where trans patients feel marginalised, misunderstood and/or discriminated against. I formulated two main research questions in response to this aim. First, I asked how trans possibilities are produced, reified and legitimated through health discourses and practices. Secondly, I asked how discourses of trans healthcare provision are *negotiated* within and between trans community groups, trans activists and health professionals. To unpack my response to these questions, I next look thematically at topics that weave through the various chapters of this book. I then conclude with some thoughts on how a better future for trans health might look.

Producing, reifying and legitimating trans possibilities

Understandings of trans and gendered possibility are shaped by clinical concepts, protocols and practices. For example, the ICD-10 definition of 'transsexualism' presupposes a male/female binary through the use of terms such as 'opposite sex' (World Health Organization, 1992: F64.0). Similar language was used until very recently within most national and/or local guidelines for gender identity services in the UK. A less overt means of defining trans possibility can be seen in the continued use of RLE in the assessment and management of trans patients. Underpinning RLE is the presumption that trans people *can* and *should* maintain a consistent (ideally cis-passing) gender identity and gendered appearance.

This kind of language draws upon and contributes to medical discourses of *trans as condition*. These understandings frame 'trans' as fixed: that is, clearly delineated and definable. In this sense, being 'trans' is *conditional*: it is only possible for a person to be 'trans' if they 'fit' clinical expectations. Condition-oriented medical understandings of trans possibility also frame 'trans' as fix*able*, that is, curable through a carefully managed transition (or through some form of therapy, depending on the perspective and approach of the practitioner).

In Chapter Two I explored how discourses of trans as condition have historically been produced through the interventions of trans people as well as through the writings and practices of health professionals. However, these discourses can also be enforced, reified and legitimated through authoritative clinical guidance (such as NHS protocols, DSM, ICD and the WPATH *Standards of Care*) and practices; a matter I expanded upon in later chapters.

Conditional notions of trans possibility have important consequences for patient subjectivity and social identities. As I showed in Chapter Four, many patients continue to draw on the discursive authority of medicalised, condition-oriented understandings of trans to reify their own identities and experiences, both within themselves and in wider social contexts such as schools, workplaces and the family. Where these understandings work to *limit* gendered possibility – for instance, through constructing gender as binary – the possibilities for constructing and reifying personal subjectivity and social identity are limited also.

Medicalised conditional models of trans possibility have consequences for trans people's health that reach well beyond physical transition. An example of this can be seen in the discourse of trans *as transition*. The idea that all trans people are necessarily transitioning, intending to transition or have transitioned, and that this defines their health needs, can lead to inappropriate care from ill-informed health professionals. This is the cause of phenomena such as Trans Broken Arm Syndrome. The discourse of trans as transition is particularly dangerous in an environment where relatively little information is easily available on trans health, as seen for instance in the limited content of the NHS Choices 'Transgender Health' web page.

Alternative 'movement'-oriented discourses of trans possibility are increasingly available, entailing less strictly categorical queer tendencies towards continual creation, fluidity and gendered world-building. They provide space for less consistent and gender-pluralist understandings of trans/gendered possibility, as well as a collective trans social movement built around diversity and solidarity rather than clear definition and the delineation of appropriate ('trans enough') identity. This can provide more room for disabled trans people and trans people of colour as well as for non-binary and genderqueer individuals; although of course, all these categories intersect (Green, 2017; Nicolazzo, 2017). Notably, however, discourses of trans as movement – including understandings of trans possibility that create space for *non*-transitioning individuals – are often defined *against* medical understandings of trans as condition.

In Chapters Two, Three and Six I examined how movement-oriented understandings of trans possibility are increasingly incorporated into international and NHS guidance, policy and practice. I attribute this to collective discursive interventions from within trans communities, bolstered by the support of activist-experts (Epstein, 1996) and insider-providers (Hanssmann, 2016), who work with sympathetic allies to build trans knowledges into everyday medical practice.

Importantly, the discursive repertoires of *both* trans as condition and trans as movement provide a 'field of intelligibility' by which gender diversity can be rendered socially *real*: and thus, possible (Steinberg, 2015a). This can work to counter cultural and professional cisgenderist norms, which may otherwise render trans subjectivities unreal, impossible or non-credible (Ansara and Hegarty, 2012; Kennedy, 2013). Rendering trans bodies, identities and experiences intelligible provides a basis for gender identity services to be publicly funded through the NHS (Combs et al, 2008), as well as a means by which trans people might be recognised and understood in everyday, non-specialist medical encounters.

Looking at trans possibilities in terms of 'condition' and 'movement' enables us to move beyond paradigmatic accounts of a discursive shift in understandings of trans health (for example, Bockting, 2009; Nieder et al, 2016). It instead enables a deeper analysis of how multiple framings of trans possibility coexist and intersect. There is no simple move from one model to another: instead, past contestations within medical literatures, trans communities and feminist theory continue to influence contemporary ideas and practices within the activist, community and practitioner spheres. From this perspective, surprising parallels can be drawn between intellectual positions that are frequently regarded as necessarily opposed, such as traditional medical accounts of transsexualism, Virginia Prince's transgenderist model and 'trans-exclusionary' radical feminist critiques of trans theory and medical practice.

This book therefore offers a response to the query raised by Jess Phillips MP when she asked what, 'clinically', 'living like a woman' or 'living like a man' *actually means*. Within the context of social and physical transition, living 'like' a woman or a man is not simply a matter of adhering to a particular model of womanhood or manhood; rather, it is about how an individual navigates the available medical *and* 'trans community' models of trans/gendered possibility in defining themselves and constructing their future.

I have demonstrated that there is no one position on what it *means* to be trans, or on how trans can be *possible*; this was observed among trans and cis people, groups and institutions across the three spheres of the ethnographic field for this project. However, lines of influence and resistance can be traced within and between all three spheres. I unpack these in the discussion of 'negotiation' that follows.

Negotiating discourses of trans health

Differences of understanding, definition and legitimation inform discursive clashes and material challenges within and between the activist, community and practitioner spheres. In this book, my analysis of these clashes and challenges focused primarily upon how they might be *negotiated* by trans patients. I looked at these negotiations on two levels: an individual level, and a collective level. I understand 'negotiation' here as the means by which trans healthcare systems might be navigated, as well as the means by which a collective agreement can be reached through extensive discussion.

Individual negotiations

In Chapter Four I explored how individual trans patients might negotiate the opportunities and limitations of condition and movement, as well as the oppressive consequences of cultural and professional cisgenderism. As previously discussed, trans patients frequently draw upon understandings of condition and/or movement to define themselves and their relation to the social world. This offers a means by which they might construct their identities and experiences as *possible* in medical encounters, thereby potentially improving their access to services. Similarly, both condition- and movement-oriented understandings of trans can be used to construct and justify trans existence in the wider social world. This is particularly important given that the high prevalence of ignorance (both innocent and malicious) among health professionals can mean that trans patients have to take a great deal of responsibility for their own care. In this way, even strictly conditional models of trans possibility can be drawn upon in an agential manner (albeit only by those who are 'trans enough' to 'fit' these models) to challenge cisgenderist assumptions and norms.

The challenges that trans patients may face in negotiating medical systems in particular were unpacked in detail in Chapters Three and Five. In Chapter Three I showed how cisgenderism and transphobia can produce barriers to care in all areas of healthcare provision. I also outlined the standard public health pathway that must be negotiated by patients seeking to transition through the NHS: a pathway defined primarily by strict assessment procedures such as RLE, as well as very long waits for treatment. Patients with access to the appropriate financial and/or social resources typically have more options for negotiating physical transition, be this through private providers or self-medication. However, these options may also be limited by political and ideological struggles within the medical professions, as seen in cases of Helen Webberley, Richard Curtis and Russell Reid.

In Chapter Five I examined how the strict assessment procedures and long waits of the NHS route can inform a collectively mediated temporality of anticipation, a queer time that offers an opportunity for mistrust and fear as well as hope and excitement to grow. The temporal and emotional disjunctures of anticipation can potentially be managed through strategic futurity, in which patients prepare carefully for clinical encounters and/or use the waiting time as an opportunity to reflect on their forthcoming transition and tell others about their plans. However, the uncertainty of waiting in the time of anticipation can be difficult to negotiate in emotional terms; this uncertainty and difficulty often leads to poor mental health and suicide ideation, as well as the aforementioned mistrust and fear of health professionals.

Collective and political negotiations

The time of anticipation can also be understood as a collective negotiation of physical transition. Individual projections of future possibility by trans patients within the time of anticipation necessarily draw on multiple experiences of past and present, in terms of challenges that people have faced and improvements that they have seen in their lives. In this way, the queer time of anticipation is mediated communally in and through the interaction of various pasts, presents and possible futures that circulate within narratives of trans health in activist and community spaces.

The collective negotiation of trans health may be further understood as a means through which material and discursive change can be sought. In Chapter Two I touched on how discourses of trans possibility constructed within the activist and community spheres might be drawn upon to influence policy and practice alike within the practitioner sphere. This theme was more fully examined in Chapter Six. In this chapter, I explored how trans patient advocates collectively construct their knowledges as *credible* through concerted and continual mutual recognition and iterative repetition across a range of social and professional contexts. These knowledges may then be drawn upon by activist-experts and insider-providers – as well as sympathetic cis professionals – in order to reconstruct the discursive and material conditions of healthcare provision, as seen in the example of the depathologisation movement.

Beyond gatekeeping

The opening pages of this book included a quotation from Catherine Meads and colleagues (2009), who noted the dearth of information on the *general* health of the trans population. Yet, having highlighted the importance of this intervention, I opened this chapter with a quote which appears to only address issues raised by gender identity services. This is not because I have sought to subsume wider issues of trans health within a project that specifically centres gender identity services (indeed, I initially set out to do entirely the opposite). Instead, it is because conversations within and between the community, activist and practitioner spheres all primarily discuss 'trans health' in terms of how it is mediated by these services. 'Trans health' is so often regarded as a synonym for transition.

I attribute this to *the major role that gender clinics play in shaping trans discourse*, in terms of both defining the scope of trans possibility and influencing the wider field of trans health. Discourses of condition and movement alike are generally defined either through or against the ideologies and practices of gender identity services. In turn, the conditions produced in and through these discourses shape how trans patients find themselves negotiating both general and specialist healthcare contexts, even if they have no intention of undergoing physical transition.

This observation has profound consequences for understandings of both trans subjectivity and trans health. My argument is that the strict management of trans/gendered possibility by 'gender experts' can work to stifle patient expression and inform harmful medical practices well beyond the boundaries of the gender clinic. This can be seen, for instance, in the historic adoption of condition-oriented perspectives on trans identity (such as the binary language of 'transsexualism') within wider health contexts, meaning that individuals with more movement-oriented identities (such as non-binary and genderqueer people) find themselves misunderstood even by health professionals who are trying to provide inclusive care.

Within NHS gender clinics, specialists who have sought to build movement-oriented understandings into their practice – for instance, through acknowledging non-binary gender – *continue to maintain the power to pronounce on their patients' gender.* The gatekeeping model of care imbues gender identity specialists with a great deal of power. This is not simply the power to advise on whether or not a patient is healthy enough to transition; it is the power to assess whether or not a patient is *appropriate* for treatment, and capable of providing a *credible* perspective on the matter of their own gender identity and potential feelings of dysphoria.

Multiple factors may shape the appropriateness and credibility of any given patient within the micro-setting of the diagnostic encounter: in addition to being 'trans enough', these might include (for instance) the intersection of gender with the patient's occupation, race, cultural background, dis/ability, family situation and/or preferred style of dress, as mediated by any given practitioners' individual biases and any given gender clinic's specific approach to conceptualising trans/gendered possibility and providing care. It is the fact that treatment *can* be delayed or denied on these grounds that informs much of the stress, anxiety, fear and mistrust that transitioning patients feel with regard to gender identity services.

It does not really matter whether or not practitioners 'relish the exercise of power, or the role of "gatekeeper"' (Richards et al, 2014: 255). Power is exercised regardless. Nor does it necessarily matter if practitioners are themselves trans, for this does not *necessarily* mean that they are challenging the fundamental nature of the clinical encounter. A majority of gender identity specialists clearly care deeply for their patients, but this is not enough to address the deep-seated and often justified fears experienced by trans patients. Questions need to be asked about how trans people are empowered and *disempowered* in making decisions about their own lives, in feeling that they *can* make decisions about their own lives.

To address these issues, we need to move beyond simply incorporating aspects of movement, such as non-binary recognition, into a more gender-pluralist form of medical practice. Rather, trans patients must be enabled to 'actualize their embodied needs rationally, euphorically perhaps, and in whatever ways they desire, without the need for psychiatric gatekeeping in the form of [gender dysphoria] diagnoses' (Davy, 2015: 1174). Gender identity services that affirm patient identities and desires in this way, centring their informed consent – rather than the authority of practitioners – have been trialled successfully in countries such as Argentina, Canada and the United States (Reisner et al, 2015; Hanssmann, 2016; Davy et al, 2018). Decentring diagnosis and gatekeeping can empower service providers 'to establish a more trusting, supportive, and facilitative relationship with patients' (Deutsch, 2012: 145). I read this more 'trusting' relationship as grounded in a regard for patient *credibility* on the micro-level of the medical appointment, with the institutional provision of such care providing an alternative to the kind of framework lottery seen in the UK's public health setting. It does not mean that medical practitioners should set aside their valuable expertise; indeed, protocols for appropriate care in line with the informed consent model have been carefully created by providers in a range of contexts (examples include Callen-Lorde Community Health Centre, 2012; Cundill and Wiggins, 2017). However, UK providers may need to discover a new humility in order to follow this path.

Looking to the future

This book does not provide a clear diagnosis for the all the challenges and difficulties inherent in the contested field of trans health, nor does it offer a firm prescription for the way forward. Numerous questions remain to be asked. For instance, how might we best introduce publicly funded models of care that emphasise the informed consent of transitioning patients? Any attempt to implement any such model in the UK would likely encounter a range of challenges, including suppression tactics similar to those encountered by Reid, Curtis and Webberley, plus the economic fall-out of austerity and Brexit. Furthermore, given that I have argued that gender identity specialists' conceptualisations of trans possibility play an important role in shaping understandings within the wider context of healthcare provision, would a shift in authority here help to inform a wider recognition of gender pluralism?

Even as new questions arise in the conclusion to this work, I hope to have provided a range of useful perspectives and analytic tools for those who follow. This book offers a broad overview of the many investments and negotiations that characterise the field of trans health in the UK, exploring the processes by which discourses and material conditions are shaped and the means by which they are conceptualised. It is my hope that these insights will prove pertinent for future sociological investigations and fully consensual experiments in practice. A range of challenges lie ahead, not least due to the exponential growth in the visible trans patient population, under-resourcing of healthcare services in general and gender identity services in particular, and rapid emergence of new trans knowledges and languages. To meet these challenges, the professional epistemic community of trans health would do well to fully recognise the contributions and insights of trans patients.

Appendix: notes on fieldwork, methods and ethics

This appendix provides some further details on the research project that informed this book. I first provide a brief description of the sites in which I undertook the ethnography, before outlining my approach to data collection and analysis.

A sketch of the field

I conducted fieldwork in a variety of online spaces, across a range of platforms: from static websites and documentation, to traditional web forums, to social media platforms Facebook and Twitter. This wide scope was intended to reflect the range of trans spaces available online, as well as the permeable boundaries of the medium itself (Postill and Pink, 2012), although of course the fieldwork sites comprised just a small part of a far wider ecology of trans content on the internet. Many of the spaces visited did not exist simply to host a discussion of trans health: however, for the purposes of this project, I sought to *specifically* examine how the topic of trans health was discussed within them. For a mostly complete list of sites visited during the project, see Pearce (2016: 229–236).

Information from these sites was 'captured' using the browser plugin NCapture, which allowed me to process it within qualitative data analysis programme NVivo. I also noted my thoughts, ideas and observations in a fieldwork diary. I then undertook a thematic analysis of this data (Braun and Clarke, 2006).

Activist sphere

For this project, I understood the activist sphere as comprising discussion groups within social media spaces, and opinion pieces written for blogs and news media platforms. I primarily observed eight Facebook groups, a Twitter hashtag and approximately 100 individual articles written for blogs and media organisations. A wide range of political tactics were discussed and/or implemented by trans individuals organising within or through these spaces, including protests/pickets, letter-writing campaigns, petitions, information/awareness drives, academic analysis, event disruption and political lobbying.

Facebook

I visited eight trans activist Facebook groups. These were accessible only to existing Facebook users. Most were either 'closed' or 'secret' groups, meaning that new members must be added or vetted by existing members: this means that they effectively operate as private spaces. 'Secret' groups are hidden from searches and can be *seen* by an individual only if they are directly invited to participate by an existing member. 'Closed' Facebook groups can be found through searches or may show on the Facebook sidebar if some of the user's friends are members. The smallest Facebook group visited for this project contained approximately 30 members and the largest contained approximately 1,000; most, however, had approximately 100–300 members.

Twitter

A majority of Twitter fieldwork for this project took place on the #transdocfail hashtag. Hundreds of Twitter users from a wide range of backgrounds were involved in #transdocfail, with most originating from the UK. Over 2,000 tweets were posted to the hashtag, a majority of which were written during the first three days (8–10 January 2013). Hashtags are used to organise discussions, automatically filing relevant tweets together. Every tweet observed on #transdocfail for this project is visible to any internet user, except where Twitter users later deleted or hid particular tweets or their entire account. I also drew on related but less popular hashtags, such as #transdocwin, and followed several hundred trans activists and health professionals from 2013 to 2017.

Blogs and activist websites

The blogs and activist websites visited during the fieldwork process are (or were, for some domain names have expired) all publicly available to any internet user. Blog articles were written in long-form prose (typically 200–2,000 words in length) by a single author, for the sake of sharing information, stimulating discussion and/or expounding a point of view.

News media

I visited a range of national UK and local media websites during the fieldwork process, most of which were associated with print newspapers and all of which are (or were) publicly available to any internet user.

Like the blog posts described above, the opinion articles on trans health issues for these websites were written in long-form prose (typically 200–2,000 words in length) by a single author, for the sake of sharing information, stimulating discussion and/or expounding a point of view.

Miscellaneous

I also looked up several Freedom of Information requests made by trans activists (and responses to these) at WhatDoTheyKnow, read numerous online petitions and played the browser game *A Trip To The Clinic*. During periods of supplementary observation that took place from April 2015, I followed the Women and Equalities Committee Transgender Equalities Inquiry, participated in e-mail, Facebook and Twitter conversations with my contacts and occasionally looked at activist conversations on the aforementioned blogs and sites such as the 'Transgender UK' sub-section of Reddit.

Community sphere

For this area of fieldwork, I observed discussions on two internet forums. Some of the activist spaces discussed in the previous section were also arguably communities in their own right (or one constituent part of a larger community). However, I use 'community' in this context to refer to the manner by which the forums *primarily* operated as social spaces: their purpose was to provide a basis for a 'community of care' (Hines, 2007). This differed from the more action-oriented nature of spaces visited within the activist sphere.

Both forums hosted a mixture of public areas (visible to any visitor) and private areas (visible only to registered members). Neither was dedicated solely to the discussion of trans health; at the same time, conversations on this topic were not confined to specific sub-forums. Instead, health was discussed *alongside* a myriad of other conversation topics, such as personal challenges, family issues, film and television, music, skills and hobbies, discrimination, ableism, racism and/or sexism.

Both forums had a large membership and were highly active as fieldwork began, with many hundreds of registered members and a more active core group of a few dozen regular users; this activity diminished over the fieldwork period as many members migrated to social media platforms. The forums were based in the UK, with memberships residing largely in the UK also. There was a great deal of diversity in terms of age, with users' ages ranging from mid-teens to late 70s. However, a majority of regular users were aged between

30 and 60, reflecting a particularly strong shift towards newer social media platforms among trans youth (Jenzen and Karl, 2014).

Forum 1

Forum 1 was, in theory, open to members from across the trans spectrum; however, the active membership predominantly identified into the 'MTF' spectrum, with trans women particularly common. I read approximately 330 pages of conversation on Forum 1. Each 'page' comprised 1–10 individual posts, with posts ranging in length from 2 to 4,000 characters. After reading the pages, I saved them to NVivo for analysis, using NCapture.

Forum 2

Forum 2 focused generally on providing space for 'FTM' spectrum experiences. However, a small number of users identified themselves as women (this included trans and cis women). Self-identified non-binary or genderqueer users were somewhat more common here than on Forum 1. I read approximately 700 pages of conversation on Forum 2, and similarly saved them to NVivo.

Practitioner sphere

The practitioner sphere largely comprised information written both by and/or for medical practitioners on the subject of trans health. However, it did include some information produced for trans patients by NHS or charitable bodies. This area of the data corpus included guidance and advice documents for NHS staff and patients, clinical guidance and protocols, GIC websites and information on public consultations. Most this material was, therefore, written by cis professionals working with trans people. However, there were a number of documents written and/or influenced by trans professionals and activists.

I acquired some materials attributed to this sphere through trans resource sites (such as UK Trans Info) and contacts made within the practitioner and activist spheres. I further obtained access to numerous letters and documents through participation in the NHS England Gender Identity Services GRC consultation process. All other materials were acquired through websites maintained by NHS organisations (such as gender clinics), public health quangos and professional bodies, which variously exist to provide and share information for patients, practitioners and/or health service managers.

Data collection

Data collection entailed immersion in the field and a subsequent capture of text(s) – as well as my own thoughts, feelings and initial insights – for later analysis. I visited relevant spaces on the internet for hours at a time: reading conversations, articles and documents, following links from one website to another. I announced my presence within every social space I visited, explicitly asking permission to conduct research. However, much of my participation from thereon in consisted of 'lurking': that is, reading interactions without generally adding my own comment (Murthy, 2008).

During the fieldwork process, I copied images and text directly from websites using the browser plugin NCapture. This enabled me to obtain a full record not only of the written discussions that are central to my analysis but also of the visual architecture of pages, thereby retaining a feel of the *visual impact* of visiting any given space. I did not conduct a formal semiotic analysis of this imagery, but the approach did enable me to re-immerse myself in the 'feel' of the spaces when later reflecting analytically upon the discussion that took place there.

I made an exception for data from Facebook groups visited during the fieldwork process. Instead of using NCapture for fieldwork on Facebook, I relied on the detailed notes made in a fieldwork diary every day during the period of immersion. This mediation of the field was performed out of respect for the very private nature of these groups and the sensitivity of conversations that took place on them.

I undertook fully immersive fieldwork – in which I dedicated most of my research time to data collection – in January–July 2013 and July 2014–April 2015. I also delved into archived forum conversations dating back to 2010 during this time. I continued to keep abreast of current affairs and undertake occasional supplementary observations and field notes into November 2017, when this book was completed.

Analysis

Thoughts, ideas and observations arising during the research process were noted in my fieldwork diary. These constituted an initial, informal stage of analysis, which informed my later thinking and the design of the more structured thematic analysis that followed.

Thematic analysis entails 'searching across a data set … to find repeated patterns of meaning' (Braun and Clarke, 2006: 91). I sought specifically to identify the (re)production, dissemination and negotiation of ideas, assumptions and meanings associated with 'trans health'. Data from social media, forums, blogs, news articles and various documents, as well as the fieldwork diary, were fed into NVivo 10, a computer program designed for qualitative data processing and analysis. I used NVivo to create a database that brought together material from across the data corpus; this material was then organised for both ease of access and thematic analysis. A key feature of NVivo is the creation of 'nodes', which facilitate the thematic coding of qualitative data. Any section of text can be coded as part of a node: I used this function to identify discursive themes across the data corpus. It is possible to undertake an automated analysis of data using NVivo, but I eschewed this in favour of using the program to *facilitate* a manual process of coding. This decision was taken in part because I feel that these automated processes lose some nuance, but also because it enabled me to maintain an immersive, feeling-based connection to the data many months after I completed the primary fieldwork.

Positionality: turning a critical lens on myself

Social research is not value neutral (Ellis, 1999). As a feminist researcher writing within the tradition of transgender studies, I have sought to centre the voices of those individuals whose words form the core of this study, and create work that might ultimately be of benefit to them. In the context of my research questions, this means that I am concerned with amplifying trans voices and promoting trans agency as well as understanding and speaking constructively to the professional context of trans health.

Furthermore, writing *as* a trans woman within a cisgenderist and frequently transmisogynistic academic world remains an important radical act. Trans people have, after all, been written *about* in an objectifying manner within many medical, feminist and sociological texts. While trans voices are finally gaining some legitimacy, cis writing about trans lives continues to contribute to an erasure of trans bodies and subjectivities in a range of contexts (Ansara and Hegarty, 2012; cárdenas, 2016; Gupta, 2018). Additionally, there are gender imbalances within transgender studies: for instance, there is a dearth of in-depth empirical social research published by trans women (Namaste, 2000; Whittle, 2006). In writing *as* a trans woman as well as *about* trans discourse, I follow the example of trans writers before me in challenging cis/male hegemony within the academic world and beyond, and hope to inspire other trans academics to follow in turn.

In social research, being an 'insider' member of a social group is increasingly recognised as advantageous for understanding social phenomena relevant within and to that group. In many respects, I approached fieldwork as a classic insider. As a woman who was coercively assigned male at birth, I am familiar with specifically trans experiences of sexual dysphoria, social and medical transition, harassment and fear, hope and fulfilment. This enabled me to empathise with trans experiences and ask pertinent questions of my findings; it also ensured that I was hyper-aware of ethical issues as they arose. As Hines (2007: 194) notes in positioning herself as a '*non*-transgender researcher' (emphasis mine), trans academics may benefit from both insider knowledge and a basis from which 'to build trust with potential participants'.

However, insider/outsider positions are not necessarily as distinct as they might seem. For example, there is no one way to be trans. My identity and experiences fit neatly into a certain *transsexual* narrative: one that differs radically from (for instance) sissy maid, drag king or non-transitioning genderqueer subjectivities. Parallels can be seen in Song and Parker's (1995) discussion of social research on race. They argue that the cultural identities of supposedly 'insider' researchers can complicate interactions with others from a supposedly *shared* background: 'the dual categories of "black/white" as well as "insider/outsider", have not only tended to obscure the diversity of experiences and viewpoints between and within various groups, but these categories have also obscured the diversity of experiences which can occur between the researcher and the researched' (Song and Parker, 1995: 243). Similarly, intersectional analysis addresses 'difference *within* groups' as well as *between* groups (Crenshaw, 1991: 1242, emphasis in original). For instance, because I am racialised (and, importantly, privileged) as white, my experience of being trans is different to that of a trans person of colour (Vidal-Ortiz, 2014).

The identity, familiarity and understandings that come with group belonging are not one-dimensional. It is therefore important to acknowledge commonalities between researchers and members of the communities they engage with, but not overemphasise them (Hines, 2007: 194). I thus consider my insider status to be of benefit to me as a researcher, but have also sought to avoid sweeping assumptions about the experiences, perspectives and discursive modes present within my findings. Instead, I have taken a reflexive approach, approaching analysis itself as an active, never-complete process of continual negotiation.

Ethics

My methodological approach raises questions of consent, privacy and authorship. The British Sociological Association (2002) recommends that researchers obtain informed consent from participants and anonymise their identities where possible to avoid the risk of harm to them. This is particularly important in research with trans participants for two central reasons. Firstly, even trans people who are 'out' on the internet may be closeted or stealth in the offline world. Any action that might unwittingly 'out' a trans individual to family, friends, work colleagues or peers is likely to place undue stress upon their mental health and leave them open to discrimination and abuse (McNeil et al, 2012). Secondly, trans people are frequently misrepresented, misgendered and othered within research (Adams, Pearce et al, 2017).

Consequently, trans people may be particularly wary of researchers' aims and intentions. During fieldwork I encountered the blog post 'Fuck you and fuck your fucking thesis', in which Anne Tagonist (2009) argues that a majority of researchers are 'self-serving' and cisgenderist, with their research interests rarely aligning with trans people's needs. The post – along with a heated debate in the attached comments thread – reflects the frequency with which trans community spaces are approached by privileged, thoughtless and/or underprepared researchers, and the distrust that can arise from this. This, coupled with the vulnerability of trans participants, means that researchers should be particularly sensitive to trans people's privacy.

At the same time, it is important to explicitly acknowledge the contribution of trans writers. Namaste (2000) argues that successive generations of trans people have been silenced by social research: in contrast, I hope to amplify trans voices. I have therefore sought to openly name participants in instances where they have explicitly sought a public audience. This need not necessarily contradict a commitment to privacy: in the context of internet research, a key issue is whether a given text was conceived of by its author as 'private' or as 'public'.

I therefore adopted the following guiding principles for ethical engagement during fieldwork and the writing of this book.

- I sought permission to acquire data from private spaces.
- I anonymised all data from these private spaces.
- I did generally did *not* anonymise data from public spaces within the activist sphere (such as public blogs); instead, I acknowledged writers openly as the author of their work, in recognition of the public statement they sought to make through writing.

- I did *not* anonymise data from the practitioner sphere, as these documents and websites were produced *as* public discourse.

In practice, implementing the first two of these principles was a complex process. As noted by the British Sociological Association (2002: 5), '[e]liciting informed consent, negotiating access agreements, assessing the boundaries between the public and the private, and ensuring the security of data transmissions are all problematic in Internet research'. This led to three issues that required careful consideration.

Firstly, while some spaces were very explicitly member only or secret, and others were explicitly aimed at a wide public audience, the distinction between 'public' and 'private' was not always clear, particularly within the activist and community spheres. For instance, tweets to #transdocfail were visible to anyone who clicked on the hashtag – a matter that regular Twitter users would be aware of – but contributors were unlikely to expect their tweet to be picked up by a researcher. As Markham (2008: 274) notes: '[s]ome users perceive publicly accessible discourse sites as private'.

Secondly, anonymisation within social research typically entails changing or omitting the reported name of participants to protect their identity (Bryman, 2004). It is possible to argue that even this is not always necessary online, as internet users frequently create pseudonyms when registering for membership of various spaces to manage their own privacy. However, there is a danger that any direct quotation from a social space online might attract undue attention regardless of pseudonym use, as readers can often uncover even 'private' locations in which conversations originally took place by copying the quote (or a section thereof) into a search engine (Kendall, 2002).

Thirdly, there were issues with consent. Seeking consent was complicated by the fluid membership and shifting activities of users within fieldwork sites in the activist and community spheres: '[o]nline discussion sites can be highly transient … Researchers gaining access permission in June may not be studying the same population in July' (Markham, 2008: 274). This, along with the sheer number of users present across multiple spaces within the field, rendered it impractical to directly seek permission from every individual whose writing is present in the data corpus for this project.

My solution to the above issues was to treat spaces with a *predominantly private* function (such as the forums) as private, and spaces with a *predominantly public* function (such as Twitter) as public. I further implemented a number of additional measures to seek consent and protect the identity of users.

I sought permission to conduct research within every private space visited for fieldwork. I posted on the forums and Facebook groups to state that I hoped to conduct research within the space. I linked to a website that provided information on myself, my research aims and methods, provided my institutional contact details and offered to answer any questions that potential participants might have. No one publicly took exception to my proposal to conduct research and I was not denied permission to conduct research in any of the spaces; however, I waited for permission from forum or group administrators before commencing data collection. In one of the two forums I was asked to restrict data collection to 'public' areas, so limited my activities accordingly; I nevertheless continued to regard this data as 'private', due to the predominantly private function of the space.

I also sought explicit consent to reproduce quotes from forums and individual Twitter users in this book, in order to address the important methodological issues raised by Markham (2008) regarding public discourse and shifting populations. I sent direct private messages or e-mails to relevant individuals to ask if they would be interested in participating in this project before (if granted permission) using their quotes.

I did not seek permission to quote from public blogs or media articles. However, I follow blogosphere etiquette – and seek to amplify trans visibility, where relevant – by openly naming writers and their blogs, and citing them as a reference if I have been influenced by their informal empirical or theoretical contributions. I also provide a list of blogs in Pearce (2016).

Where this book quotes from blogs, media articles and Twitter, I use the name or pseudonym chosen by the author. In this way, I aim to respect the choice made by the author in selecting a username that may have an important personal meaning. Where this book quotes from forums, I use a pseudonym selected by myself to protect the identity of the author. Some quotes (particularly those from public areas of forums I have treated as private) have undergone small edits – with permission from the participant – to protect the author from discovery via search engine (I am grateful to Karen Throsby for her advice on this measure). When taking this step, I have sought to retain the intent, spirit and 'feel' of the original quote.

I therefore sought to adopt a nuanced approach to the sensitive ethical issues that arose from my methodological approach. Applying a single, inflexible principle in matters of consent, privacy and authorship might have served to undermine the privacy and/or autonomy of participants. Instead, I adapted and responded to specific circumstances within different spaces in the field.

List of key terms

activist sphere
One of the three primary research sites for this book. I use this term to refer to trans social spaces on the internet which prioritise the discussion of political issues and activism.

activist-experts
Campaigners who have worked to establish themselves as credible experts through formal or informal scholarship and often also an adherence to certain professional norms, with the aim of being able to influence policy and/or practice.

anticipation
Trans people's access to specialist gender identity services is frequently defined by long periods of waiting. I use the term 'anticipation' to highlight transitioning patients' orientation towards the future in response to the deferral of treatment and resultant feelings of being caught in limbo. This can inform hope and excitement for a better future, but may also result in a growing mistrust and fear of healthcare practitioners (see: Chapter Five).

autoethnography
A qualitative research method that draws on a formal analysis of personal experience in order to acquire insights about the social world. Some elements of my discussion in this book draw upon autoethnographic data.

binarist
A way of thinking that relies on binary oppositions. Examples include the assumption that gender is female *or* male and the premise that social gender and biological sex are necessarily distinct categories.

bridging hormones
Hormone therapy overseen by GPs while their trans patients are waiting for a first appointment at a gender clinic. At present, bridging prescriptions are most often provided in the UK as a harm reduction measure for individuals who are perceived to be at risk due to self-medication and/or self-harm.

cis

A Latin-derived word meaning 'on the same side', which contrasts with 'the prefix *trans*-, meaning "across from"' (Ansara and Hegarty, 2012: 152). I use the term 'cis' to refer to individuals whose gendered identity *and* gendered appearance generally align with the gender they were assigned at birth. The term is also commonly used to refer to people who are 'not trans'. However, a growing number of trans scholars caution against the creation of a simplistic trans/cis binary.

cisgenderism

Cisgenderism describes the structuring of social norms and institutions around the assumption that everyone has 'cis' bodies and experiences. Cisgenderist attitudes do not necessarily arise from anti-trans prejudice, but do nevertheless work to create substantial difficulties for trans people (see also: cultural cisgenderism, professional cisgenderism).

community sphere

One of the three primary research sites for this book. I use this term to refer to trans social spaces on the internet which facilitate the casual discussion of shared experiences in healthcare settings and beyond.

cultural cisgenderism

A tacit form of cisgenderism that arises from the implicit assumption that everyone moves through the world as cis. This can lead to trans experiences and needs being ignored or not being taken seriously (see also: cis, cisgenderism).

depathologisation

If an identity, experience or behaviour is 'pathologised', it is treated or represented as a pathology: an abnormality, illness or disease. The process of 'depathologisation' therefore represents a shift away from this. For example, the trans depathologisation movement seeks to represent trans identities, experiences and behaviours as an aspect of human diversity. Similarly, 'depsychopathologisation' represents a move away from representing something as a psychiatric problem.

discourse

A term that refers to the authoritative ways in which we talk about ideas in a society, and the manner in which these ideas can also work to reproduce how the world is seen and experienced.

epistemic community
A collection of individuals and/or groups who jointly develop particular kinds of knowledge. A 'professional' epistemic community may comprise of clinical researchers or academics working in a particular field. A 'lay' epistemic community may comprise activists or independent scholars with a shared interest.

epistemic politics
The politics of knowledge production. Epistemic politics may centre around questions such as: who is capable of producing knowledge? and how might knowledge be produced? (see: Chapter Six).

Equality Act 2010
A British law which primarily applies in England, Scotland and Wales. Its aim is to ensure equal access to employment and both public and private services for people from a range of social groups, including trans people.

ethnography
A qualitative research method requiring immersive participant observation in a specific social setting. Qualitative methods are concerned with looking at social relations in depth to answer questions that cannot always be answered using statistics, such as 'why does this happen?' and 'how does this happen?' I undertook an internet ethnography to produce the primary data discussed in this book.

futurity
A temporal experience of – or engagement with – the present in which an individual's attention is focused on their vision of a possible, desired or feared future (see also: anticipation, temporality).

gatekeepers
In trans healthcare settings, gatekeepers control access to gender identity services. The role – and power – of the gatekeeper can differ enormously between (and even within) different institutions and practices. Under the 'gatekeeper model' of treatment, gender identity specialists ultimately decide if, when and how a transition should proceed.

gender clinics
Specialist multidisciplinary centres that exist to manage medical transitions. In the UK, gender clinics are also commonly known as Gender Identity Clinics, or GICs.

gender dysphoria
A term used in both medical literatures and trans communities to describe experiences of distress that arise from the apparent incongruence of an individual's social gender role and/or physical body. Gender dysphoria is also a psychiatric diagnosis in DSM-5 (see: Chapter 3).

gender identity services
Specialist healthcare services that exist to support and/or guide trans people through a transition. These include (but are not limited to) gender clinics, counselling and therapeutic services, hair removal clinics and surgery providers.

gender pluralism
An approach to gender diversity which acknowledges that people may take different routes to understanding and embodying gender. Gender pluralism prioritises social and political collaboration, rather than philosophical debates over the importance of one categorical approach or another.

Gender Recognition Act 2004 (GRA)
A UK law that enables trans people to change the sex on their birth certificate, and obtain a Gender Recognition Certificate (GRC). The law was groundbreaking in 2004, but has been criticised by trans people for adhering to binary gender norms and being unnecessarily bureaucratic.

genderqueer
The term 'genderqueer' may be used to refer to a gendered identity that sits between or beyond the binary gendered categories of 'female' or 'male'; it is also used by people who wish to refuse the notion of a gendered (or sexual) identity altogether (see also: non-binary).

Health and Social Care Act 2012
A law which restructured the NHS in England and Wales. One consequence of this Act is that most gender identity services are now

commissioned nationally (by NHS England or NHS Wales), rather than locally.

hormone time
A linear, utopian experience of time 'directed toward the end of living full time in the desired gender', which enables trans people to imagine or anticipate a better future (Horak, 2014: 580) (see also: anticipation, temporality).

informed consent model
An emerging paradigm for the provision of physical transition through gender identity services. In this model of care, the role of gender identity specialists is to empower trans people to make their own decisions about physical transition.

insider–providers
Healthcare practitioners who work with a marginalised patient group of which they themselves are a member.

invert
A sexological term from the late 19th and early 20th centuries. Inverts did not conform to sexual and gender norms. Experiences and behaviours that were historically described as 'inverted' might today be referred to as lesbian, gay, bisexual, trans, intersex or queer.

negotiation
An ongoing process of social contestation in which 'there is no rest'; according to Pereira (2017: 61), the negotiation of meaning and understanding is 'continuous and never complete'.

non–binary
The term 'non-binary' aims to acknowledge that gendered identities, experiences, behaviours and appearances cannot be divided strictly into one of two categories (female/male). During the 2010s, a growing number of trans people came to describe their gender as 'non-binary' (see also: genderqueer).

practitioner sphere
One of the three primary research sites for this book. I use this term to refer to a variety of online information, documentation and literatures on trans health, written by and/or for medical practitioners and administrators.

professional cisgenderism
An explicit form of cisgenderism that leads to the erasure of trans experiences in professional settings, such as academia and healthcare services, through the intentional imposition of cis ideologies and norms (see also: cis, cisgenderism).

queer time
An experience of time that may involve alternative ways of growing up, embodying age or engaging in culture. This contrasts with a normative linear progression through 'straight' life stages such as adolescence, marriage and reproduction (see also: temporality).

Real Life Experience (RLE)
A period of time during which transitioning individuals are expected to demonstrate to healthcare professionals that they are capable of living permanently in their preferred social gender role, as part of the 'gatekeeping model' of care. The WPATH *Standards of Care* require a year of RLE prior to genital surgery (Coleman et al., 2012). Some UK gender clinics require RLE prior to the commencement of other medical interventions, such as hormone therapy (see also: gatekeeper).

temporality
A term that is used to highlight the feeling of being caught within time, and to describe how time may be felt or experienced differently by people under various social circumstances.

traditional transsexual narrative
Historically, it was widely assumed that a transsexual should undertake a permanent, physical transition from 'female to male' or 'male to female'. This narrative was reinforced through medical practices and trans community discourses, which often encouraged transsexuals to conform to stereotypical gender roles.

trans
An umbrella term that refers to a range of gender variant identities, experiences, and ways of moving through the world. Trans language has emerged from both medical discourse and social movements (see: Chapter Two).

trans as condition
A range of understandings that provide definitive explanations for what 'trans' is, and how it might be resolved or fixed (such as through a specific way of living or a certain medical pathway).

trans as movement
A range of understandings that provide fluid and/or multiple means by which 'trans' might be, which tend to emphasise a process of change and contestation rather than any necessary outcome.

trans as transition
An approach to service provision in which all trans health needs are associated (often inappropriately or unnecessarily) with physical transition.

trans knowledges
Understandings of trans needs and what it means to be or live as trans, which emerge initially from personal experience and are further developed within trans communities, trans activism and trans scholarship.

#transdocfail
A Twitter hashtag that represented the first mass, collective and *public* online expression of dissatisfaction with healthcare services by trans patients in the UK. A research site for this book, positioned within the activist sphere.

transgender
An umbrella term for gender variant identities and experiences. 'Transgender' is often used as a synonym for the stand-alone 'trans', but may be associated with a more limited range of meanings. For instance, some individuals who have transitioned physically argue that they cannot be 'transgender' because it is their body – rather than their gender identity – which has changed. Consequently, the stand-alone 'trans' became increasingly popular through the 2000s and 2010s.

transition
A process of social and/or physical change, which a trans person may undergo in order to inhabit a more comfortable or authentic feeling gender role and/or body.

transitional time
A non-linear experience of time in which elements of the past, present and future co-exist and interact, with movements 'forward, backward, sideways, [and] tangential[ly]' (Carter, 2013: 141) (see also: temporality).

transphobia
A prejudiced attitude towards trans people. Transphobic actions include the use of offensive language, active discrimination, harassment and violence.

transsexualism
A term that has historically been used in both medical literatures and trans communities to refer to the desire for and/or practice of transitioning from one gender to another (see also: 'traditional transsexual narrative).

transvestitism
A term that has historically been used both in medical literatures and trans communities to refer to gender variant behaviour. Most typically, a 'transvestite' is an individual who cross-dresses, or wears clothes associated with the 'opposite' gender. However, writers such as Magnus Hirschfeld and Virginia Prince used the language of transvestism to refer to a wider range of individuals and social behaviours (see: Chapter 2).

understandings
In this book I use 'understandings' to refer to the *multiple* ways in which ideas such as 'trans identity' and 'trans health' are conceptualised, practiced and contested. The book's title is an intentional play on my observation that there is more than one way of understanding trans health.

References

Action For Trans Health (2015a) 'Demand #16: Action for Trans Health – Democratise trans healthcare now! Stop cis gatekeeping of essential treatment', Demanding the Future, 24 March.

Action For Trans Health (2015b) 'Written evidence submitted by Action For Trans Health to the Inquiry into Transgender Equality', data.parliament.uk, 21 August.

Action For Trans Health (nd) 'Join' (web page).

Adams, N., Hitomi, M. and Moody, C. (2017) 'Varied reports of adult transgender suicidality: synthesizing and describing the peer-reviewed and gray literature', *Transgender Health*, 2(1): 60–75.

Adams, N., Pearce, R., Veale, J., Radix, A., Castro, D., Sarkar, A. and Thom, K.C. (2017) 'Guidance and ethical considerations for undertaking transgender health research and institutional review boards adjudicating this research', *Transgender Health*, 2(1): 165–175.

Ahmad, S., Barrett, J., Beaini, B.Y., Bouman, W.P., Davies, A., Greener, H.M., Lenihan, P., Lorimer, S., Murjan, S., Richards, C., Seal, L.J. and Stradins, L. (2013) 'Gender dysphoria services: a guide for general practitioners and other healthcare staff', *Sexual and Relationship Therapy*, 28(3): 172–185.

Ahmed, S. (2016) 'An affinity of hammers', *TSQ: Transgender Studies Quarterly*, 3(1–2): 22–34.

Aizura, A.Z. (2012) 'Transnational transgender rights and immigration law', in Enke, A.F. (ed) *Transfeminist Perspectives in and beyond Transgender and Gender Studies*. Philadelphia: Temple University Press, pp. 133–150.

Aizura, A.Z. (2017) 'Unrecognizable: on trans recognition in 2017', *South Atlantic Quarterly*, 116(3): 606–611.

Akrich, M. (2010) 'From communities of practice to epistemic communities: health mobilizations on the internet', *Sociological Research Online*, 15(2).

American Psychiatric Association (2013) *Diagnostic and Statistical Manual of Mental Disorders: DSM-5*. Arlington: American Psychiatric Association.

Amin, K. (2014) 'Temporality', *TSQ: Transgender Studies Quarterly*, 1(1–2): 219–222.

Anderson, B. (1991) *Imagined Communities: Reflections on the Origin and Spread of Nationalism*. London: Verso.

Anderson, L. (2006) 'Analytic autoethnography', *Journal of Contemporary Ethnography*, 35(4): 373–395.

Ansara, Y.G. (2010) 'Beyond cisgenderism: counselling people with non-assigned gender identities', in Moon, L. (ed) *Counselling Ideologies: Queer Challenges to Heteronormativity*. Farnham: Ashgate, pp. 167–200.

Ansara, Y.G. (2015) 'Challenging cisgenderism in the ageing and aged care sector: meeting the needs of older people of trans and/or non-binary experience', *Australasian Journal on Ageing*, 34(S2): 14–18.

Ansara, Y.G. and Hegarty, P. (2012) 'Cisgenderism in Psychology: pathologizing and misgendering children from 1999 to 2008', *Psychology and Sexuality*, 3(3): 137–160.

Arcelus, J., Bouman, W.P., Jones, B.A., Richards, C., Jimenez-Murcia, S. and Griffiths, M.D. (2017) 'Video gaming and gaming addiction in transgender people: an exploratory study', *Journal of Behavioral Addictions*, 6(1): 21–29.

Bailey, L. and McNeil, J. (2013) *Monitoring and Promoting Trans Health Across the North West*. Manchester: NHS North West. [Online]. Available at: http://www.traverse-research.com/wp-content/uploads/2012/12/Trans-Health-GP-Practices-Report-March-2013.pdf.

Barrett, J. (2007) *Transsexual and Other Disorders of Gender Identity*. Oxford: Radcliffe.

Barrett, J. (2016) 'Doctors are failing to help people with gender dysphoria', *BMJ*, 352: i1694.

Batty, D. (2013) 'Doctor under fire for alleged errors prescribing sex-change hormones', *Observer*, 6 January.

Bauer, G.R., Hammond, R., Travers, R., Kaay, M., Hohenadel, K.M. and Boyce, M. (2009) '"I don't think this is theoretical; this is our lives": how erasure impacts health care for transgender people', *Journal of the Association of Nurses in AIDS Care*, 20(5): 348–361.

Belcher, H. (2014) *TransDocFail: The Findings*. Challenging Journeys (Phase 2). [Online]. Available at: http://uktrans.info/attachments/article/342/transdocfail-findings.pdf.

Belfast Health and Social Care Trust (nd) 'Regional Gender Identity Service at Brackenburn Clinic Frequently Asked Questions'. [Online]. Available at: http://www.belfasttrust.hscni.net/pdf/BrackenburnClinic-FAQ.pdf.

Benjamin, H. (1954) 'Transsexualism and transvestism as psycho-somatic and somato-psychic syndromes', in Stryker, S. and Whittle, S. (eds) (2006) *The Transgender Studies Reader*. London: Routledge, pp. 45–52.

Benjamin, H. (1966) *The Transsexual Phenomena*. New York: The Julian Press.

Bettcher, T. M. (2007) 'Evil deceivers and make-believers: on transphobic violence and the politics of illusion', *Hypatia: A Journal of Feminist Philosophy*, 22(3): 43–65.

Bettcher, T. M. (2009) 'Feminist perspectives on trans issues', *Stanford Encyclopaedia of Philosophy*. Available at: http://plato.stanford.edu/entries/feminism-trans/.

Bhanji, N. (2013) 'Trans/criptions: homing desires, (trans)sexual citizenship and racialized bodies', in Stryker, S. and Aizura, A.Z. (eds) *The Transgender Studies Reader 2*. New York: Routledge.

Bindel, J. (2009) 'The operation that can ruin your life', *Standpoint*. Available at: http://www.standpointmag.co.uk/the-operation-that-can-ruin-your-life-features-november-09-julie-bindel-transsexuals.

Bishop, J.-A. (2013) *Trans* Patients' Experiences of their GP Surgery – Annual Survey 2013*. Manchester: TransForum.

Bockting, W.O. (2009) 'Transforming the paradigm of transgender health: a field in transition', *Sex and Relationship Therapy*, 24(2): 103–107.

Bockting, W. O., Fraser, L., Knudson, G., Whittle, S., Botzer, M., Brown, G., DeCuypere, G., Green, J., Rachlin, K., Winter, S., and Wylie, K. (2010) *De-psychopathologisation Statement*. World Professional Association For Transgender Health. [Online]. Available at: http://www.wpath.org/site_announcements_detail.cfm?pk_association_announcement =6302#.

Bonifacio, H.J. and Massarella, C. (2017) *Adolescence: Moving Forward with Gender-affirming Care for Youth*. Workshop at CPATH Pre-Conference in Vancouver, Canada, 26 October [2017].

Bonifacio, H.J. and Rosenthal, S.M. (2015) 'Gender variance and dysphoria in children and adolescents', *Pediatric Clinics of North America*, 62(4): 1001–1016.

Bornstein, K. (1994) *Gender Outlaw: On Men, Women and the Rest of Us*. London: Routledge.

Bornstein, K. and Bergman, S.B. (2010) *Gender Outlaws: The Next Generation*. Berkeley: Seal Press.

Bouman, W.P., Bauer, G.R., Richards, C. and Coleman, E. (2010) 'World Professional Association for Transgender Health consensus statement on considerations of the role of distress (Criterion D) in the DSM Diagnosis of Gender Identity Disorder', *International Journal of Transgenderism*, 12: 100–106.

Bouman, W.P., Richards, C., Addinall, R.M., Arango de Montis, I., Arcelus, J., Duisin, D., Esteva, I., Fisher, A., Harte, F., Khoury, B., Lu, Z., Marais, A., Mattila, A., Nayarana Reddy, D., Nieder, T.O., Robles Garcia, R., Rodrigues, O.M., Roque Guerra, A., Tereshkevich, D., T'Sjoen, G. and Wilson, D. (2014) 'Yes and yes again: are standards of care which require two referrals for genital reconstructive surgery ethical?', *Sexual and Relationship Therapy*, 29(4): 377–389.

Bradley, J. and Myerscough, F. (2015) 'Transitional demands', *Action For Trans Health*. [Online]. Available at: http://actionfortranshealth. org.uk/2015/03/30/transitional-demands/.

Braun, V. and Clarke, V. (2006) 'Using thematic analysis in psychology', *Qualitative Research in Psychology*, 3(2): 77–101.

British Sociological Association (2002) *Statement of Ethical Practice for the British Sociological Association*. [Online]. Available at: https://www. britsoc.co.uk/media/23902/statementofethicalpractice.pdf.

Bryman, A. (2004) *Social Research Methods*. New York: Oxford University Press.

Bunch, M. (2013) 'The unbecoming subject of sex: performativity, interpellation, and the politics of queer theory', *Feminist Theory*, 14(1): 39–55.

Burke, M.C. (2011) 'Resisting pathology: GID and the contested terrain of diagnosis in the transgender rights movement', in McGann, P.J. and Hutson, D.J. (eds) *Sociology of Diagnosis*. Bingley: Emerald Group Publishing Limited, pp. 183–210.

Burns, C. (2006) *Collected Essays in Trans Healthcare Politics: Documenting the Scandal of How Medicine Lost the Trust of Trans People*. London: Press For Change. [Online]. Available at: http://www.changelingaspects. com/PDF/essays-transhealth.pdf.

Burns, C. (2008) *Trans: A Practical Guide for the NHS*. London: Department of Health Publications.

Burns, C. (2013) *Pressing Matters (Vol 1)*. Amazon Media.

Butler, J. (1993) *Bodies that Matter: On the Discursive Limits of 'Sex'*. New York: Routledge.

Butler, J. (1999) *Gender Trouble: Feminism and the Subversion of Identity*. 2nd edition. New York: Routledge.

Cabral, M., Suess, A., Ehrt, J., Seehole, T.J. and Wong, J. (2016) 'Removal of a gender incongruence of childhood diagnostic category: A human rights perspective', *Lancet Psychiatry*, 3(5): 405–406.

Callen-Lorde Community Health Centre (2012) *Protocols for the Provision of Cross-Gender Hormone Therapy*. [Online]. Available at: http://www.tmeltzer.com/assets/callen-lorde-revised-protocols.pdf.

Capuzza, J.C. (2014) 'Who defines gender diversity? Sourcing routines and representation in mainstream U.S. news stories about transgenderism', *International Journal of Transgenderism*, 15(3–4): 115–128.

cárdenas, M. (2016) 'Pregnancy: reproductive futures in trans of color feminism', *TSQ: Transgender Studies Quarterly*, 3(1–2): 48–57.

Carpenter, E. (1919) *Intermediate Types among Primitive Folk: A Study in Social Evolution*. London: George Allen & Unwin Limited.

Carter, J. (2013) 'Embracing transition, or dancing in the folds of time', in Stryker, S. and Aizura, A.Z. (eds) *The Transgender Studies Reader 2*. New York: Routledge, pp. 130–143.

Catalano, D.C.J. (2015) '"Trans enough?" The pressures trans men negotiate in higher education', *TSQ: Transgender Studies Quarterly*, 2(3): 411–430.

Cauldwell, D.O. (1949) 'Psychopathia transexualis', *Sexology*, 16: 274–280.

Chang, H. (2016) 'Autoethnography in health research: growing pains?', *Qualitative Health Research*, 26(4): 443–451.

Chen, D., Hidalgo, M.A., Leibowitz, S., Leininger, J., Simons, L., Finlayson, C. and Garofalo, R. (2016) 'Multidisciplinary care for gender-diverse youth: a narrative review and unique model of gender-affirming care', *Transgender Health*, 1(1): 117–123.

Clune-Taylor, C. (2016) 'Intersex movement', *The Wiley Blackwell Encyclopedia of Gender and Sexuality Studies*. [Online]. Available at: http://onlinelibrary.wiley.com/doi/10.1002/9781118663219.wbegss219/full.

Coleman, E., Bockting, W., Botzer, M., Cohen-Kettenis, P., DeCuypere, G., Feldman, J., Fraser, L., Green, J., Knudson, G., Meyer, W.J., Monstrey, S., Adler, R.K., Brown, G.R., Devor, A.H., Ehrbar, R., Ettner, R., Eyler, E., Garofalo, R., Karasic, D.H., Lev, A.I., Mayer, G., Meyer-Bahlburg, H., Hall, B.P., Pfaefflin, F., Rachlin, K., Robinson, B., Schechter, L.S., Tangpricha, V., van Trotsenburg, M., Vitale, A., Winter, S., Whittle, S., Wylie, K.R. and Zucker, K. (2012) 'Standards of care for the health of transsexual, transgender and gender nonconforming people, version 7', *International Journal of Transgenderism*: 165–232.

Collins, H. and Pinch, T. (1998) *The Golem: What You Should Know about Science*. Cambridge: Cambridge University Press.

Combs, R., Turner, L. and Whittle, S. (2008) *Gender Identity Services in England: The Mapping Project Report*. London: Press For Change. [Online]. Available at: http://www.pfc.org.uk/pdf/UK_GIC_%20 Mapping&ServicesProject%204DoH.pdf.

Crenshaw, K. (1991) 'Mapping the margins: intersectionality, identity politics, and violence against women of color', *Stanford Law Review*, 43(6): 1241–1299.

Cundill, P. and Wiggins, J. (2017) *Protocols for the Initiation of Hormone Therapy for Trans and Gender Diverse Patients*. Melbourne: Victorian Aids Council. [Online]. Available at: http://vac.org.au/site/assets/uploaded/b3e096c2-equinox-informed-consent-guidelines.pdf.

Curson, N. (2010) 'Transgender Identities: towards a Social Analysis of Gender eds. Sally Hines and Tam Sanger', *Graduate Journal of Social Science*, 7(2): 141–145.

Curtis, R., Levy, A., Martin, J., Zoe-Jane, P., Wylie, K., Reed, T. and Reed, B. (2008) *Guidance for GPs, other Clinicians and Health Professionals on the Care of Gender Variant People*. London: Department of Health Publications.

Davies, A., Bouman, W.P., Richards, C., Barrett, J., Ahmad, S., Baker, K., Lenihan, P., Lorimer, S., Murjan, S., Mepham, N., Robbins-Cherry, S., Seal, L.J. and Stradins, L. (2013) 'Patient satisfaction with gender identity clinic services in the United Kingdom', *Sexual & Relationship Therapy*, 28(4): 400–418.

Davy, Z. (2010) 'Transsexual agents: negotiating authenticity and embodiment within the UK's medicolegal system', in Hines, S. and Sanger, T. (eds) *Transgender Identities: Towards a Social Analysis of Gender Diversity*. Oxford: Routledge, pp. 106–126.

Davy, Z. (2011) *Recognizing Transsexuals: Personal, Political and Medicolegal Embodiment*. Surrey: Ashgate.

Davy, Z. (2015) 'The DSM-5 and the politics of diagnosing transpeople', *Archives of Sexual Behaviour*, 44(5): 1165–1176.

Davy, Z. (2018) 'Genderqueer(ing): "on this side of the world against which it protests"', *Sexualities*. Pre-published 30 January 2018. Available at: https://doi.org/10.1177/1363460717740255.

Davy, Z., Sørlie, A. and Schwend, A.S. (2018) 'Democratising diagnoses? The role of the depathologisation perspective in constructing corporeal trans citizenship', *Critical Social Policy*, 38(1): 13–34.

De Cuypere, G., Knudson, G. and Green, J. (2013) *WPATH Consensus Process Regarding Transgender and Transsexual-Related Diagnoses in ICD-11*. [Online]. World Professional Association for Transgender Health. Available at: http://www.wpath.org/uploaded_files/140/files/ICD%20Meeting%20Packet-Report-Final-sm.pdf (Accessed 31 July 2016).

Delemarre-van de Waal, H.A. and Cohen-Kettenis, P.T. (2006) 'Clinical management of gender identity disorder in adolescents: a protocol on psychological and paediatric endocrinology aspects', *European Journal of Endocrinology*, 155(suppl 1): S131–S137.

Denzin, N.K. (1994) 'Evaluating qualitative research in the poststructural moment: the lessons James Joyce teaches us', *International Journal of Qualitative Studies in Education*, 7(4): 295–308.

Department of Health (2010) *Equity and Excellence: Liberating the NHS.* [Online]. Available at: https://www.gov.uk/government/uploads/system/uploads/attachment_data/file/213823/dh_117794.pdf.

Department of Health (2012) 'Gender dysphoria services – an English protocol', draft document for consultation (26 July).

Deutsch, M.B. (2012) 'Use of the informed consent model in the provision of cross-sex hormone therapy: a survey of the practices of selected clinics', *International Journal of Transgenderism*, 13(3): 140–146.

Dewey, J.M. (2008) 'Knowledge legitimacy: how trans-patient behaviour supports and challenges current medical knowledge', *Qualitative Health Research*, 18(10): 1345–1355.

Drescher, J., Cohen-Kettenis, P.T. and Reed, G.M. (2016) 'Gender incongruence of childhood in the ICD-11: controversies, proposal, and rationale', *The Lancet Psychiatry*, 3(3): 297–304.

Dutta, A. and Roy, R. (2014) 'Decolonizing transgender in India: some reflections', *TSQ: Transgender Studies Quarterly*, 1(3): 320–337.

Ekins, R. and King, D. (2006) *The Transgender Phenomenon.* London: Sage Publications.

Ekins, R. and King, D. (2010) 'The emergence of new transgendering identities in the age of the internet', in Hines, S. and Sanger, T. (eds) *Transgender Identities: Towards a Social Analysis of Gender Diversity.* London: Routledge, pp. 25–42.

Elliot, P. (2009) 'Engaging trans debates on gender variance: a feminist analysis', *Sexualities*, 12(1): 5–32.

Ellis, C. (1999) 'Heartful autoethnography', *Qualitative Health Research*, 9(5): 669–683.

Ellis, S.J., Bailey, L. and McNeil, J. (2015) 'Trans people's experiences of mental health and gender identity services: a UK study', *Journal of Gay & Lesbian Mental Health*, 19(1): 4–20.

Enke, A.F. (2012) 'The education of little cis: Cisgender and the discipline of opposing bodies', in Enke, A.F. (ed) *Transfeminist Perspectives in and beyond Transgender and Gender Studies.* Philadelphia: Temple University Press, pp. 60-77.

Epstein, S. (1996) *Impure Science: AIDS, Activism and the Politics of Knowledge.* London: University of California Press.

Fae, J. (2013) '#TransDocFail: the trans community rises', *The F Word*, 9 January.

Fae, J. (2015) 'Sound and fury ...', *British Journalism Review*, 26(4): 5–7.

Feinberg, L. (1992) 'Transgender liberation: a movement whose time has come', in Stryker, S. and Whittle, S. (eds) (2006) *The Transgender Studies Reader*. New York: Routledge, pp. 205–220.

Feinberg, L. (1999) *Trans Liberation: Beyond Pink or Blue*. Boston, MA: Beacon Press.

Feinberg, L. (2006) *Drag King Dreams*. New York: Carroll & Graf.

Fish, J. (2007) *Trans People's Health*. London: Department of Health.

Foucault, M. (1978) *The Will to Knowledge: The History of Sexuality: 1*. Translated by Hurley, R. London: Penguin Books.

Franklin, S. (1997) *Embodied Progress: A Cultural Account of Assisted Conception*. London: Routledge.

G3 – Gender Governance Group (2009) 'Minutes of meeting held on Wednesday 25 March 2009'.

G3 – Gender Governance Group (2010) 'G3 meeting held on Wednesday 13 October 2010'.

GMC (General Medical Council) (2016) *Treatment Pathways*. [Online]. Available at: http://www.gmc-uk.org/guidance/ethical_guidance/28852.asp.

Glass, P.G. (2016) 'Using history to explain the present: the past as born and performed', *Ethnography*, 17(1): 92–110.

Goh, J. and Kananatu, T. (2018) 'Mak Nyahs and the dismantling of dehumanisation: framing empowerment strategies of Malaysian male-to-female transsexuals in the 2000s', *Sexualities*. Pre-published 30 January 2018. Available at: https://doi.org/10.1177/1363460717740256.

Goldberg, J.M. (2006) 'Training community-based clinicians in transgender care', *International Journal of Transgenderism*, 9(3–4): 219–231.

Gramling, D. and Dutta, A. (2016) 'Introduction', *TSQ: Transgender Studies Quarterly*, 3(3–4): 333–356.

Green, K.M. (2017) 'Trans★ movement/trans★ moment: an afterword', *International Journal of Qualitative Studies in Education*, 30(3): 320–321.

Greer, G. (1999) *The Whole Woman*. London: Doubleday.

Gupta, K. (2018) 'Response and responsibility: mainstream media and Lucy Meadows in a post-Leveson context', *Sexualities*. Pre-published 30 January 2018. Available at: https://doi.org/10.1177/1363460717740259.

Haas, P.M. (1992) 'Introduction: epistemic communities and international policy coordination', *International Organization*, 46(1): 1–35.

Halberstam, J. (1998) 'Transgender butch: butch/FTM border wars and the masculine continuum', *GLQ: A Journal of Lesbian and Gay Studies*, 4(2): 287–310.

Halberstam, J. (2005) *In a Queer Time and Place: Transgender Bodies, Subcultural Lives*. New York: New York University Press.

Hall, R. (1926) *The Well of Loneliness*. London: Virago Modern Classics.

Hallam, C. (2013) 'As the #transdocfail hashtag showed, many trans people are afraid of their doctors', *New Statesman*, 9 January.

Hanssmann, C. (2016) 'Passing torches? Feminist inquiries and trans-health politics and practices', *TSQ: Transgender Studies Quarterly*, 3(1–2): 120–136.

Haraway, D. (1991) *Simians, Cyborgs and Women: The Reinvention of Nature*. New York: Routledge.

Hausman, B. (1995) *Changing Sex: Transsexualism, Technology, and the Idea of Gender*. Durham, NC: Duke University Press.

Hess, D.J. (2004) 'Medical modernisation, scientific research fields and the epistemic politics of health social movement', *Sociology of Health & Illness*, 26(6): 695–709.

Heyes, C. (2007) 'Feminist solidarity after queer theory: the case of transgender', in Stryker, S. and Aizura, A.Z. (eds) (2013) *The Transgender Studies Reader 2*. New York: Routledge, pp. 201–212.

Hill, D.B. and Willoughby, B. (2005) 'The development and validation of the genderism and transphobia scale', *Sex Roles*, 53(7–8): 531–544.

Hill, R. (2013) 'Before transgender: *Transvestia*'s spectrum of gender variance', in Stryker, S. and Aizura, A.Z. (eds) *The Transgender Studies Reader 2*. New York: Routledge, pp. 364–379.

Hills, M. (2009) 'Participatory culture: mobility interactivity and identity', in Creeber, G. and Martin, R. (eds) *Digital Cultures: Understanding New Media*. Maidenhead: Open University Press, pp. 107–116.

Hine, C. (2000) *Virtual Ethnography*. London: Sage.

Hines, S. (2007) *TransForming Gender: Transgender Practices of Identity, Intimacy and Care*. Bristol: Policy Press.

Hines, S. (2013) *Gender Diversity, Recognition and Citizenship: Towards a Politics of Difference*. Basingstoke: Palgrave Macmillan.

Hird, M.J. (2003) 'A typical gender identity conference? Some disturbing reports from the therapeutic front lines', *Feminism & Psychology*, 13(2): 181–199.

Hirschfeld, M. (1910 [1991]) *The Transvestites: The Erotic Drive to Cross-Dress*. Translated by Lombardi-Nash, M.A. Amherst, MA: Prometheus Books.

Home Office (2011) *Advancing Transgender Equality: A Plan for Action*. [Online]. Available at: http://www.homeoffice.gov.uk/publications/equalities/lgbt-equality-publications/transgender-action-plan?view=Binary.

Horak, L. (2014) 'Trans on YouTube: intimacy, visibility, temporality', *TSQ: Transgender Studies Quarterly*, 1(4): 572–585.

Hunt, J. (2014) 'An initial study of transgender people's experiences of seeking and receiving counselling or psychotherapy in the UK', *Counselling and Psychotherapy Research*, 14(4): 288–296.

Jackson, P.A. (2004) 'Gay adaptation, tom-dee resistance, and kathoey indifference: Thailand's gender/sex minorities and the episodic allure of queer English', in Leap, W.L. and Boellstorff, T. (eds) *Speaking in Queer Tongues: Globalization and Gay Language*. Chicago: University of Illinois Press, pp. 202–230.

Jacobs, S.-E., Thomas, W. and Lang, S. (1997) *Two-Spirit People: Native American Gender Identity, Sexuality and Spirituality*. Urbana: University of Illinois Press.

Jacques, J. (2010) 'I was looking for a trans counter-culture', *Guardian*, 16 June.

Jain, S.L. (2007) 'Living in prognosis: toward an elegiac politics', *Representations*, 98(1): 77–92.

Jeffreys, S. (2014) *Gender Hurts: A Feminist Analysis of the Politics of Transgenderism*. London: Routledge.

Jenzen, O. and Karl, I. (2014) 'Make, share, care: social media and LGBTQ youth engagement', *Ada: A Journal of Gender, New Media, and Technology*, 5.

Jewkes, E.V. (2017) 'My journey through transition', in Bouman, W.P. and Arcelus, J. (eds) *The Transgender Handbook: A Guide for Transgender People, Their Families and Professionals*. New York: Nova Science, pp. 387–398.

Kendall, L. (2002) *Hanging Out in the Virtual Pub: Masculinities and Relationships Online*. Berkeley: University of California Press.

Kennedy, N. (2013) 'Cultural cisgenderism: consequences of the imperceptible', *Psychology of Women Section Review*, 15(2): 3–11.

Kennedy, N. and Hellen, M. (2010) 'Transgender children: more than a theoretical challenge', *Graduate Journal of Social Science*, 7(2): 25–42.

Kessler, S.J. and McKenna, W. (1978) *Gender: An Ethnomethodological Approach*. Chicago: University of Chicago Press.

Koyama, E. (2002) *Cissexual/Cisgender: Decentralizing the Dominant Group*. [Online]. Available at: http://eminism.org/interchange/2002/20020607-wmstl.html.

Koyama, E. (2004) *Whose Feminism Is it Anyway? And Other Essays from the Third Wave*. Portland: Confluere Publications.

Krafft-Ebing, R. v. (1877 [2006]) 'Selections from Psychopathia Sexualis with special reference to contrary sexual instinct: a medico-legal study', in Stryker, S. and Whittle, S. (eds) (2006) *The Transgender Studies Reader*. London: Routledge, pp. 21–27.

Kristensen, Z.E. and Broome, M.R. (2015) 'Autistic traits in an internet sample of gender variant UK adults', *International Journal of Transgenderism*, 16(4): 234–245.

Kruijver, F.P.M., Zhou, J.-N., Pool, C.W., Hofman, M.A., Gooren, L.J.G. and Swaab, D.F. (2000) 'Male-to-female transsexuals have female neuron numbers in a limbic nucleus', *The Journal of Clinical Endocrinology & Metabolism*, 85(5): 2034–2041.

Lamble, S. (2008) 'Retelling racialized violence, remaking white innocence: the politics of interlocking oppressions in transgender day of remembrance', *Sexuality Research and Social Policy*, 5(1): 24–42.

Lancet, The (2011) 'The end of our National Health Service', *The Lancet*, 377(9763): 353.

Landzelius, K. (2006) 'Introduction: patient organization movements and new metamorphoses in patienthood', *Social Science & Medicine*, 62: 529–537.

Layard, R., Banerjee, S., Bell, S., Clark, D., Field, S., Knapp, M., Meacher, M., Naylor, C., Parsonage, M., Scott, S., Strang, J., Thornicroft, G. and Wessely, S. (2012) *How Mental Illness Loses Out in the NHS*. [Online]. Available at: http://cep.lse.ac.uk/pubs/download/special/cepsp26.pdf.

Leeds and York Partnership NHS Foundation Trust (2012) Letter, attachment to Freedom of Information request, 'Registered doctors involved in FoI response'.

Lester, C. (2017) *Trans Like Me: A Journey for All of Us*. London: Virago.

Lev, A.I. (2009) 'The ten tasks of the mental health provider: recommendations for revision of the World Professional Association of Transgender Health's Standards of Care', *International Journal of Transgenderism*, 11(2): 74–99.

Lohman, K. (2017) *The Connected Lives of Dutch Punks: Contesting Subcultural Boundaries*. London: Palgrave Macmillan.

Lyons, K. (2016) 'UK doctor prescribing cross-sex hormones to children as young as 12'. [Online]. *Guardian*. Available at: https://www.theguardian.com/society/2016/jul/11/transgender-nhs-doctor-prescribing-sex-hormones-children-uk.

Markham, A.N. (2008) 'The methods, politics and ethics of representation in online ethnography', in Denzin, N.K. and Lincoln, Y.S. (eds) *Collecting and Interpreting Qualitative Materials*. London: Sage, pp. 793–820.

Matte, N., Devor, A.H. and Vladicka, T. (2009) 'Nomenclature in the World Professional Association for Transgender Health's Standards of Care: background and recommendations', *International Journal of Transgenderism*, 11(1): 42–52.

McNeil, J., Bailey, L., Ellis, S., Morton, J. and Regan, M. (2012) *Trans Mental Health Study 2012*. Edinburgh: Equality Network.

Meads, C., Pennant, M., McManus, J. and Bayliss, S. (2009) *A Systematic Review of Lesbian, Gay, Bisexual and Transgender Health in the West Midlands Region of the UK Compared to Published UK Research*. Birmingham: West Midlands Health Technology Assessment Collaboration.

Meyer, W., Bockting, W.O., Cohen-Kettenis, P., Coleman, E., DiCeglie, D., Devor, H., Gooren, L., Hage, J.J., Kirk, S., Kuiper, B., Laub, D., Lawrence, A., Menard, Y., Patton, J., Schaefer, L., Webb, A. and Wheeler, C.C. (2001) 'The standards of care for gender identity disorders – sixth version', *International Journal of Transgenderism*, 5(1).

Meyerowitz, J. (2002) *How Sex Changed: A History of Transsexuality in the United States*. Cambridge, MA: Harvard University Press.

Mills, C.W. (1959) *The Sociological Imagination*. New York: Oxford University Press.

Monro, S. (2005) 'Beyond male and female: poststructuralism and the spectrum of gender', *International Journal of Transgenderism*, 8(1): 3–22.

Monro, S. (2007) 'Transmuting gender binaries: the theoretical challenge', *Sociological Research Online*, 12(1).

Moon, I (2018) '"Boying" the boy and "girling' the girl": From Affective Interpellation to Trans-emotionality', *Sexualities*. Pre-published 30 January 2018. Available at: https://doi.org/10.1177/1363460717740260.

Morgan, J. (2016) 'Self-determining legal gender: transgender right, or wrong?', *The Lancet Diabetes & Endocrinology*, 4(3): 207–208.

Muñoz, J.E. (2007) 'Cruising the toilet: LeRoi Jones/Amiri Baraka, radical black traditions, and queer futurity', *GLQ: A Journal of Lesbian and Gay Studies*: 353–367.

Munt, S. (ed) (1998) *Butch/Femme: Inside Lesbian Gender*. London: Cassell.

Murthy, D. (2008) 'Digital ethnography: an examination of the use of new technologies for social research', *Sociology*, 42(5): 837–855.

Namaste, V.K. (2000) *Invisible Lives: The Erasure of Transsexual and Transgendered People*. Chicago: University of Chicago Press.

Nestle, J., Howell, C. and Wilchins, R. (2002) *Genderqueer: Voices from Beyond the Sexual Binary*. New York: Alyson Books.

Ngunjiri, F.W., Hernandez, K.-A.C. and Chang, H. (2010) 'Living autoethnography: connecting life and research', *Journal of Research Practice*, 6(1): Article E1.

NHS and Department of Health (2007) *A Guide for Young Trans People in the UK*, April. Available at: http://www.mermaidsuk.org.uk/assets/media/17-15-02-A-Guide-For-Young-People.pdf.

NHS Coventry (2010) *Advice Process for Changing Name and Gender in Primary Care*.

NHS England (2013a) *Interim NHS England Gender Dysphoria Protocol and Service Guideline 2013/14*. Available at: https://www.england.nhs.uk/wp-content/uploads/2013/10/int-gend-proto.pdf.

NHS England (2013b) 'Clinical commissioning policy: the provision of gender dysphoria services', draft document for consultation (1 January).

NHS England (2015a) *Experiences of People from, and Working with, Transgender Communities within the NHS – Summary of Findings, 2013/14*. Available at: https://www.england.nhs.uk/commissioning/wp-content/uploads/sites/12/2015/11/gend-ident-clnc-exprnc-rep-nov15.pdf.

NHS England (2015b) *Treatment and Support of transgender and Non-binary People across the Health and Care Sector: Symposium Report*. Available at: https://www.england.nhs.uk/commissioning/wp-content/uploads/sites/12/2015/09/symposium-report.pdf.

NHS England (2015c) *Operational Research Report Following Visits and Analysis of Gender Identity Clinics in England*. Available at: https://www.england.nhs.uk/commissioning/wp-content/uploads/sites/12/2015/11/gender-ident-clncs-rep-nov15.pdf.

NHS England (2015d) 'Clinical commissioning policy: [gender identity services]', consultation document (24 March).

NHS England (2017a) *Guide to Consultation: Specialised Gender Identity Services for Adults*. Available at: https://www.engage.england.nhs.uk/survey/gender-identity-services-for-adults/user_uploads/gender-identity-consultation-guide-1.pdf.

NHS England (2017b) 'Gender identity services for adults (non-surgical interventions)', draft document for consultation (7 July).

NHS Scotland (2012) *Gender Reassignment Protocol*. Edinburgh: NHS Scotland. Available at: http://www.sehd.scot.nhs.uk/mels/CEL2012_26.pdf.

NHS Wales (2012) *Specialised Services Policy: CP21 Specialised Adult Gender Identity Services.* [Online]. Available at: http://www.whssc. wales.nhs.uk/sitesplus/documents/1119/CP21%20Gender%20 Services%20Specialies%20Services%20Policy%20%20Approved%20 1209251.pdf.

Nicolazzo, Z. (2017) *Trans* in College: Transgender Students' Strategies for Navigating Campus Life and the Institutional Politics of Inclusion.* Sterling: Stylus.

Nieder, T.O. and Strauss, B. (2015) 'Transgender health care in Germany: participatory approaches and the development of a guideline', *International Review of Psychiatry*, 27(5): 416–426.

Nieder, T.O., Elaut, E., Richards, C. and Dekker, A. (2016) 'Sexual orientation of trans adults is not linked to outcome of transition-related health care, but is worth asking', *International Review of Psychiatry*, 28(1): 103–111.

NIGB (2011) *Advice Process for Changing Name and Gender in Primary Care.* [Online]. Available at: http://webarchive.nationalarchives.gov. uk/20130513181011/http://www.nigb.nhs.uk/advice/changename/ process-for-changing-name-and-gender-in-primary-care.

Nirta, C. (2018) *Marginal Bodies, Trans Utopias.* London: Routledge.

Patel, N. (2017) 'Violent cistems: trans experiences of bathroom space', *Agenda*, 31(1): 51–63.

Payton, N. (2015) 'Feature: the dangers of trans broken arm syndrome', *Pink News*, 9 July.

Pearce, R. (2012) 'Inadvertent praxis: what can "genderfork" tell us about trans feminism?', *MP: An Online Feminist Journal*, 3(4): 87–129.

Pearce, R. (2016) '(Im)possible patients: negotiating discourses of trans health in the UK'. PhD thesis. Department of Sociology, University of Warwick.

Pearce, R. (2018) 'Trans temporalities and non-linear ageing', in King, A., Almack, K., Westwood, S. and Suen, Y-T. (eds) *Older LGBT* People: Minding the Knowledge Gaps.* Abingdon: Routledge.

Pearce, R. and Lohman, K. (2018) 'De/constructing DIY identities in a trans music scene', *Sexualities*. Pre-published 5 February 2018. Available at: https://doi.org/10.1177/1363460717740276.

Pearce, R., Steinberg, D.L. and Moon, I. (2018) 'The emergence of "trans"', *Sexualities*. Pre-published 30 January 2018. Available at: https://doi.org/10.1177/1363460717740261.

Pereira, M.d.M. (2012) '"Feminist theory is proper knowledge, but...": the status of feminist scholarship in the academy', *Feminist Theory*, 13(3): 283–303.

Pereira, M.d.M. (2017) *Power, Knowledge and Feminist Scholarship: An Ethnography of Academia*. London: Routledge.

Plummer, K. (1995) *Telling Sexual Stories: Power, Change and Social Worlds*. London: Routledge.

Postill, J. and Pink, S. (2012) 'Social media ethnography: the social researcher in a messy web', *Media International Australia*, (145): online only.

Prince, V. (1973 [2005]) 'Sex vs. gender', *International Journal of Transgenderism*, 8(4): 20–24.

Prince, V. (1978 [2005]) 'The "transcendents" or "trans" people', *International Journal of Transgenderism*, 8(4): 39–46.

Prosser, J. (1998) *Second Skins: The Body Narratives of Transsexualism*. New York: Columbia University Press.

Pyne, J. (2014) 'The governance of gender non-conforming children: a dangerous enclosure', *Annual Review of Critical Psychology*, 11: 79–96.

Raha, N. (2017) 'Transfeminine Brokenness, Radical Transfeminism', *South Atlantic Quarterly*, 116(3): 632-646.

Ravine, J.A. (2014) 'Toms and zees: locating FTM identity in Thailand', *TSQ: Transgender Studies Quarterly*, 1(3): 387–401.

Raymond, J. (1979) *The Transsexual Empire: The Making of the She-Male*. Boston, MA: Beacon Press.

Reed, B., Rhodes, S., Schofield, P. and Wylie, K. (2009) *Gender Variance in the UK: Prevalence, Incidence, Growth and Geographic Distribution*. [Online]. Available at: http://www.gires.org.uk/assets/Medpro-Assets/GenderVarianceUK-report.pdf.

Reisner, S.L., Poteat, T., Keatley, J., Cabral, M., Mothopeng, T., Dunham, E., Holland, C.E., Max, R. and Baral, S.D. (2016) 'Global health burden and needs of transgender populations: a review', *The Lancet Transgender Health*, 1(1): 32–56.

Reisner, S.L., Bradford, J., Hopwood, R., Gonzalez, A., Makadon, H., Todisco, D., Cavanaugh, T., VanDerwarker, R., Grasso, C., Zaslow, S., Boswell, S.L. and Mayer, K. (2015) 'Comprehensive transgender healthcare: the gender affirming clinical and public health model of Fenway Health', *Journal of Urban Health*, 92(3): 584–592.

Richards, C. and Lenihan, P. (2012) 'A critique of Trans people's partnerships: towards an ethics of intimacy, by Tam Sanger (2010)', *Sexual and Relationship Therapy*, 27(1): 63–68.

Richards, C., Bouman, W. and Barker, M.-J. (eds) (2017) *Genderqueer and Non-Binary Genders*. Basingstoke: Palgrave Macmillan.

Richards, C., Barker, M.-J., Lenihan, P. and Iantaffi, A. (2014) 'Who watches the watchmen? A critical perspective on the theorization of trans people and clinicians', *Feminism & Psychology*, 24(2): 248–258.

Richards, C., Bouman, W.P., Seal, L., Barker, M.-J., Nieder, T.O. and T'Sjoen, G. (2016) 'Non-binary or genderqueer genders', *International Review of Psychiatry*, 28(1): 95–102.

Richards, C., Arcelus, J., Barrett, J., Bouman, W.P., Lenihan, P., Lorimer, S., Murjan, S. and Seal, L. (2015) 'Trans is not a disorder – but should still receive funding', *Sexual and Relationship Therapy*, 30(3): 309–313.

Richardson, D. and Monro, S. (2010) 'Intersectionality and sexuality: the case of sexuality and transgender equalities work in UK local government', in Taylor, Y., Hines, S. and Casey, M.E. (eds) *Theorizing Intersectionality and Sexuality*. Basingstoke: Palgrave MacMillan, pp. 99–118.

Rivera, S. (2002) 'Queens in exile, the forgotten ones', in Nestle, J., Howell, C. and Wilchins, R. (eds) *Genderqueer: Voices from Beyond the Sexual Binary*. New York: Alyson Books.

Roberts, A. (2015) *NHS funding projections*. London: The Health Foundation. [Online]. Available at: http://staging.healthfoundation. apps.awsripple.com/sites/default/files/FundingOverview_ NHSFundingProjections.pdf (Accessed 5 July 2016).

Roen, K. (2001) 'Transgender theory and embodiment: the risk of racial marginalisation', *Journal of Gender Studies*, 10(3): 253–263.

Royal College of Psychiatrists (2013) *Good Practice Guidelines for the Assessment and Treatment of Adults with Gender Dysphoria*. [Online]. Available at: http://www.rcpsych.ac.uk/files/pdfversion/CR181_ Nov15.pdf.

Rubin, H. (2003) 'The Logic of Treatment', in Stryker, S. and Whittle, S. (eds) (2006) *The Transgender Studies Reader*. New York: Routledge.

Rumbelow, H. (2017) 'The doctor who helps kids to change gender'. [Online]. *The Times*. Available at: https://www.thetimes.co.uk/ article/the-doctor-who-helps-kids-to-change-gender-xsw6dxc7n.

Sanger, T. (2010) *Trans People's Partnerships*. Basingstoke: Palgrave Macmillan.

Schonfield, S. and Gardner, C. (2008) *Survey of Patient Satisfaction with Transgender Services*. London: NHS Audit, Information and Analysis Unit. [Online]. Available at: http://www.gires.org.uk/assets/ Medpro-Assets/AIAUSatisfactionAuditJune2008.pdf.

Serano, J. (2007) *Whipping Girl: A Transsexual Woman on Sexism and the Scapegoating of Femininity*. Emeryville: Seal Press.

Shapiro, E. (2004) '"Trans"cending barriers: transgender organizing on the internet', *Journal of Gay & Lesbian Social Services*, 16(3–4): 165–179.

Song, M. and Parker, D. (1995) 'Commonality, difference and the dynamics of disclosure in in-depth interviewing', *Sociology*, 29(2): 241–256.

Spack, N.P., Edwards-Leeper, L., Feldman, H.A., Leibowitz, S., Mandel, E., Diamond, D.A. and Vance, S.R. (2012) 'Children and adolescents with gender identity disorder referred to a pediatric medical center', *Pediatrics*, 129(3): 418–425.

Speer, S.A. (2013) 'Talking about sex in the gender identity clinic: implications for training and practice', *Health*, 17(6): 622–639.

Steinberg, D.L. (1997) 'Technologies of heterosexuality: eugenic reproductions under glass', in Steinberg, D.L., Epstein, D. and Johnson, R. (eds) *Border Patrols: Policing the Boundaries of Heterosexuality*. London: Cassell, pp. 66–97.

Steinberg, D.L. (2015a) *Genes and the Bioimaginary: Science, Spectacle, Culture*. Farnham: Ashgate.

Steinberg, D.L. (2015b) 'The bad patient: estranged subjects of the cancer culture', *Body & Society*, 21(3): 115–143.

Steinberg, D.L., Epstein, D. and Johnson, R. (1997) *Border Patrols: Policing the Boundaries of Heterosexuality*. London: Cassell.

Stone, S. (1991) 'The empire strikes back: a posttranssexual manifesto', in Stryker, S. and Whittle, S. (eds) (2006) *The Transgender Studies Reader*. New York: Routledge, pp. 221–235.

Stryker, S. (1994) 'My words to Victor Frankenstein above the village of Chamounix: performing transgender rage', *GLQ: A Journal of Lesbian and Gay Studies*, 1(3): 237–254.

Stryker, S. (2005) 'Foreword', *International Journal of Transgenderism*, 8(4): xv–xvi.

Stryker, S. (2006) '(De)subjugated knowledges: an introduction to transgender studies', in Stryker, S. and Whittle, S. (eds) *The Transgender Studies Reader*. New York: Routledge, pp. 1–17.

Stryker, S. (2008) *Transgender History*. Berkeley: Seal Press.

Stryker, S. and Aizura, A.Z. (eds) (2013) *The Transgender Studies Reader 2*. New York: Routledge.

Stryker, S. and Whittle, S. (2006) 'Editorial to "Sappho by Surgery: The Transsexually Constructed Lesbian-Feminist" by Janice Raymond', in Stryker, S. and Whittle, S. (eds) *The Transgender Studies Reader*. New York: Routledge.

Tagonist, A. (2009) 'Fuck you and fuck your fucking thesis', *Huck Finn on Estradiol*. [Online]. Available at: http://tagonist.livejournal.com/199563.html.

Titman, N. (2014) 'How many people in the United Kingdom are nonbinary?' *Practical Androgyny*. [Online]. Available from: http://practicalandrogyny.com/2014/12/16/how-many-people-in-the-uk-arenonbinary.

Tosh, J. (2011) '"Zuck off!" A commentary on the protest against Ken Zucker and his treatment of childhood gender identity disorder', *Psychology of Women Section Review*, 13(1): 10–16.

Tosh, J. (2016) *Psychology and Gender Dysphoria: Feminist and Transgender Perspectives*. London: Routledge.

Toze, M. (2015) Written evidence submitted by Michael Toze to the Inquiry into Transgender Equality, data.parliament.uk, 17 July.

UCL Institute of Health Equity (2012) *The Impact of the Economic Downturn and Policy Changes on Health Inequalities in London*. [Online]. Available at: https://www.instituteofhealthequity.org/Content/FileManager/pdf/london-full-rep-medium-res.pdf.

UK Trans Info (2015) *Imperial College Healthcare NHS Trust (Charing Cross) GRS Waiting Times*. Available at: http://uktrans.info/ichnt.

UK Trans Info (2016) *Current Waiting Times and Patient Population for Gender Identity Clinics in the UK*. [Online]. Available at: http://uktrans.info/attachments/article/341/patientpopulation-oct15.pdf.

Vähäpassi, E. (2013) 'Creating a home in the borderlands? Transgender stories in the original plumbing magazine', *Journal of Queer Studies in Finland*, 7(1–2): 30–41.

Valentine, D. (2007) *Imagining Transgender: An Ethnography of a Category*. Durham, NC: Duke University Press.

Valentine, V. (2016) *Specific Detriment: A Survey into Non-binary People's Experiences in the UK*. Conference paper presented at Beyond the Binaries of Sex and Gender: Non-Binary Identities, Bodies, and Discourses, University of Leeds, UK, March 2016.

Van Der Miesen, A.I.R., Hurley, H. and De Vriesa, A.L.C. (2016) 'Gender dysphoria and autism spectrum disorder: a narrative review', *International Review of Psychiatry*, 28(1): 70–80.

Vance, S.R., Ehrensaft, D. and Rosenthal, S.M. (2014) 'Psychological and medical care of gender nonconforming youth', *Pediatrics*, 134(6): 1184–1192.

Vek, L. (2010) *Crossing Sex and Gender in Latin America*. London: Palgrave Macmillan.

Vidal-Ortiz, S. (2014) 'Whiteness', *TSQ: Transgender Studies Quarterly*, 1(1–2): 264–266.

Vincent, B.W. (2016) 'Non-Binary Gender Identity Negotiations: Interactions with Queer Communities and Medical Practice'. PhD thesis. School of Sociology and Social Policy, University of Leeds. Available at: http://etheses.whiterose.ac.uk/15956/.

Ware, S.M. (2017) 'All power to all people? Black LGBTTI2QQ activism, remembrance, and archiving in Toronto', *TSQ: Transgender Studies Quarterly*, 4(2): 170–180.

Weinand, J.D. and Safer, J.D. (2015) 'Hormone therapy in transgender adults is safe with provider supervision; a review of hormone therapy sequelae for transgender individuals', *Journal of Clinical & Translational Endocrinology*, 2(2): 55–60.

Weiner, K. (2009) 'Lay Involvement and legitimacy: the construction of expertise and participation within HEART UK', *Journal of Contemporary Ethnography*, 38(2): 254–273.

Wesley, S. (2014) 'Twin-spirited woman: Sts'iyóye smestíyexw slhá:li', *TSQ: Transgender Studies Quarterly*, 1(3): 338–351.

West, C. and Zimmerman, D.H. (1987) 'Doing gender', *Gender & Society*, 1(2): 125–151.

Whittle, S. (1998) 'The trans-cyberian mail way', *Social Legal Studies*, 7(3): 389–408.

Whittle, S. (2006) 'Foreword', in Stryker, S. and Whittle, S. (eds) *The Transgender Studies Reader*. New York: Routledge, pp. xi–xvi.

Whittle, S. (2016) *The End of Gender; Invalidating the Trans-identity and the Need to Be Someone*. Conference paper presented at Trans Studies: Reflections and Advances, University of Leeds, UK, March 2016.

Whittle, S., Turner, L. and Al-Alami, M. (2007) *Engendered Penalties: Transgender and Transsexual People's Experiences of Inequality and Discrimination*. Wetherby: Communities and Local Government publications.

Williams, C. (2014) 'Transgender', *TSQ: Transgender Studies Quarterly*, 1(1–2): 232–234.

Winter, S. (2009) 'Cultural considerations for the World Professional Association for Transgender Health's Standards of Care: the Asian perspective', *International Journal of Transgenderism*, 11(1): 19–41.

Women and Equalities Committee (2015) *Transgender Equality Inquiry: fourth oral evidence session*. See exchange 14:48 minutes in. Available at: http://www.parliament.uk/business/committees/committees-a-z/commons-select/women-and-equalities-committee/news-parliament-2015/transgender-inquiry-ministers-evidence-15-16/.

Women and Equalities Committee (2016) *Transgender Equalities*. London: House of Commons. [Online]. Available at: http://www.publications.parliament.uk/pa/cm201516/cmselect/cmwomeq/390/390.pdf.

World Health Organization (1992) *International Classification of Diseases 10*. Geneva: World Health Organization.

Yeadon-Lee, T. (2016) 'What's the story? Exploring online narratives of online non-binary gender identities', *Interdisciplinary Social and Community Studies*, 11(2): 19–34.

Zinck, S. and Pignatiello, A. (2015) *External Review of the Gender Identity Clinic of the Child, Youth and Family Service in the Underserved Populations Program at the Centre for Addiction and Mental Health*. Toronto: Centre for Addition and Mental Health.

Acts of Parliament

Gender Recognition Act 2004. Available at: http://www.legislation.gov.uk/ukpga/2004/7/contents.

The Sex Discrimination (Amendment of Legislation) Regulations 2008. Available at: http://www.legislation.gov.uk/uksi/2008/963/contents/made.

Equality Act 2010. Available at: http://www.legislation.gov.uk/ukpga/2010/15/contents.

Health and Social Care Act 2012. Available at: http://www.legislation.gov.uk/ukpga/2012/7/contents/enacted.

Index

A

A Trip To The Clinic (game) 159–60, 172
Action For Trans Health 120, 178–80
activist groups
  action research 176–7
  alternative approaches 177–80
  anticipation 126
  on bridging hormones 74–5
  collective interventions 175–80
  and collective social movement 37
  and concept of trans 4
  depathologisation 185–7, 192
  discourses of trans as condition 89–90
  guidance documents 57, 177, 187,
    188–9, 190
  inclusivity 45, 104
  internet 39–40
  intersex community 116n2
  knowledge 160–1, 181, 194
  language 41–4, 184, 191
  militant 37
  misgendering 109
  mistrust of health professionals 75, 133,
    134
  other patient activism 6, 162
  social media 11, 170, 210–11*app*
  trans journalists 173
activist sphere 11–12, 149, 151, 161, 168,
  189, 209, 219*gl*
activist-experts 161–4, 174, 182, 188,
  194, 201, 204, 219*gl*
adolescent patients, hormone blockers 65,
  67–8, 167
age, chronological and trans 124–5
agency
  exercise of 133
  loss of 14, 152, 162
  negotiations and 203
  and power 10, 52, 166
  private treatment 73, 78
  protocols and 191
  and temporality 122, 123, 154, 155
  and trans identity 97, 98
  and waiting times 128, 131
Ahmed, Sara 142
AIDS activism 162
Aizura, Aren 17, 186
Akrich, Madeleine 164

*American Psychiatric Association, Diagnostic
  and Statistical Manual of Mental Disorders*
  (DSM) 26, 28, 30, 58–60, 97, 184–7,
  199, 222
Ansara, Y Gavriel 43–4, 142
  and Hegarty, Peter 29, 43, 86, 113–15,
  144
anticipation 219*gl*
  anticipating difficulty 120–1, 137–44
  hope 144–7
  and mistrust 131–7
  narratives of 126–7
  'not-yet' 152, 154
  and temporality 124, 125–6, 130–1
  and waiting 127
appropriate trans behaviour, hierarchies
  of 107
Arcelus, Jon 188
  and colleagues 94, 195n2
Argentina 46, 192
Asscheman, Henk 73
assessment procedures
  documentation for 139
  as gatekeeping 28, 92, 113, 136–9,
    162–3, 198–9
  and gender binary 59, 71
  hope and 146, 147
  pathway 60–1, 64–7
  in Scotland 69–70, 190
  and self-medication 73
  'trans enough' 27, 60, 92, 137–44, 149,
    150, 201, 206
  in Wales 71
  see also RLE ('Real Life Experience')
'assigned at birth' (non-consensual gender
  assignment) 38, 183, 184
assimilationist approach 37
austerity, impact of 72, 207
Australia 46
authority, international 188–92
autistic spectrum conditions 91
autobiography 13, 34
autoethnography 13, 219gl
aversion therapy 22

B

Bailey, Louie and McNeil, Jay 54, 56, 87,
  91, 109

Barrett, James 60, 63, 65, 68, 113, 115, 136, 139, 164–5, 168, 170, 182
Batty, David 165–6
'behavioural modification' 33
Belcher, Helen 55, 152, 175
Belfast Health and Social Care Trust 141
see also Brackenburn Clinic, Belfast
belonging 38, 102, 105, 106–8, 116, 215
Benjamin, Harry 30, 31, 32, 178
The Transsexual Phenomenon 24–6, 34
Bettcher, Talia Mae 24, 42
Bhanji, Nael 103, 105–6, 159
binarist 219gl
binarist language 59, 60, 184–5, 188, 205
binary gender discourse
cisgenderism and 85–86, 110, 114–15
conditional discourse and 9
and diagnosis 26, 59–60, 136
gatekeeping and 113
Gender Recognition Act 69
HBS movement 178
ICD-10 59, 60, 200
NHS Choices 92
'trans-exclusionary' radical feminism and 32
transgenderists 30
treatment 61, 95–6
WPATH Standards of Care 46
Bindel, Julie 32
biological determinism 32
birth certificates, new 130
Bockting, Walter 9
Bornstein, Kate 34, 40, 42
and Bergman, S. Bear, Gender Outlaws: The Next Generation 45
Gender Outlaw 36, 39
Bouman, Walter and colleagues 68, 164
boundaries 9, 10, 43, 89, 95–6, 103–7, 193
Bowers, Marci 43, 46
Boys Don't Cry (film) 122
Brackenburn Clinic, Belfast 64, 72, 79n3, 141
Bradley, Jess and Myerscough, Francis 119, 120, 123, 127, 128, 129, 130, 137, 147
bridging hormones 74–5, 219gl
British Sociological Association 216app, 217app
Brown, Sarah 75
Burchill, Julie 196n5
Burns, Christine 57, 70, 172, 174–5, 176
Trans: A practical guide for the NHS 57, 70
Butler, Judith 6, 35, 36, 44, 83, 85

C

Callen-Lorde Community Health Centre, New York 188
Canada 46, 61
Carpenter, Edward 48n1
Carter, Julian 123–4, 127, 128, 154, 155
Cauldwell, David 25, 27
CCGs (Clinical Commissioning Groups) 70
Centre for Addiction and Mental Health, Toronto 49n10
Chalmers clinic, Edinburgh 72
Chang, Heewon 13
Charing Cross Gender Identity Clinic, London 5, 51–2, 62–4, 66, 71, 74, 141, 146–7
children 85–7, 117n4
restricting gender expression 29, 49–50n10
cis 42–4, 220gl
cisgenderism 43–4, 85–6, 96, 114–15, 220gl
cultural 85–6, 88, 97, 99, 109, 110, 111, 113, 220gl
counter-discourse 101, 102, 103, 202
institutional cisgenderism 57
professional 86, 95, 106, 113, 115, 116, 224gl
civil rights 99, 173
class 17, 22, 37, 78, 106
Clinical Commissioning Groups see CCGs
Clinical Reference Groups see CRGs
cliniQ 54, 90
clothing 23–4
Coalition Government 72
Equity and Excellence: Liberating the NHS 169
Transgender Action Plan 190
Coleman, Eli 188
collective social movements 9, 36–41, 175–82
alternatives to transsexualism 102–3
negotiations 204
preparation for assessment 139
and Standards of Care 188, 189
see also epistemic community
Colombia 192
Combs, Ryan and colleagues 63, 109
'coming out' 83–7
community sphere 12, 220gl
age and 125
anticipation and 126
on assessment 139, 143
authority and 94
depathologisation 186
forums 104, 108

conditional discourses 9, 20–33, 89–101,
225*gl*
alternative approaches 177–8
authoritative discourse and 112–16, 149
binary model and 43
butches and 103–4
contradictory discourses 108–9
depathologisation 185–6
DSM 185
gatekeeping and 60, 92–6, 141–2, 171,
205
Gender Recognition Act 69
historical 17, 21–6, 29–31
irreversibility 66
and movement 38–9, 45–6, 102
'trans-exclusionary' radical feminism
and 31–3
and trans possibilities 200–3
countdown timers 145
'counter-expertise' 163
Cox, Laverne 16
CRGs (Clinical Reference Groups) 70,
93–4, 190, 191–2
Curson, Natasha 39
Curtis, Richard 72, 149–50, 165–7
cyborg feminism 35

D

Davidson, Liam 115
Davy, Zowie 28, 73, 77–8, 101, 186,
187, 195, 206
Dean, John 192
'deceptive transsexual' trope 25, 49n7
Defosse, Dana Leland 42–4
depathologisation 28, 182–93, 220*gl*
depsychopathologisation 185, 186, 187,
190, 220
'Stop Trans Pathologization!'
campaign 186
Whittle and 175
WPATH Standards of Care 187–92
diagnosis
binary discourse 26, 59–60, 136
classificatory systems 97
criteria 58–60, 92, 94, 114, 142, 143
discursive shifts 182–6
pathologising model 46
power of 26–9, 48, 98–9, 206
waiting time for 64–7, 90
see also DSM; gatekeeping; ICD
discourse 7–10, 47–8, 220*gl*
discrimination 16, 28, 42, 53–5, 57, 169,
216
discursive feedback loop 34
Dorsey, Sean 123–4
drag 37

DSM see *American Psychiatric Association,
Diagnostic and Statistical Manual of
Mental Disorders*
'dual role transvestism' 30, 60, 114
dyke bands 123

E

Ekins, Richard and King, David 88, 178
Ellis, Havelock 21, 23
Ellis, Sonja-J. and colleagues 51, 60, 67,
144
empowerment 179, 181, 206
endocrinology 22, 61, 67, 74
Engendered Penalties study 2007 53
England 63, 66, 70–2, 87, 183, 190 *see
also* NHS England
Enke, Finn 41, 42–4
epistemic community 161, 164, 168,
182–5, 207, 221*gl*
lay epistemic community 181, 182
epistemic hierarchies 27–8, 100
epistemic politics 161–4, 221*gl*
Epstein, Stephen 160, 162
Equality Act 2010 16, 40, 52, 57, 77,
169, 170, 221*gl*
essentialist approach 39, 85, 105, 109–11,
136
ethnocentrism 29, 115, 188 *see also* race;
whiteness
ethnographic research 10–14, 221*gl*
expert knowledge
alternative 103–4
and conditionality 9, 101
as gatekeepers 27–8, 30, 92–6, 112–16
individual 108
non-trans 31, 33
power of 47, 48, 60–1, 98–100, 181–2,
186
'expert patients' 134, 137

F

Facebook 11–13, 99, 109–10, 126, 133,
169, 210*app*, 213*app*
Fae, Jane 105–6
Feinberg, Leslie 36–9, 41, 42, 45, 102,
104, 106
*Transgender Liberation: A Movement Whose
Time Has Come* 33, 40–1
female sexuality 22
female to male transsexualism *see* FTM
feminist approaches 8, 23, 28, 202*app*,
214–15*app*
'trans-exclusionary' radical
feminism 31–4m 49n7
trans feminism 32, 34–5, 38, 214–15*app*
see also intersectionality
'femiphile' transvestism 30
'fetishistic' transvestism 30

Field, Steve 192
Fish, Julie 91
Frankenstein, Victor and his monster 35
FTM (female-to-male) transsexualism 22, 30, 49n4, 103–4, 212*app*
'Fuck you and fuck your fucking thesis' 216*app*
funding 46, 61–4, 70, 72, 128, 164, 169, 186
futurity 123, 133–4, 221*gl*

G

Garfinkel, Harold 23
gatekeeping 27–8, 221*gl*
  assessment procedures 28, 92, 113, 136–9, 162–3, 198–9
  binary gender discourse 113
  conditional model 60, 92–6, 141–2, 171, 205
  expert knowledge 27–8, 30, 92–6, 112–16
  gender norms 113–14, 171
  and power 47, 60, 78, 205–6
  'Real Life Experience' 61, 64–6, 94–5, 113, 189, 198–9, 200
  Richard Curtis and 166–7
gender clinics 58, 222*gl see also* gender identity services
gender dysphoria 26, 58, 183–5, 222*gl*
Gender Dysphoria Clinic and Treatments, Edinburgh 149
gender fluidity 34
Gender Governance Group 95, 170
'Gender GP' Online Transgender Medical Clinic 72, 167
Gender Identity Research and Education Society (GIRES) 170–1
gender identity services 4, 5, 58–72, 222*gl*
  Clinical Reference Group 70, 93, 190, 191–2
  diagnostic criteria 58–60
gender incongruence 59, 185
gender outlaws 37
gender performativity 34, 35, 36
gender pluralism 21, 44–5, 48, 107, 222*gl*
gender reassignment surgery
  decision not to undertake 95, 107
  denial of 55
  early 24
  and gender performativity 34
  gender recognition 69
  private medical care 148
  Real Life Experience 66, 68, 70, 165–6
  waiting times 72
gender recognition 69, 99, 192–3
Gender Recognition Act 2004 (GRA) 40, 57, 58, 69, 99, 192, 222*gl*

GenderCare, London 72, 149
Gendered Intelligence 91, 148, 177
gendered violence 35, 42, 49n7, 54
genderqueer 41, 222*gl*
  in academic literature 45–6, 71
  autistic spectrum conditions and 91
  binary discourse 61
  individual identity 170
  trans as movement 89, 102
  see also non-binary
GIC *see* gender clinics
GIRES *see* Gender Identity and Research Education Society
GMC (General Medical Council) 55–6, 74
  Fitness to Practice Panel 164
GPs (general practitioners)
  bridging hormones 74–5
  denial of possibility of trans 87, 109
  direct referral to gender clinics 71, 120
  forum users' advice on 133–4
  evidence base 91
  experiences with 51–6
  hormone therapy 67
  'luck' and 78, 148, 149
  misgendering 181
  name and gender markers 91, 99–100
  pathway 61, 63, 130
  transphobia 77, 97, 153, 154
  waiting times 152
GRA *see* Gender Recognition Act
GRC *see* gender recognition
Green, Jamison 188
Greer, Germaine 32

H

Haas, Peter 164
hair removal services 61, 67, 71, 119–20, 153–5, 190
Halberstam, Jack 39, 103, 122–3, 124, 154, 155
Hall, Radclyffe, *The Well of Loneliness* 22–3
Hallam, Charlie 151
Hanssmann, Christoph 163
harassment 16, 42, 57, 154
Haraway, Donna, 'Cyborg Manifesto' 35
Harry Benjamin International Gender Dysphoria Association (later World Professional Association for Transgender Health (WPATH)) *Standards of Care* 26, 88
Harry Benjamin Syndrome (HBS) movement 177–8, 180, 186
Hausman, Bernice 32
Health and Social Care Act 2012 70, 174, 182, 222*gl*–223*gl*
'healthy body,' disruption of 93, 109

Hess, David 163–164, 167
heterosexism 95, 142
Hines, Sally 69, 103, 146, 215*app*
Hirschfeld, Magnus 24, 25, 29
  The Transvestites 23–4
homophobia 42, 84
Horak, Laura 125, 126, 140, 145, 223
hormone blockers 65, 67–8, 167
hormone therapy
  early 22, 26
  feminist approaches 32, 38
  gatekeeping 143, 165–7
  historical 49n3
  NHS pathway 61–2
  pathologisation and 46
  Scottish protocol 70, 190
  self-medication 73–5
  waiting lists 64–8
  youthful appearance 124
  see also RLE ('Real Life Experience')
hormone time 125–7, 140, 145–6,
  149–50, 152, 154, 223*gl*
House of Commons Women and
  Equalities Committee, Transgender
  Equality Inquiry 51, 55–6, 77, 163,
  180, 197–9
Hunt, Jane 111
Huxter, Will 197
'hysteria' 22

I

ICD (*International Classification of Diseases*)
  (World Health Organization) 26, 30,
  58–9, 93, 114, 184–5, 187, 200
identity
  hierarchies of 26–7
  and medical discourse 96–101
imagined community 105
Indigenous gender identities 48n1–49n1
information and publications 90–2
informed consent model 46, 75, 165,
  180, 206–7, 223*gl*
insider-providers 163, 223*gl*
Institut für Sexualwissenschaft (Institute
  for Sexual Science), Berlin 24
International Classification of Diseases see
  ICD
internet 10–14, 39–42, 209–13, 216–19
internet-based pharmacies 73
intersectionality 39, 106, 141–2, 179–80,
  201, 215*app*
intersex 88, 100, 116n2, 117n3, 178
invert 21–3, 223*gl*
Ireland 192

J

Jacques, Juliet 104–5
Jeffreys, Sheila 32

Jorgensen, Christine 17, 24–5
Just Plain Sense (blog) 174

K

Kaveney, Roz 45
Kennedy, Natacha 43, 85, 86, 110, 117n4
Kessler, Suzanne and McKenna,
  Wendy 23–4
Khoosal, Deenesh 95–6
Krafft-Ebing, Richard von 21, 22
  Psychopathia Sexualis 23

L

Landzelius, Kyra 10
language 39–42, 76, 84, 95–6
'The Laurels', Exeter 64
lay epistemic community 181
Leeds and York Partnership NHS
  Foundation Trust 189
Leeds Gender Identity Service 62, 188–9
Lees, Paris 175
legal rights 17, 27, 99, 186
legislation 40, 52, 57, 69, 130–1, 170
'LGBT Health … Who Cares?'
  seminar 3–5
LGBT news websites 174
Liberty 40, 170–1
'Live Well' series, NHS 91–2
Lou (dance work) 123

M

Majority World gender identities 48n1–
  49n1
'male-to-female' transsexualism *see* MTF
malpractice 55, 134–7, 176–7
Malta 192
marginalisation
  economic 56
  and gatekeeping 27
  intersectional 141, 142, 179, 182, 194
  language and 42–4
  pathologisation 28
  shared 4
  and solidarity 36–7, 39, 179–80
Marxism 178
McNeil, Jay and colleagues 53, 91, 128,
  152, 153
Meads, Catherine and colleagues 4, 205
media portrayals, negative 83, 93
mental health
  and diagnosis 58
  funding 169
  genital reconstruction surgery 68
  and hormone therapy 74
  literature on 91
  and mistrust 132, 135
  name and gender markers 100
  pathway 60–1, 63, 71

power and 66–7, 179
Trans Broken Arm Syndrome 111
transsexualism and 25, 27, 56, 64, 97,
    152
    waiting times and 128, 204
    WPATH *Standards of Care* 187, 190,
        191
methodology 209–18*app*
Meyerowitz, Joanne 88, 98, 100, 178
Miller, Maria MP 197–8
Mills, C. Wright 3, 5
misgendering 29, 86, 109–11, 181
mistreatment, fear of 131–3
mistrust of health professionals 75–8,
    131–7
Monro, Surya 44–5, 48, 50n16, 95, 96
Moore, Suzanne 196n5
movement-oriented discourse 9–10,
    38–9, 45–6, 89, 102–8, 201, 212*app*,
    225*gl*
MTF (male-to-female) transsexualism 24–
    5, 29–30, 101
Muñoz, José Esteban 125–6, 127, 134
myths 141–4

N

Namaste, Viviane K. 8, 38, 39, 216*app*
name and gender markers, change of 91,
    99–100, 181
names, ambiguity of 114–15
The National Trans Youth Network 18n1
negotiation 10, 223*gl*
    collective and political 204
    individual 203–4
    and knowledge 168
    and movement 20
Nestle, Joan and colleagues,
    Genderqueer 41, 45
Netherlands, hormone therapy 195n3
neuroscience 100–1
New Labour government 169
New Statesman 151, 196n5
NHS
    institutional cisgenderism 57
    patient advocacy bodies 52, 56
    patient rights 56–8
    positive experiences 56, 146–7
    pros and cons 148–9
    restructure of 70, 169, 190
    transphobia 54, 57
NHS Barking and Dagenham 91
NHS Choices, 'Transgender Health' web
    page 91–2, 201
NHS Coventry, *Advice Process for Changing
    Name and Gender in Primary Care* 181
NHS England 70–1, 172, 174, 183–4,
    190–2, 197–9

Gender Identity Clinical Reference
    Group 93–4
Interim Gender Protocol 71, 120, 192
NHS gender identity services 60–72
    based on WPATH *Standards of Care* 60,
        188–92
    child and adolescent services 62
    cultural cisgenderism 93
    geographic and funding issues 63–4
    increase in the visible trans
        population 62–3
    institutional approach 61
    legal entitlement to 86–7
    legal recognition of trans identity 69
    mental health assessment 60
    non-specialist practitioners 63
    pathway of care 199
    referral and waiting time 62–7
    reform and austerity 69–72
    self-referral to 63
    variation in policies 66
    waiting lists 62–4, 72
NHS Scotland 69, 190
NHS Wales 71
Nirta, Caterina 123, 130–1
non-binary 223*gl*
non-binary people
    and autistic spectrum conditions 91
    diagnosis as unnecessary 102
    diversity of 30, 48n1, 73, 89, 104, 105
    Equality Act 57, 170
    identity 6, 8
    inclusivity 41, 45–6, 195
    language 40–1, 184
    protocols 71, 96, 187
    rejection of concept 114
    see also genderqueer
Northamptonshire Gender Dysphoria
    Service 71, 72, 79n3
Northern Ireland 63, 79n3 *see also*
    Brackenburn Clinic, Belfast
Nottingham Centre for Transgender
    Health 62, 64–5, 136, 142–3
    clinical research 66, 162–3, 195n2
    gatekeeping 162–3, 188
    'Harry Benjamin Standards of Care' 71
    patient satisfaction survey 66
    'Real Life Experience' 66, 94
NVivo software 214*app*

O

The Observer 165, 196n5
Orange Is The New Black (TV series) 16
orchidectomy 68
osteoporosis 167
'outing' 216

P

paternalism of medical profession 45, 162
pathologisation 22, 26, 29, 46
patient advocates 181
patient groups, UK 161
patient knowledges 168–82
  action research 176–7
  alternative approaches 177–80
  collective activism 175–80
  guidance documents 177
  individual interventions 169–72
  trans journalists 173–4
  see also activist-experts
patriarchy 31, 35
Payton, Naith 111
PCTs (Primary Care Trusts) 64, 70
Pereira, Maria do Mar 10, 225*gl*
phallocentrism 31, 95
Phillips, Jess MP 197–8, 202
Plummer, Kenneth 39, 126
'postcode lottery' 5, 78
  framework lottery 206
poststructuralist approach 8, 31, 38
posttranssexualism 35, 87–9
power, differential of
  and agency 10, 52, 166
  in assessment and diagnosis 26–9, 60,
    65, 66, 67–8, 136–7, 185, 205–6
  discourse and 7–8, 48
  interpretation of guidelines and 94
  journalists' 173–4
  legislation and 58, 169, 170
  of non-specialists 63
  patriarchal 35
  and privilege 106
  and trans knowledge 161, 181, 182,
    192–5
  waiting time 131
  see also gatekeeping
practitioner sphere 11, 12, 223*gl*
Press For Change 40, 170–1, 174, 176,
  181
primary care *see* GPs (general
  practitioners)
Primary Care Trust *see* PCTs
Prince, Virginia 29–31, 36
private medicine 72–5, 78, 147–51
privilege 17, 37, 42, 43, 106, 179,
  215–16
pronouns, use of 7, 22, 29, 40, 52, 100
Prosser, Jay 23, 38, 42
Protocol for Scotland 69–70, 190, 192
psychoanalysis 22
psychological distress 28
public awareness 17
public spending cuts 169 *see also* austerity,
  impact of

Q

queer subcultural production 123
queer theory 38–9, 44
queer time 122–3, 124, 127, 224*gl*
Queer Youth Network 18n1

R

race 17, 37, 106, 142, 215
racism 106, 142
Radix, Asa 188
Raymond, Janice 31
  The Transsexual Empire 31–45
Reid, Russell 164–5, 168
Reisner, Sari and colleagues 53, 91
respect 37, 52, 78, 110, 148–9
Richards, Christina and colleagues 27,
  28, 46, 47, 60, 71, 135, 182, 206
RLE ('Real Life Experience') 224*gl*
  and adolescent patients 68
  gatekeeping 61, 64–6, 94–5, 113, 189,
    198–9, 200
  private clinics 73
  Scottish protocol 62, 70
  variation in period 68
  waiting time 129
Royal College of Psychiatrists 74
Rubin, Henry 21, 22, 24, 29, 33, 88, 98

S

Sandyford Clinic, Glasgow 62, 177
Scotland 62, 63, 69–70, 192
  Gender Reassignment Protocol 69, 70
  see also NHS Scotland
Scottish National Party 192
Scottish Trans Alliance 190
  Trans Mental Health Study 176
Seal, Leighton 28, 74
self-harm 91, 128
self-medication 72, 73–4, 129, 147,
  150–1
self-referral to private clinics 73
Serano, Julia 6, 34, 38, 39, 50n16, 100,
  101
  Whipping Girl 43
Sex Discrimination (Amendment of
  Legislation) Regulations 2008 57, 169
sexism 31–5, 84
sexual inversion *see* invert
Shapiro, Eve 40
social media 75–6, 170–1 *see also*
  Facebook; Twitter
speech therapy 67, 70, 190
'stealth' 89
Steinberg, Deborah Lynn 50n17, 85, 95,
  161
stereotypes 31–2, 34, 54

Stone, Sandy 19, 31, 39, 87–8, 89, 95, 106, 115
  The Empire Strikes Back: A Posttranssexual Manifesto 33–5
'straight time' 122
Stryker, Susan 9, 26, 30, 31, 33, 35–6, 39, 184
substance abuse 53, 91
suicide and suicidal ideation 91, 97, 129, 135, 151–3, 204
Sullivan, Lou 123

T

Tavistock and Portman Gender Identity Clinic *see* Charing Cross Gender Identity Clinic
Teena, Brandon 122–3
temporality 119–55, 224*gl*
  anticipation 119–22, 126–47
  futurity 123, 133–4
  hope 144–7
  mistrust 131–7
  queer time 122–3
  straight time 122
  transitional time 123–6
  waiting time 127–31
Terrence Higgins Trust 91
Time (magazine) 16
Tosh, Jemma 22
Toze, Michael 162–3
TPATH (Transgender International Association for Transgender Health) 188
traditional transsexual narrative 34–5, 38, 87–9, 224*gl*
trans 4, 36, 224*gl*
Trans Activist Takes On World (blog) 191
trans as transition 90–2, 107, 111–12, 225*gl*
'Trans Broken Arm Syndrome' 111–12
trans communities 103–6
trans discourse 19–48
  curing 21–33
  as historically located 19
'trans enough' 27, 60, 92, 137–44, 149, 150, 201, 206
trans knowledges 189–90, 225*gl*
  international authority 188–92
  authority and expertise 181–2
Trans Media Watch 175
Trans Mental Health Study 2012 *see* McNeil, Jay and colleagues
Trans Youth Network 3–4
TransForum (Manchester) 176
transgender 36–7, 225*gl*
Transgender International Association for Transgender Health *see* TPATH
transgender rage 35–6

transgender studies 14, 18n3, 27, 28, 214*app*
  emergence of 33
'transgender tipping point' 16–17
Transhealth 72, 149–50, 167
transition 4–5, 225*gl*
  mental health after 152
transitional time 123–4, 126, 128, 226*gl*
transphobia 42, 55–6, 57, 76, 226*gl*
transsexualism 23–6, 38–9, 226*gl*
transsexualism diagnosis
  DSM 26
  ICD-10 59
Transvestia (magazine) 30
transvestism 17, 23–7, 30, 102, 226*gl*
Turing, Alan 49n3
Twitter 12, 54, 127, 132, 172, 195n5, 209, 210
  #transdocfail 54, 75, 86, 95, 105–6, 111, 112, 114, 115, 127, 132, 137, 152, 166, 171–2, 174, 196n5, 210, 225*gl*

U

UK Trans Info 79n1, 79n3
understandings 7, 43–7, 108–15, 200–3, 226*gl*
  autoethnography 14
  condition-oriented 20–1, 69, 171, 187, 200–1
  movement-oriented 9, 20–1, 102, 160, 177, 182, 201, 205
  transition-oriented 87, 89
US (United States) 17, 37, 46, 91, 173, 187

V

Vähäpassi, Emmi 39, 185
validation 97, 100, 102, 106–8
violence 42, 49n7, 53, 53, 91, 154
Volcano, Del LaGrace 122, 123

W

waiting times 64–8, 72, 90, 127–31, 149
Wales 63, 64, 70–1
Walsh, Reubs J. 114–15
Webberley, Helen 167
West London Mental Health Trust Gender Identity Clinic *see* Charing Cross Gender Identity Clinic
Whittle, Stephen 4, 18n3, 39, 40, 175, 176, 187–8
women's liberation movement 29
World Health Organization 59, 114, 200
  see also ICD (*International Classification of Diseases*)

WPATH (World Professional Association
    for Transgender Health) 26, 175,
    187–8
  and depathologisation 187, 191
  representation of women 50n12
WPATH *Standards of Care*
  on bridging hormones 74
  built in waiting times 149
  depathologisation 28, 186
  interpretation 60, 71, 72, 136, 165, 167
  on non-binary 46
  revision 175, 187–92
  'Real Life Experience' 66
  Scottish protocol 69, 70, 190
  on surgery 68
'wrong body' narrative 88, 100

Y

York gender clinic 62
YourGP, Edinburgh and Aberdeen 72

Z

Zucker, Kenneth, 'invisible college' 29,
    49n10